RAPPACCINI'S DA

The only play by Latin
dramatic poem about
was first st

D1488306

'Paz's writing allows us to glimpse a distant and future
place . . . liberating and affirming.' *Guardian*

NIGHT OF THE ASSASSINS ■ JOSÉ TRIANA

Cuban José Triana outraged Fidel Castro's government with
this stunningly macabre portrayal of rebellious youth. This
translation first staged in Britain in 1994.

'The atmosphere of oppression is almost tangible . . . in the
hysteria and power games of three siblings enacting or re-enacting
the murder of their parents . . . utterly compelling.' *Scotsman*

SAYING YES ■ GRISELDA GAMBARO

This shocking story of an everyday trip to the hairdresser's is by
the leading Argentine woman playwright. This translation first
staged in Britain in 1996.

'One of the most innovative and powerful writers in the world
today, . . . she is singularly perceptive about the criminal
machinations of the authoritarian governments she lived
under . . . ' Diana Taylor

ORCHIDS IN THE MOONLIGHT ■ CARLOS FUENTES

Set in Venice, the day Orson Welles died, this extraordinary play
relentlessly stretches the imagination with artistic reveries and
supernatural fantasies. This version first staged in Britain in 1992.

'Rich in language and movement, fantasy and reality, sensuality
and cruelty; as iconoclastic as the magic realist boom of
the 1960s.' *Scotland on Sunday*

MISTRESS OF DESIRES ■ MARIO VARGAS LLOSA

Peru's most acclaimed writer sets his play in a 1940s desert town
where machismo and sexual desire lead to the mysterious
disappearance of a beautiful young girl. This translation
first staged in Britain in 1992.

'In the star-studded world of Latin American literature,
Mario Vargas Llosa is a supernova.' *Wall Street Journal*

Other volumes in the International Collection

AUSTRALIA PLAYS
ed. Katharine Parsons
Jack Davis: No Sugar
Alma de Groen: The Rivers of China
Michael Gow: Away
Louis Nowra: The Golden Age
David Williamson: Travelling North
ISBN 1 85459 056 1

CZECH PLAYS
ed. Barbara Day
Václav Havel: Tomorrow!
Ivan Klíma: Games
Josef Topol: Cat on the Rails
Daniela Fischerová: Dog and Wolf
ISBN 1 85459 074 X

DUTCH PLAYS
ed. Della Couling
Lodewijk de Boer: The Buddha of Ceylon
Judith Herzberg: Wedding Party
Arne Sierens: Drummers
Frans Strijards: The Stendhal Syndrome
Karst Woudstra: Burying the Dog
ISNB 1 85459 289 0

HUNGARIAN PLAYS
ed. László Upor
András Nagy. The Seducer's Diary
Andor Szilágyi: Unsent Letters
Ákos Németh: Muller's Dances
Péter Kárpáti: Everywoman
ISBN 1 85459 244 0

SOUTH AFRICAN PLAYS
ed. Stephen Gray
Anthony Akerman: Somewhere on the Border
Maishe Maponya: Tile Hungry Earth
Susan Pam-Grant: Curl Up and Dye
Paul Slabolepszy: Over the Hill
Pieter-Dirk Uys: Just Like Home
ISBN 1 85459 148 7

STARS IN THE MORNING SKY
ed. Michael Glenny
Alexander Chervinsky: Heart of a Dog
Alexander Galin: Stars in the Morning Sky
Alexander Gelman: A Man with Connections
Grigory Gorin: Forget Herostratus!
Ludmila Petrushevskaya: Three Girls in Blue
ISBN 1 85459 020 0

LATIN AMERICAN PLAYS

New Drama from Argentina, Cuba, Mexico and Peru

Rappaccini's Daughter ■ Octavio Paz

Night of the Assassins ■ José Triana

Saying Yes ■ Griselda Gambaro

Orchids in the Moonlight ■ Carlos Fuentes

Mistress of Desires ■ Mario Vargas Llosa

Selected, translated and introduced by

Sebastian Doggart

THE INTERNATIONAL COLLECTION

NICK HERN BOOKS
London
in association with

Visiting Arts

A Nick Hern Book

Latin American Plays first published in Great Britain in 1996
as an original paperback by Nick Hern Books Limited,
14 Larden Road, London W3 7ST

Cover image by Oliver Gaiger

The authors of the original plays and the translator have asserted
their moral rights

Typeset by Country Setting, Woodchurch, Kent TN26 3TB
Printed and bound in Great Britain by Athenaeum Press Ltd.,
Gateshead, Tyne and Wear

A CIP catalogue record for this book is available from
the British Library

ISBN 1 85459 249 1

Contents

An Introduction to Latin American Theatre

by Sebastian Doggart

Latin American theatre is an untapped goldmine for the English-speaking world. While the region's novels and poetry are widely read and respected, its theatre remains largely unknown. Few Latin American plays are published or produced in English, and these often suffer from unsympathetic translations. School and university courses mostly ignore Latin American theatre and there is a dearth of critical studies on the subject. The main purpose of this book, therefore, is to encourage the reading, study and staging of Latin American drama.

The book has three sections. First, it presents original translations of five contemporary Latin American plays, which have been prepared in collaboration with the playwrights themselves, and chosen for their high literary and dramatic quality. Although they have specifically 'Latin American' features, they retain qualities that give them a universal accessibility. To test this, all five plays were staged in the UK by English-speaking performers, and these productions have yielded fresh insights into the authors' intentions, which have been incorporated into the translations. The plays' broad range of styles and subject matter is representative of the rich diversity of drama written since the 1950s. The chosen writers represent four of the most historically vibrant centres of Latin American theatre – Cuba, Mexico, Argentina and Peru – and their work is concerned with many of the issues and patterns that have preoccupied Latin American dramatists for over five centuries. The second section of the book contains interviews with the playwrights, giving the writers a chance to explain to an English-speaking audience the intentions behind their plays, and to reveal some of their literary and personal sources. The third section is this introduction which contextualises the plays through a historical survey of drama in Cuba, Mexico, Argentina and Peru, and then discusses some of the challenges involved in translating and staging Latin American drama in English.

A Brief History of Latin American Theatre: Pre-1492

Our knowledge of the pre-Columbian period is very limited. Europeans who discovered indigenous spectacles judged them to be primitively heretical, banned public performances, and destroyed local records. What information we do have comes from Catholic missionaries,

whose reports agreed that throughout the region there was theatre
in the form of 'ritual spectacles', such as Cuban *areitos*, in which
Arawak Indian actors dressed up to enact historical and religious
stories using dialogue, music and dance, until they were prohibited
by the Spanish colonial administration in 1511. The Aztecs in Mexico
used a mixture of dance, music and Nahuatl dialogue to depict the
activities of their gods. According to Fray Diego Durán, a Dominican
friar, one Aztec festival required a conscripted performer to take on
the role of the god Quetzalcoátl. As such, he was worshipped for 40
days, after which, to help Huitzilopochtli, god of daylight, fight the
forces of darkness, his heart was removed and offered to the moon.
His flayed skin was then worn as the god's costume by another
performer. While the Incas ruled Peru, the Quechua are reported to
have performed ritual spectacles involving dance, costumes and music,
but probably not dialogue, to purify the earth, bring fertility to women
and the soil, and worship ancestral spirits. The Inca Tupac Yupanqui
used his warriors to re-enact his son's victorious defence of the
Sacsahuamán fortress above Cuzco against 50,000 invaders.

The only pre-Columbian 'script' to survive the European campaign
against indigenous culture, the *Rabinal Achí* of the Maya-Quiché
Indians of Central America, is the story of a Quiché Warrior who is
captured after a long war by his sworn enemy the Rabinal Warrior
and, when he refuses to bow down to the Rabinal Warrior's king,
is sacrificed. The story was told through sung formal challenges,
interspersed with music and dance, with each actor wearing an ornate
wooden mask which was so heavy that the actors had to be replaced
several times during the performance. The last actor playing the
Quiché warrior was sacrificed. The work was preserved through oral
tradition, until 1855 when it was recorded in writing by Charles
Brasseur, a French priest in the Guatemalan village of Rabinal. It is
still performed there every January – omitting the final sacrifice.

1492-1550

The arrival of the Spaniards led to a blending, or *mestizaje*, of local and
European influences, which has since become one of the most distinctive features of Latin American theatre. Catholic missionaries identified the theatre as an effective tool for converting the local people to
Christianity, and in Mexico, the Franciscans sought to transform the
religious beliefs of the Aztecs by learning Nahuatl and studying their
rituals and ceremonies. In doing so, they found that Aztec and Christian religions had much in common: the Aztecs associated the cross
with Quetzalcoatl, 'baptised' newly-born children, 'confessed' to the
gods when they transgressed, and practised 'communion' through the
eating of human sacrifices. The Franciscans dramatised such symbols
and rituals in the local language, so that the Aztecs would become
more open to conversion through identification with the characters.

Theatrical presentations were usually staged in 'open chapels', built on the site of indigenous places of worship, with wooden platforms resembling end-on stages. Mass preceded performances, which were based on local dance and song, and celebrated European religious and secular authority. In the early 1500s, the Church turned to a more effective technique for storytelling and evangelising: a modified version of the Spanish *auto sacramental*, a one-act religious allegory which was performed on feast days, especially Corpus Christi. Such Indo-Hispanic *autos* are the first theatrical works to be described legitimately as 'plays', in that they were formally scripted. The Catholic missions also put on large-scale productions for mass conversions and to foster new communities revolving around the Church. One of the most spectacular of these events was the Franciscan production of the *auto, The Conquest of Rhodes* (*La Conquista de Rodas*, 1543) in the Mexican town of Tenochtitlán, where construction of the set alone required the work of some 50,000 Indians.

1550-1750

From the mid-16th century Indo-Hispanic evangelical theatre began to wane as secular authorities wrested influence away from the Catholic missionaries. Radical demographic changes contributed to this: by 1600, the Indian population in Latin America was estimated to be only one tenth of what it had been 100 years earlier. Many immigrants were arriving from Europe, and there was a growing *mestizo* (part Indian, part European) population whose idea of entertainment was far removed from evangelising theatre in indigenous languages. European influences became dominant. Spanish baroque dramatists like Lopé de Vega, Calderón de la Barca and Tirso de Molina refined the *auto sacramental*, and developed two other dramatic forms which they combined with the *auto*: the *loa*, a short dramatic prologue in praise of visiting dignitaries or to celebrate royal anniversaries; and the *sainete*, a musical sketch, inserted between acts, which made fun of local customs or of the *auto* itself.

Such innovations encouraged the emergence of Latin American dramatists like Mexican-born Juan Ruiz de Alarcón, Peruvian Juan del Valle y Caviedas and the Argentine Antonio Fuentes del Arco whose best-known play, *Loa* (1717), celebrated the repeal of a tax imposed in Argentina on the importation of the herb *mate* from Paraguay. Particularly notable is the work of the Mexican nun, poet, intellectual, scientist, and early 'feminist' Sor Juana Inés de la Cruz. She wrote seventeen *loas*, three *autos*, two *sainetes,* and two secular comedies. Formally her theatre fits within the conventions of the Spanish baroque, and her comedies were particularly influenced by Calderón; yet the content of her work shows an independent mind verging on the subversive. For a Mexican woman in a colonial, male-dominated society, it was a remarkable achievement just to have had her plays performed. Her treatment of subject matter and characterisation boldly questioned colonial, religious, and male power. In her secular comedy of errors, *The Desires of a Noble House* (*Los empeños de una casa*, c. 1683), for example, she dressed up a male character in women's clothes to ridicule the way men expected women to assume subservient roles. She also became one of the first Latin American dramatists to confront the scorn shown by the Spaniards for indigenous cultures, particularly in the *loa* to her *auto*, *The Divine Narcissus* (*El Divino Narciso*, c.1680), where two characters discuss whether such 'primitive' culture as Aztec dance and music would be suitable for performance at the Spanish court.

Sor Juana's drama is the first example of Latin American 'autonomous theatre', which is defined as theatre attempting to establish personal or cultural identity by using dramatic forms to question, ridicule or resist an oppressive status quo, or to celebrate the beliefs and customs of an oppressed culture or social group. The emergence of autonomous theatre coincided with a growing desire for independence from Spain, which was clearly demonstrated in the Mexican and Cuban insurrections of 1692 and 1717; and the concept of the 'autonomous' was to play a major role in subsequent Latin American theatre, including the five plays in this volume.

1750-1900

The reign of the *autos* in Latin American theatre came to an abrupt end in 1765 when the Spanish king Charles III banned them for being religiously corrupt. They were largely replaced by European-inspired neo-classical and romantic plays. In general, the use of European forms stunted the development of home-grown Latin American theatre, perpetuating the region's cultural dependence on the Old World. The Spaniards contributed more positively, however, by implementing a region-wide programme of theatre construction. Their buildings were generally of a classical style, using proscenium arch stages, and were intended to glorify their colonial sponsors. In the early 19th century, the Cuban Governor Tacón set out to build the biggest theatre in Latin America by levying a hefty tax on slaves imported into the island. The eponymous theatre seated 4000 and had 150 boxes.

This was also the period when much of Latin America gained its independence from Spain: Mexico in 1810, Argentina in 1816, Peru in 1822 and Cuba in 1898. Theatre contributed to and fed off these social and political upheavals, with many plays depicting the Spaniards negatively, especially historical figures like Cortés and Pizarro, while indigenous and local life was celebrated through *costumbrismo*. Cuban playwrights were probably the most outspoken critics of the Spaniards during the last decades of colonial rule. José María Heredia used classical stories to draw parallels with the corrupt tyranny of Spanish rule. His *The Frightened Peasant* (*El Campesino espantado*, 1820) is a one-act *sainete* about a man from the country abused by the urban colonial authorities, while *The Last Romans (Los Ultimos Romanos*, 1829) symbolises the decaying Spanish empire. Heredia's work angered the Cuban authorities so much that he was forced into exile – as was his compatriot José Triana 150 years later.

Bufo, another example of Cuban autonomous theatre, developed out of the tradition of the *sainete* and was influenced by the North American minstrel groups that toured the island between 1860 and 1865. *Bufo* shows had three main characters: the *gallego* (a white Galician immigrant), the *negrito* (a white actor with a black face) and the *mulata* (an Afro-Cuban woman fought over by the two men). They used a distinctive mixture of Spanish, French, English and Yoruba and were often critical of the colonial authorities. At one show in 1869, a *bufonero* called Jacinto Valdés was bold enough to shout "*Viva Céspedes*", the name of a revolutionary leader. Spanish officials reprimanded him, but Valdés defied them by arranging the next show as a special benefit to raise money for Céspedes' forces. This time, when Valdés incited the audience to chant "*Cuba Libre!*", colonial soldiers broke into the theatre and opened fire on the audience, killing many, and forcing Valdés to flee the country. The following day, the newspaper *La Patria Libre* published *Abdala*, a one-act dramatic poem by the 16-year-old poet and subsequent political activist José Martí. *Abdala* tells of a Nubian soldier who, against his mother's wishes, leaves home to help save his people from invading Arabs, and dies in battle – a tragic prophesy of Martí's own violent death fighting the Spaniards in 1895. Like Heredia, Martí's theatre used historical analogy to encourage resistance to colonial rule.

A key development in the Argentine theatre, meanwhile, was the emergence of the *gaucho*, the cowboy of the pampas, as a symbol of cultural autonomy. The *gaucho* fiercely resisted any constraints on his personal freedom, particularly those imposed by the colonial authorities, and then, after Independence, by the urban government. From these seeds grew the *teatro gauchesco*, epitomised by the theatrical adaptation of *Juan Moreira*, a popular serialised novel by Eduardo Gutiérrez. The plot is relatively simple: Juan wants a comfortable family life but a provincial official desires his wife. A shopkeeper reneges on a debt to Juan, and is supported by the covetous official. Angry and dishonoured, Juan kills them both and becomes an outlaw. Although he helps the poor and cleverly avoids capture, he is eventually surrounded and killed. Two different productions were staged. The first version, in 1884, had no dialogue and featured a famous Uruguayan clown, José J. Podestá, in the leading role. It was performed in the round as a pantomime, with horses, musicians and dancers. Two years later, Podestá produced another version, also in the circus ring, adding dialogue in the authentic *gaucho* dialect. It was hugely popular, ran for five years and inspired a host of other *gaucho* plays, notably Martiniano Leguizamón's *Calandria* (1896).

Just as the *teatro gaucho* stood for a particular way of life, other Latin American playwrights used *costumbrista* theatre to celebrate local colour and customs. Mexican audiences applauded the social comedy of its *sainetes,* while in Peru the playwright Manuel Ascencio Segura caricatured the army in *Sergeant Canute (El Sargentin Canuto*, 1839) and delighted audiences with his portrait of a Lima matchmaker, *Na Catita* (1856).

1900-1920

Argentina and Uruguay became the hub of Latin American theatre in the early 20th century. Industrialisation was under way and European immigrants flooded into Buenos Aires which saw a population explosion from 187,000 in 1869 to 1.6 million in 1914. Uruguayan-born Florencio Sánchez powerfully portrayed the way urbanisation was changing everyday life. Sánchez shared with his *teatro gauchesco* predecessors a preoccupation with the conflicts between the individual and society and between urban and rural lives; but he condemned the idealisation of the *gaucho*. His two most performed plays are *La gringa* (1904), about a young European immigrant girl's struggle to survive in the New World, and *Down the Gully (Barranca abajo,* 1905), a three-act rural tragedy about an old *gaucho* whose ranch is threatened by legal action from an immigrant city-dweller. His wife and daughters pester him to allow them to socialise more. When he resists, one daughter starts a relationship with the immigrant. The other, Cordelia-like, remains loyal to him, but when she dies of tuberculosis, the *gaucho* decides to commit suicide.

The conflict between immigrants and locals, or creoles, also lay at the heart of new urban *sainetes*, which explored the social, cultural and linguistic contradictions of life in Buenos Aires. Throughout Latin America the *sainete* had become established as a genre in its own right, and the urban form had one act and two central characters, the immigrant and the creole, who usually spoke different dialects. The styles ranged from political satire to social caricature and melodrama, and the most successful writers of urban *sainetes* were Alberto Vacarezza and Nemesio Trejo.

In Cuba, dramatists were confronting significant political changes. Cuba obtained nominal independence from Spain in 1898, but in 1901 the USA inserted the so-called 'Platt amendment' into the Cuban Constitution, authorising US intervention 'as necessary'. The USA also forced economic dependence on Cuba by monopolising sugar exports for the US market and by securing free access for US capital and goods. One of the plays which gave vent to the growing resentment to US neo-colonialism was *Rebel Soul (Alma Rebelde,* 1906) by José Antonio Ramos.

In Mexico, the cosy cultural conservatism of the Porfirio Diaz regime exploded with the revolution of 1910. The only notable theatrical activity in the ensuing civil war was the emergence of political revue, in which performers used local language to satirise the new leaders. The 1917 Mexican Constitution put education high on the social and political agenda, and with it came the promise of theatrical renewal.

1920-1940

Conflicting desires to create autonomous Latin American theatre and to yield to the powerful influences of European and US theatre dominated this period. On the one hand, theatres like Teatro Orientación in Mexico and Luis A. Baralt's Teatro de la Cueva in Cuba staged works by writers like Pirandello, Chekhov, Shaw, O'Neill, Cocteau and Strindberg, European ideas about the role of the director gained widespread acceptance, as did Stanislavski's acting 'system', and theatres throughout the region were relying on imports for technical innovations in staging, lighting and sound. On the other hand, artists and intellectuals throughout the region were searching for national identities and making determined efforts to free themselves from cultural dependence on Europe and the USA. Nationalist sentiment was strongest in Mexico. Like the Catholic missionaries, the new revolutionary rulers saw theatre as an effective tool of mass education. One of the first big state projects was the construction of a 9000-seater open-air theatre which staged Erfrén Orozco Rosales' aptly titled *Liberation* (*Liberación*, 1929), which set out to teach the glorious story of Mexico City from its conquest by the wicked Spaniards to its triumphant salvation through the revolution. The production had a cast of over 1000 performers, echoing the mass evangelical productions of the 16th century. Pleased with the success of the project, the government instigated an incredible two-year construction programme during which some 4000 new theatres were built in both urban and rural areas. Orozco Rosales continued to write strongly nationalist drama which either celebrated the revolution, as in *Land and Liberty* (*Tierra y Libertad*, 1933), or extolled the power of the Aztec spirit, such as *Creation of the Fifth Sun* (*Creación del Quinto Sol*, 1934), which used a cast of 3000 to tell the story of two Aztec gods who saved the world by throwing themselves into fire in order to create a new sun and moon.

The desire to create autonomous theatre in Argentina led to a new form, the 'creole-grotesque'. As in the *teatro gauchesco*, the urban *sainetes* and the work of Florencio Sánchez, the main conflict in the creole-grotesque is between the individual and society. The form arose out of the work of two Argentine playwrights – Francisco Defilippis Novoa and Armando Discépolo. Both were influenced by a mixture of anarchist thought and the promise of Christian mercy. Their definition of the 'grotesque' can be described as the discrepancy between a character's inner self and his outer mask. The dramatists heightened this tension by calling for exaggerated sets, lighting, costumes, and make-up, and by the use of deforming mirrors and masks. Nevertheless, both writers encouraged ways of overcoming 'grotesque' human traits: Discépolo called on society to reject hypocrisy and to show greater compassion for the struggling individual, particularly the immigrant; while, in contrast, Defilippis Novoa suggested that redemption was in the hands of the individual and could only be achieved by accepting God. His Christian fable, *I Have Seen God* (*He Visto a Dios*, 1930), which illustrates this hope, is the story of a cruel and dishonest pawnbroker, Carmelo, who loses the one thing he loves, his son Chico. Carmelo gets drunk and is tricked by his assistant, Victorio, disguised as a vision of God, into handing over his money. When Chico's pregnant girlfriend also attempts to rob him, Carmelo's Bible-selling tenant intervenes to save him: sober again, Carmelo forgives all, gives away his business and leaves to find God in himself.

Discépolo and Defilippis Novoa have had a significant influence on Griselda Gambaro's work. This period of Argentine theatre also produced a precursor for, if not a direct influence on, Carlos Fuentes and Mario Vargas Llosa, in the form of the playwright and novelist Roberto Arlt. Arlt was inspired by literary works like *Don Quijote* and by the paintings of Goya, Brueghel and Dürer. In plays such as *Saverio the Cruel* (*Saverio el cruel*, 1935) and *The Desert Island* (*La Isla Desierta*, 1937) conventional reality is combined with the world of dreams – dimensions which are similarly interwoven in *Mistress of Desires* and *Orchids in the Moonlight*.

1940-1959

During this period there was a temporary lull in the debate among Latin American theatre practitioners about whether or not a truly national drama should reject European cultural influences. The Cuban writer Fernando Ortiz suggested that ideas borrowed from another culture set off a complex process of 'transculturation', leading to the creation of entirely new cultural phenomena: such a view made the question of influences largely redundant. At the same time there was a growing awareness of the need for better financed theatre companies and for training. Governments throughout the region responded by setting up drama colleges and national theatres and by funding independent groups. The Cuban Academia de Artes Dramáticas was founded in 1941 to provide actor training, and in 1949 Havana University set up the Teatro Experimental to encourage the development of national playwrights through an awareness of international theatre traditions. In Mexico, many new theatre companies were formed in the 1940s. The Instituto Nacional de Bellas Artes was created in 1947 to train actors, maintain repertory theatres and organise annual drama festivals. Meanwhile, two important new institutions were established in Peru: a national theatre company, the Compañía Nacional de Comedias, and a national drama college, the Escuela Nacional de Arte Escénica.

In this supportive environment play-writing thrived. In Mexico, actor, translator, producer, teacher and playwright Rodolfo Usigli emerged as the bright new star of the national theatre. Although his plays are deeply Mexican in their passionately critical exploration of the national psyche, Usigli admired European dramatists and 'acculturated' some of their formal techniques, especially those of his friend George Bernard Shaw. Usigli's best-known play is *The Impostor* (*El Gesticulador*, 1947), a complex satire of social hypocrisy and deception revolving around a history professor who distorts Mexican history for his own political ends. The play caused a scandal when it was published, provoking a cabinet crisis, and it remained unproduced for ten years. Since then, it has been performed regularly and successfully throughout the Americas and Europe. Usigli's influence on Mexican theatre is difficult to over-estimate. His plays showed audiences how Latin America represented the 'Other' to Europe's 'Self'. Playwright Luisa Josefina Hernández whose profound characterisations and unusual story-telling talent is best shown in the collection of dialogues called *Big Deal Street* (*La Calle de la Gran Ocasión*, 1962), acknowledges him as her mentor.

In Argentina, the search for a national drama remained intense, as shown in the plays of Osvaldo Dragún, a leading writer of 'autonomous theatre' of this period. Like Usigli, he sought to expose the hypocrisy of politicians and the middle classes. He was deeply concerned with the social injustices that Peronism had failed to address. The political content of Dragún's work is well illustrated in *The Plague Comes from Melos* (*La Peste Viene de Melos*, 1956), which, though set in Ancient Greece, is an implicit critique of the USA for the way its ostensibly anti-Communist foreign policies masked darker imperialist ambitions. It had particular resonance in the wake of the CIA-backed coup which overthrew Guatemalan president Jacobo Arbenz in 1954. Dragún also experimented with formal techniques: in *Stories to Be Told* (*Historias para ser contados*, 1957) he used songs, dialogue and mime in a succession of one-act plays to explore the dehumanising effects of materialism. During successful productions in the USA and Europe, critics compared him to Brecht and his theatre conventions to the *commedia del arte*; but Dragún's work is essentially Argentine, rooted in the urban *sainete* and the creole-grotesque.

Another playwright who used classical settings to explore local reality was Virgilio Piñera. He vividly exposed the fear behind Cuba's cheerful facade. His first work, *Electra Garrigó* (1948), was an absurdist parody of Sophocles' *Electra*, reinterpreted in a vein of black humour. A flavour of Piñera's wit can be gained from a summary of the plot of *Jesús* (1950) in which a barber named Jesus Barcia, son of Joseph and Mary, is rumoured to be the Messiah, despite his protestations to the contrary, and is eventually stabbed to death for refusing to work miracles. (Both the grotesque humour and the hairdresser's setting are echoed in this volume in Gambaro's *Saying Yes*.)

Peru emerged from 50 years of theatrical stagnation in these years with some fine new playwrights. Sebastián Salazar Bondy wrote with nationalist intent and met with international acclaim. He experimented with forms ranging from satirical farce, as in *Love, the Great Labyrinth (Amor, gran laberinto*, 1947), to historical drama, with *Flora Tristrán* (1958). Salazar Bondy was also a noted poet, and shared with many Latin American dramatists since Sor Juana the ability to combine theatrical work with poetry and prose fiction. Such creative breadth is of special relevance to our understanding of the theatre of Octavio Paz, Fuentes and Vargas Llosa, who are not generally identified primarily as playwrights.

Poet, essayist, teacher, editor, diplomat, and Nobel laureate, Paz is a central figure in contemporary Latin American literature. He was born in 1914 in Mexico City, where he grew up. He fought on the Republican side in the Spanish Civil War and moved to the USA in 1943. In 1945 he joined the Mexican diplomatic service, which led to extensive travel. In 1950, Paz shot to international literary fame with his essay on Mexican character and culture, *The Labyrinth of Solitude*. Five years later, he published a seminal essay on poetics, *The Bow and the Lyre*, and in 1956 turned his attention to an exploration of the role of poetry in the theatre. He gathered together Mexican writers and artists, including the painter Leonora Carrington, and set up the experimental theatre group Poetry Out Loud (*Poesía en Alta Voz*). The group rejected realism, instead defining theatre as a kind of game, and produced eight programmes of plays, ranging from Greek and Spanish classics to modern Mexican works, the most notable of which was *Rappaccini's Daughter*, the only play written by Paz. Poetry Out Loud also gave Elena Garro her big career break, by producing her play *The Lady on Her Balcony (La Señora en Su Balcón*, 1963), a poetic and disturbing portrayal of an elderly woman haunted by the illusions of her past. Garro's imaginative use of physical images to depict external realities made her a leading Mexican dramatist of the 1960s and 1970s.

The symbiosis of prose fiction and theatre is best illustrated by the work of Guatemalan-born Miguel Angel Asturias. Winner of the 1967 Nobel Prize for Literature, he is best known for his novels *Mr. President* and *Men of Maize*, and for his anthropological study of Guatemalan legends; but he also wrote four plays in which he combined fantasy and psychology, the modern and the mythical. *Soluna* (1955), for example, is a dream play which starts as a naturalistic drama, and is then transformed by masks, music and dance into a ritual spectacle of pre-Columbian magic.

1959-1980

These were the most fertile years thus far in Latin American theatre, marked by unprecedented achievements in both quality and volume. The number of locally written plays produced increased sharply during this period: for example, while only 40 Cuban plays were put on in Havana between 1952 and 1958, 281 were staged in 1967 alone. All over the region new playwrights were seeing their work produced and were attracting international critical and public acclaim. These plays grew out of a period of confrontation and transition. The 1959 Cuban revolution encouraged people throughout the region to believe that political transformation could overcome social inequalities, corruption, and US imperialism. The Catholic Church gave its support to social change, and Gustavo Gutierrez and his 'theology of liberation' inspired Paulo Freire and others to set up 'base communities' to transform society from the grass roots. But aspirations for a region-wide revolution died with Ché Guevara, and public expressions of political opposition were met with violence. Authoritarian governments took control in Argentina and Peru, the Cuban revolution ossified, the USA implemented neurotic anti-Communist policies, and the Vatican retreated into the ultra-conservatism of John Paul II's papacy. Against this turbulent backdrop, the theatre often provided the only place where people could freely express their hopes for change.

José Triana ranks among the most significant writers of Latin American autonomous theatre. Triana was born in Bayamo in 1932, studied in Cuba, and was inspired by José Martí as a student. He became a friend of Virgilio Piñera, who encouraged him to publish his poems in Cuban literary magazines. Triana took an active stance against the Batista government and, following a number of failed rebellions, was forced into exile in Spain, where he became involved in the theatre, saw many plays, and started writing his own. He returned to Cuba after the revolution and, inspired by Piñera's *Electra Garrigó*, completed *Medea in the Mirror* (*Medea en el espejo*, 1960), which placed classical tragedy figures in a humble Cuban setting. His fifth play, *Night of the Assassins* is, in social and political terms, undoubtedly the most significant work of the period. Writing started in 1957 and the play had its Havana premiere in 1965. It won the prestigious Casa de las Américas award, and was subsequently performed throughout the Americas and Europe. It is an unsettling and complex work, which elicited many interpretations: some took its 1950s setting as an attack on pre-revolutionary society under Batista, others picked up on Lalo's last lines to argue that the play was a clarion call for the redemptive power of Love, while the Cuban Ministry of Culture interpreted the play as a direct attack on the incompetence and complacency of Fidel Castro's government. This was indeed one of Triana's intentions and he was to suffer dearly for it. The Ministry judged him to be "outside the revolution", denied him the resources to stage plays like *War Ceremonial* (*Ceremonial de Guerra*, 1968-73) and *Frolic on the Battle Field (Revolico en el campo de marte*, 1971), and marginalised him from active cultural life. In 1980, Triana emigrated with his wife to Paris.

Another seminal writer of autonomous theatre to emerge during this period was Griselda Gambaro. Born in Buenos Aires in 1928, she worked in accounting and business until she got married and, in her words, her husband 'emancipated' her. She wrote her first play aged 24, since when there have been over 30 further plays, as well as several novels. Gambaro's work paints a deformed and unnerving portrait of a tragic period in Argentine history. Starting with the military coup that ousted Perón in 1955, these years were marked by an uneasy succession of military and constitutional regimes. Perón's return to power in 1973 was short-lived, and his death in 1974 unleashed a rash of political violence from left-wing guerrilla groups and right-wing death squads. In 1976 the ruling military junta vowed to rid the country of 'subversion' and instigated the 'Dirty War', during which the army crushed both the guerrilla movements and its civilian opponents. Gambaro herself was forced to flee to Spain after her novel *Earning Death (Ganarse la Muerte*, 1976) was banned as 'subversive, amoral and harmful to the family', and after she had received death threats. Her nightmarish portrayals of abductions in *The Walls (Las Paredes*, 1963) and fascist excesses in *The Camp (El Campo*, 1967) grimly predicted the summary executions and torture which were to 'disappear' an estimated 15,000 Argentines. In *The Blunder (El Desatino*, 1965) she exposes the passive compliance with which many accepted military repression. In later plays like *Antígona Furiosa* (1986) female characters take on more central roles and often take bold steps to resist patriarchal oppression. Gambaro's work mines a human propensity to victimise others, and is directly descended from the creole-grotesque dramatists of the 1920s. Gambaro's language is an extraordinary hybrid of Argentine slang, the encoded dialects of tyrannised people, and diverse cultural references: in her promenade play *Information for Foreigners (Información para Extranjeros*, 1973), for example, she seamlessly interweaves *porteño* jokes with a lullaby from Lorca's *Blood Wedding*, an account of Stanley Milgram's experiments on the human capacity for violence, and extracts from *Othello*.

A very different form of autonomous theatre to have a big impact between 1960 and 1980 was 'New Theatre'. Pioneered by Enrique Buenaventura's Teatro Experimental de Cali in Colombia, and rooted in the base groups of liberation theology and a version of Brechtian epic theatre, New Theatre's ideological objective was to create a radical alternative to 'bourgeois' drama. New Theatre was to be based on five principles. First, it would be the product of collective work rather than the imagination of an individual author; although there would be one overseeing director, an egalitarian structure would be established so that every participant would be simultaneously actor, writer, researcher and technician. Second, New Theatre would perform theatre for, and to, communities unfamiliar with the theatre. Third, whereas the messages of bourgeois theatre were passively received by the public, the audiences of New Theatre would be invited to participate actively in the performances; in this way, a play would be rewritten at each performance. Fourth, New Theatre would seek to transform reality not just to interpret it, not to preach ideas but to set up dialectical situations and then engage audiences in debating them. Fifth and finally, whereas bourgeois drama valued the cultured, the eternal and the universal, New Theatre sought the immediate and the popular: plays would use local colour, language and music, and would be a theatre of theatricality rather than of staged literary texts.

These principles were rigorously applied by Cuba's Teatro Escambray, set up by director Sergio Corrieri in 1968 as 'an effective weapon at the service of the Revolution'. The production of *The Judgment (El Juicio*, 1973) was inspired by a real-life counter-revolutionary insurrection in a small mountain community where the group had settled. Interview data was collected from the area, with questions concentrated on how society should treat an individual opposed to the revolution. Corrieri then developed a script with the actors through improvisations. The actual performance was in the form of a trial, with the audience seated in a semi-circle. Before the start of the show, six members of the audience were chosen as a 'jury' and came on stage to listen to witnesses and to 'judge' a man accused of counter-revolutionary activities. After the hearing, the 'jury' met backstage to decide his fate and deliver its 'verdict'.

There have been numerous variations of New Theatre, the most notable by the Brazilian Augusto Boal and the Nicaraguan Alan Bolt. But New Theatre and 'collective creation' techniques have been attacked on many grounds. A common criticism (and one which Mario Vargas Llosa voices in his interview in this volume) is that neglect of the text produces an ephemerality in the work that impoverishes the theatre. A second criticism has been that egalitarianism within groups rarely existed, since the 'power' that was wrested from the writer was merely transferred to the director. Alienation from the community/ audience was a further problem, in that most of the dramatised situations were chosen and set up by groups with their own agendas in mind. Such criticisms significantly weakened the New Theatre movement during the 1980s.

The 'boom' in Latin American novels during this period gave new impetus to the cross-fertilisation between theatre and other literary genres. Gabriel García Márquez' *One Hundred Years of Solitude*, published in 1967, was the first of a series of worldwide successes for novelists like Isabel Allende, Mario Vargas Llosa and Carlos Fuentes. It sent shock-waves throughout Latin American culture, which had shown itself capable of competing independently on a world stage. 'Magic realism' managed to touch nerves that were both universal and specifically Latin American, and became an inspiration for painters and film-makers. Theatrical adaptations of novels and short stories were produced throughout the region, as playwrights and directors sought to appropriate the language, images and structures of prose fiction.

Poetry continued to influence the theatre, often through the collective-creation methods applied by the New Theatre groups. Experimental and university groups used techniques ranging from ballet to Stanislavski's system to devise adaptations of works by popular Latin American poets like Gabriela Mistral and Nicolas Guillén. This was also the time when poet Pablo Neruda's only play *The Gleam and Death of Joaquín Murieta* (*El Fulgor y Muerte de Joaquín Murieta*, 1966) was first produced. It tells the story of a Chilean folk hero who travels to California in the late 19th-century Gold Rush. The 'Yankees' mistreat Joaquín in the mines and rape and murder his beloved wife, Teresa. Joaquín becomes a bandit and with his gang steals the Yankees' gold. Joaquín is ambushed and shot when he visits Teresa's grave. The Yankees then charge the public a fee to gaze at his decapitated body. This story is told in six scenes through a mixture of verse narration, choral interludes, prose dialogue, and song. Joaquín only appears once in the play, after his death, when his head begs Pablo Neruda to sing for him. In his preface, Neruda says: 'This is a tragedy, but it is also partly written as a joke. It seeks to be a melodrama, an opera and a pantomime.' Neruda says the inspiration for the play was a funeral scene he saw in a Noh play, adding: 'I never had any idea what that Japanese play was about. I hope the same thing happens to the audience of this tragedy.'

1980-1996

Most of Latin America embraced liberal democracy in the 1980s and 1990s, and by 1996 only Cuba remained outside this political fold. Some theatre practitioners could not cope with the new pluralism after years of rigid regulation. Those who had harboured hopes of popular revolutions despaired as socialism crumbled in Eastern Europe. Other dramatists used the changes and actively supported democratisation, usually by turning theatrical spotlights onto the horrors of past military dictatorships, a trend exemplified in Ariel Dorfman's *Death and the Maiden* (*La Muerte y La Doncella*, 1991), a film version of which was directed by Roman Polanski in 1994.

Thematic concerns shifted with the times. Issues such as class conflict, military oppression, revolution, and US imperialism no longer excited dramatists as they had done in the 1960s and 1970s. The focus moved from the socio-political to the inter-personal, concentrating on themes of sexuality, gender, personal identity, and the influence of the mass media, as reflected in the plays by Fuentes and Vargas Llosa in this volume.

Carlos Fuentes was born in Mexico City in 1929, grew up in
Washington DC and studied at universities in Mexico and Switzerland.
He is an extraordinary polymath: a highly acclaimed novelist, writer of
screenplays, editor, historian, political thinker, teacher and ambassador
for his country. The first of his three plays, *All the Cats Are Lame*
(*Todos los gatos son pardos*, 1970), is a complex socio-historical
portrayal of the Spanish invasion of Mexico, revolving around the
conflict between the Aztec leader Montezuma II and Hernán Cortés.
The Blind Man is King (*El Tuerto es rey*, 1970) concerns a blind lady
and her blind servant, who await the return of the lady's husband, both
of them terrified that the other has sight. The third play, *Orchids in the
Moonlight*, is a stunning portrait of the intricacies of human fantasy
and the impact of the moving image.

Mario Vargas Llosa was born in Arequipa, Peru in 1936. He spent
his first ten years in Bolivia where his grandfather was a diplomat,
and later studied law at the University of San Marcos in Lima. Like
Paz and Fuentes, he has many professional identities: novelist,
critic, essayist, TV journalist, and Peruvian presidential candidate.
He has written five plays to date. No copy survives of *El Inca*, his
first play which he wrote while studying in Peru. His second, written
some 25 years later, is *The Young Lady from Tacna* (*La Señorita de
Tacna*, 1981), a dramatisation of the process of storytelling. It was
followed by *Kathie and the Hippopotamus* (*Kathie y el Hipopótamo,*
1983), a comedy about a Parisian housewife who hires a writer to
record her invented memories. *Mistress of Desires* was written two
years later. Finally, *The Madman of the Balconies* (*El Loco de los
Balcones*, 1993) tells the story of an old professor whose obsession
with preserving the colonial balconies of Lima drives his beloved
daughter to desert him – an interesting parallel to the storyline of
Paz's *Rappaccini's Daughter*.

The self-searching that preoccupied dramatists like Vargas Llosa and
Fuentes in the 1980s and 1990s marked a change in the nature of
'autonomous theatre'. The use of anthropology as a method of
exploring both personal and cultural identity proved to be a rich new
source of inspiration. This was encouraged by the activities of three
European-based institutions: Eugenio Barba's International School of
Theatre Anthropology which was founded in Denmark; Jerzy
Grotowski's Laboratory Theatre in Poland; and Peter Brook's International Centre of Theatre Research in France. Many Latin Americans
read about, or worked at, these establishments, and then developed
their own related ideas. The Cuban theatre group Teatro Buendía
places anthropology at the centre of its rehearsal method. During its
investigation of the Afro-Cuban religion of *santería*, the group found
that the rhythms of the *batá* drums, which *santería* believers consider
to be the intermediaries between the human and the divine, can induce
a state of trance. The group now uses trance as a preparation technique
for creating a form of theatre that is both in close contact with its own

cultural roots and which can communicate successfully across national
boundaries, as demonstrated in the critical and public acclaim that
greeted its tours in Europe and the Far East in the 1990s.

A few of these anthropological projects have resulted in written texts.
The Mexican Compañía Nacional de Teatro collaborated with the
playwright Sergio Magaña to record *The Enemies* (*Los Enemigos*,
1990). This extraordinary text portrays the attempts of the 19th-
century priest Charles Brasseur to stage the *Rabinal Achí*. The story
begins just after Brasseur's first transcription of the piece from oral
tradition. Proud of his work, Brasseur wants to see the play staged in
an 'authentic' way, as opposed to the folkloric representations of the
time. The Indians refuse to participate until he agrees to pay them and
to allow the performance to be staged in the nave of the local church.
The Indians then perform an 'authentic' version of the *Rabinal Achí*,
which ends in the actual sacrifice of the actor playing the Quiché
Warrior on the church altar. Appalled by what he has done, Brasseur
flees the village while the locals honour the sacrificed actor. The
production was based on extensive anthropological research into the
dress, music, dance and gestural languages both of the 19th century
and of the *Rabinal Achí* itself, and on European understanding and
portrayal of the Mayans. The story was told through the eyes of
Brasseur, a European, so that the rituals took on an exotic and
primitive quality. For the mainly Mexican audience, it was only
'authentic' in the sense that it depicted the ways Europeans perceived
indigenous cultures.

Some of the work that has come out of anthropological research can be
properly described as 'post-modern'. Post-modernism, according to
Jean-François Lyotard who coined the term, means a sceptical attitude
towards overarching explanations of the world. In the theatre, this
scepticism is directed at any universalising theories of drama, such as
the Christian or socialist suggestions that theatre should be used as a
tool for social change, or the Aristotelian notion that effective drama
can only be produced if the unities of time, place and action are
maintained. Post-modernism is also characterised by linguistic
playfulness and by referentiality, which tends to mean multiple
quotations from other texts, genres, and from the works themselves.
A good example of a post-modern Latin American play is *Timeball*
(1991) by the Cuban Joel Cano. This mosaic-like work shows radical
scepticism towards theatrical norms. Instead of a logical narrative
progression, there are 52 scenes which must be 'shuffled' before each
performance, so that they will always be presented in a different order.
Cano describes this genre as 'theatrical fortune-telling'. The play
contains many cultural references, including 'appearances' by Charlie
Chaplin, John Lennon, Lenin, and Marilyn Monroe. Cano also
expresses an ironic attitude towards the dramatic unities, setting the
play in 1933, 1970 and 'no time', and alternating the action between a
stable, a park, a circus and a stadium.

In the 1990s Latin America once again flourishes as a rich seedbed for exciting new plays; but the region's theatre also faces enormous problems. As in most parts of the world, no problem is more acute than the shortage of funding. In the 1980s and 1990s, governments cut back finance for the theatre, especially for training. It is difficult for a Latin American playwright to make a living as runs are short, and revenues divided many ways. Financial temptations lure many good writers into television and to richer pastures in Europe or the USA. In addition, Latin American audiences remain generally conservative in their tastes, and a playwright devoted to non-commercial or 'autonomous' theatre always risks alienating the very people whose material support he depends on. Economic self-censorship has, at the end of the 20th century, taken the place of the almost extinct direct political censorship of the theatre.

Selecting and Translating the Plays

The five plays included in this book may all be described as being within the tradition of autonomous theatre. Their principal characters express a desire for freedom and a spirit of resistance to oppressive authority: Lalo in *Night of the Assassins* and Beatrice in *Rappaccini's Daughter* share a yearning for a life outside the suffocating confines of their homes; La Chunga in *Mistress of Desires* and Dolores in *Orchids in the Moonlight* bravely search for dignity in the face of violent male chauvinism; and the Man in *Saying Yes* strives to overcome his cowardice and passivity and to confront the hairdresser's callousness. Although the characters often fail tragically in their bids for freedom, they encourage the belief that we are all capable of changing our lives for the better if we overcome fear.

The playwrights make bold formal choices, some of them remarkably similar. They all reject straightforward naturalism, and they avoid a linear narrative in favour of broadly circular structures, so that in every play the ending mirrors the beginning in some way: the Boys repeat their ritual song at the end of *Mistress of Desires*, the Hairdresser is reading his magazine again in *Saying Yes*, the Messenger re-addresses the audience in *Rappaccini's Daughter*, Beba prepares to lead a new game in *Night of the Assassins*, and Dolores repeats her opening complaint in *Orchids in the Moonlight*. Such endings resolve nothing, and the writers run the risk that their audiences will accept the ambiguities left at the end at face value; yet such ambiguities provide audiences with questions that they must try to answer for themselves in order to finish the plays: Where is Meche? Are Maria and Dolores awake or dreaming? Does the antidote kill Beatrice or release her into the outside world? Could the siblings really kill their parents? Why does the Hairdresser kill the Man? The plays also have certain images in common, particularly those of the mirror and the labyrinth. Labyrinths feature in all the plays except *Saying Yes*, and have fascinated Latin American writers stretching back to Sor Juana and her secular comedy *Love is the Greater Labyrinth* (*Amor es Más Laberinto*, 1688).

The plays are also individually distinctive in many respects. Their sources, language, and action are as individual as the writers themselves. Moreover, since each play was written at a different time during the second half of the 20th century, each reflects the social and political concerns of its particular moment. *Rappaccini's Daughter* mirrors the terror of technological progress and the nuclear threat that stalked the 1950s; the 1960s hope of revolution is a principal theme of *Night of the Assassins*; the political violence and global terrorism of the 1970s provides the dark backdrop to *Saying Yes*; and social scientists, writers and film-makers were exploring issues concerning personal identity and sexuality when *Orchids in the Moonlight* and *Mistress of Desires* were written.

The starting point for translation of the plays was always the individual words, and they have been translated as transparently as possible. The translation of Spanish poetry in the plays treats the word as more significant than the rhyme or metre: this is especially reflected in *Rappaccini's Daughter* and in the blank verse translation of Sandoval y Zapata's sonnet in *Orchids in the Moonlight*. Words which are peculiar in the original Spanish, moreover, are translated that way into English, as in the use of 'marmots' in *Saying Yes*, or in Catholic expletives like 'Holy Whore!' in *Mistress of Desires*.

The English versions have benefited enormously from being read and amended by the playwrights themselves, all of whom are familiar with the English language. The authors' insights have helped ensure accurate renderings of the actual Spanish words, which also echo the intentions behind the original texts. Mario Vargas Llosa, for example, explained that the name La Chunga refers to a strong, lower-class woman in 1940s Peru; while discussions with Carlos Fuentes excavated many of the cinematic references in *Orchids in the Moonlight*.

Sometimes a literal translation cannot convey a sound or rhythm essential to the original. In these cases, alternative choices have been made, retaining associations to the original. This 'associative' approach was taken in the translation of the Boys' song in *Mistress of Desires*, and in the allusions to nursery rhymes in *Night of the Assassins*. The actual staging of the plays was always viewed as an integral part of the translation process, and production has enriched all these texts. Hearing the words onstage opened the way for a greater immediacy in the translation.

Select Bibliography:

J.J. Arrom, *Historia del Teatro hispanoamericano: época colonial*, Mexico, 1967; P. Beardsell, *A Theatre for Cannibals: Rodolfo Usigli and the Mexican Stage*, London & Toronto, 1992; W. Benjamin, *Illuminations*, Fontana, 1992; Raul H. Castagnino, *El Teatro de Roberto Arlt*, Buenos Aires, 1964; F. Colecchia & J. Matas, *Selected Latin American One-Act Plays*, Pittsburg, 1973; Sor Juana Ines de la Cruz, *Obras Completas*, Mexico, 1992; W.K. Jones, *Behind Spanish American footlights*, Austin, 1966; *Latin American Theatre Review*; *New Theatre Quarterly*; R. Leal, *Breve Historia del Teatro Cubano*, Havana 1980; O. Paz, *Sor Juana or The Traps of Faith*, Harvard, 1988; C. Solorzano, *El teatro latinoamericano en el siglo XX*, Mexico, 1964; D. Taylor, *Theatre of Crisis: Drama and Politics in Latin America*, Kentucky, 1991; R. Unger, *Poesía en alta voz in the Theatre of Mexico*, Missouri, 1981; A. Versényi, *Theatre in Latin America*, Cambridge, 1992.

Acknowledgments

Thanks are due to numerous people for their support and assistance over this four-year project. I am especially grateful to the playwrights for their advice and collaboration on the translations and stagings.

Many thanks also to a number of people who gave generously of their time to read and make suggestions on drafts of the text, particularly Kate Berney, Caroline Voûte, Mark Hawkins-Dady, Catherine Boyle, Montserrat Guibernau, Tilly Franklin, William Brandt, Tom Hiney, Gaye Wilkins, Jeremy White, Eliot Weinberger and Zoë Crawshaw.

In addition, I am indebted to all the performers, designers, musicians, producers and technicians who channelled their creative energies into the staging of the plays and brought them to life in the process. I am also deeply grateful to those institutions and individuals who provided the material resources for the productions, especially Tony Doggart, the Southern Development Trust, Drama King's, the Gertrude Kingston Fund, the Esmée Fairbairn Trust and Ann Toettcher.

Thank you, finally, to all those who gave encouragement and inspiration of a personal nature particularly Jane Toettcher, Dadie Rylands, Rupert Gatti, Susan Melrose, Graham McCann, David Lehmann, Nike Doggart, Hugo Jackson, Flora Lauten, Carlos Celdrán and Natalia Gil Torner.

This book is dedicated to my parents and grandparents.

S.D., May 1996

RAPPACCINI'S DAUGHTER

by Octavio Paz

La Hija de Rappaccini was written in 1956. This translation of *Rappaccini's Daughter* was first performed at the Gate Theatre, London on 21 January 1996, with the following cast:[1]

MESSENGER	Gabrielle Jourdan
ISABELA (*an old servant*)	Kay D'Arcy
RAPPACCINI (*a famous scholar*)	Kevin Colson
BEATRICE (*his daughter*)	Sarah Alexander
BAGLIONI (*a university doctor*)	John O'Byrne
GIOVANNI (*a student from Naples*)	Jud Charlton

Director Sebastian Doggart
Designer Tom Harrison

A one-act play, based on a short story by Nathaniel Hawthorne.

To Leonora Carrington

Prologue

The garden of DR. RAPPACCINI. *At one side, part of an old
building where* GIOVANNI's *room is. The stage is set so that
the audience can see inside the room: tall and narrow, a large
mirror covered with dust, a desolate atmosphere. Flanked by
worn curtains, a balcony opens on to the garden. A magical
tree stands centre stage. As the curtain rises, the stage remains
in darkness, except in the space occupied by* THE MESSENGER,
*a hermaphroditic character dressed like one of the Tarot figures,
though not any particular one.*

THE MESSENGER. My name does not matter. Nor does my
origin. In fact, I don't have a name, or a sex, or an age, or a
country. Man or woman; young or old; yesterday or
tomorrow; north or south; the two genders, the three tenses,
the four ages and the four cardinal points converge in me
and in me dissolve. My soul is transparent: if you peer into it
you will sink into a cold and dizzy clarity; and you will find
nothing of me at the bottom. Nothing except the image of
your desire, that until now you did not know. I am the
meeting place; all roads lead to me. Space! Pure space, null
and void! I am here, but I am also there; everything is here,
everything is there; I am at every electric point in space and
in every charged fragment of time: yesterday is today;
tomorrow, today; everything which was, everything which
shall be, is happening right now, here on earth or there in the
heavens. The meeting: two gazes which cross until they are
no more than a glowing point, two wills which entwine and
form a knot of flames.

Unions and separations: souls that unite and form a
constellation which sings for a fraction of a second in the
centre of time, worlds which break up like the seeds of a
pomegranate scattered on the grass.

Takes out a Tarot card.[2]

And here, at the centre of the dance, as the constant star,
I have the Queen of the Night, the lady of hell, who governs

the growth of the plants, the pull of the tides and the shifting of the sky; moon huntress, shepherdess of the dead in the underground valleys; mother of harvests and springs, who sleeps for half the year and then awakes resplendent in bracelets of water, sometimes golden, sometimes dark.

Takes out two cards.

And here we have her enemies: the King of this world, seated on a throne of manure and money, the book of laws and the moral code lying on his trembling knees, the whip within his reach – the just and virtuous King, who gives to Caesar what is Caesar's and denies the Spirit what is the Spirit's. And facing him the Hermit: worshipper of the triangle and the sphere, learned in Chaldean writings and ignorant of the language of blood, lost in his labyrinth of syllogisms, prisoner of himself.

Takes out another card.

And here we have the Minstrel, the young man; asleep, his head resting on his own childhood. He hears the Lady's night-time song and wakes. Guided by that song, he walks over the abyss with his eyes shut, balancing on the tightrope. He walks with confidence in search of his dream and his steps lead towards me, I who do not exist. If he slips, he will fall headlong. And here is the last card; the Lovers. Two figures, one the colour of day, the other the colour of night. Two paths. Love is choice: death or life?

THE MESSENGER *exits.*

Scene I

The garden remains in darkness. The room is lit by a dim light; the balcony curtain is drawn.

ISABELA (*comes in and shows the room*). We're here at last, my young sir. (*Reacting to his dispirited silence.*) It's years since anyone has lived here, which is why it feels abandoned. But you will give it life. The walls are strong . . .

GIOVANNI. Perhaps too strong. High and thick . . .

ISABELA. Good for keeping out the noise from the street. Nothing better for a young student.

GIOVANNI. Thick and damp. It will be hard to get used to the damp and the silence, though there are some who say thought feeds on solitude.

ISABELA. I promise that you'll soon feel at home.

GIOVANNI. In Naples my room was big and my bed was as tall and spacious as a ship. Every night when I closed my eyes, I sailed over nameless seas, unsettled lands, continents of shadow and fog. At times, I was frightened by the idea of never coming back and I saw myself lost and alone in the middle of a black ocean. But my bed slid with silent certainty over the crest of the night, and every morning I was deposited on the same happy shore. I slept with the window open; at daybreak the sun and the sea breeze would spill into my room.

ISABELA. Well, there's no sea in Padua. But we've got gardens. The most beautiful in Italy.

GIOVANNI (*to himself*). The sea and the sun on the sea. This room is too dark.

ISABELA. That's because the curtains are closed. When they're open, the light dazzles you.

She opens the curtains, and the garden appears before the audience, lit up.

GIOVANNI (*dazzled*). Now that is something! What a golden light! (*Walks to the balcony.*) And there's a garden. Does it belong to the house?

ISABELA. It used to be part of the palace. Now it's owned by the famous Doctor Rappaccini.

GIOVANNI (*leaning over the balcony*). That is not a garden. At least, not a Neapolitan garden. It's like a bad dream.

ISABELA. A lot of people say that, sir. But don't be alarmed. Doctor Rappaccini doesn't grow ordinary flowers; everything you see is medicinal plants and herbs.

GIOVANNI. And yet the air is delicious. Cool and warm at the same time, subtle and light; it has no weight and scarcely any fragrance. I must admit that even if he knows nothing of the art of pleasing the eye, this Rappaccini certainly understands the secrets of perfume. What kind of a man is he?

ISABELA. A wise man, a very wise man. They say there's no other doctor like him. And they say other things . . .

GIOVANNI. What things?

ISABELA. You must judge for yourself, sir. You'll see him today or tomorrow, from this balcony. Every day he goes out to tend to his plants. Sometimes his daughter goes with him.

GIOVANNI. No, I'm certain I won't like him. (*Draws the curtain.*) And Rappaccini's daughter? Is she like her father?

ISABELA. Beatrice is one of the most beautiful creatures these old eyes have ever seen. Many men admire her, but from far away, because her father doesn't let them near her. And she is shy. The minute she sees a stranger, she disappears. Can I do anything else for you, sir? I'd be happy to serve you in any way I can. You're so young and handsome. And you must feel so lonely . . .

GIOVANNI. Thank you but no, Isabela. Solitude does no harm.

ISABELA *exits.*

Scene II

GIOVANNI. I shall try to get used to this cave. As long as it doesn't turn me into a bat.

He goes over to the mirror and blows away a layer of dust. He imitates the movements of a bat, laughs, then is serious. At this moment ISABELA *comes in, which surprises him.*

ISABELA. Excuse the interruption, sir. I felt so bad leaving you all alone, so I decided to bring you this bouquet of roses. Maybe they'll cheer you up. I picked them myself this morning.

GIOVANNI (*takes the flowers*). Thank you, Isabela, thank you very much.

ISABELA *exits.*

GIOVANNI. What a kind gesture! They are beautiful, but I don't have anyone to give them to.

He throws them into the air, smiles, picks them up, goes over to the mirror, looks at himself with delight, bows, offers the flowers to an imaginary girl and pirouettes. Motionless, he hesitates; then he jumps up, opens the curtains and leans over the balcony. He spots RAPPACCINI, *and positions himself so that he can spy on the garden unobserved.*

Scene III

RAPPACCINI *examines the plants. Leans over a flower.*

RAPPACCINI. Just looking at you makes you blush like a shy little girl. What sensitivity! And what a flirt you are! You're going red but you're well armed: if someone touches you, they would soon see their skin covered in a rash of blue spots. (*Jumps up and sees some other plants, intertwined.*) The lovers, kissing like an adulterous couple. (*Separates them and picks one.*) You are going to be very lonely from now on, and your fierce desire will provoke a restless, parched madness in anyone that smells you: the madness of mirrors! (*Jumps up and sees another plant.*) Are you life or death? (*Shrugs his shoulders.*) Who knows? And aren't they the same thing? When we are born our body starts to die; when we die, it starts to live . . . a different sort of life. Who could dare say that a corpse is dead? You should ask the worms' opinion. They will say that they have never enjoyed better health. Poisons and antidotes, they are one and the same. Deadly nightshade, monkshood, hemlock, black henbane, hellebore. What an endless wealth of forms and what a variety of effects. The poisonous milk caps, the lecherous mandrake, mildew, the false Morel, the hypocritical coralline, the death cap and Satan's boletus. And by their side, separated by a millimetre on the scale of the species, the lycopodium and the lungwort, oriental moss and verdigris agaric, terror of all cooks. And yet the principle remains the same: a small change, a slight alteration and a poison becomes an elixir of life. Death and life: names, names![3] (*Jumps up again and stands in front of the tree.*) Beatrice, child!

BEATRICE *appears at the door and comes forward.*

BEATRICE. Here I am, father.

RAPPACCINI. Look how our tree has grown. Every day taller and more elegant. And heavy with fruit.

BEATRICE (*in front of the tree*). He's so beautiful! So handsome! My little brother, how you have grown. (*Hugs the tree, placing her cheek against the trunk.*) You don't speak but you answer in your own way: your sap flows faster. (*To her father.*) I can hear it throbbing, as if he were alive.

RAPPACCINI. He is alive.

BEATRICE. I meant alive like you and me. Alive like a child. (*Holds up a leaf and inhales it.*) Let me breathe in your perfume and steal some of your life!

RAPPACCINI. I was just saying to myself: what is life to some is death to others. We only see half the sphere. But the sphere is made of life and death. If I could hit on the right measures and proportions, I could infuse portions of life into death; then the two halves could unite and we would be as gods. If my experiment . . .

BEATRICE. No! Don't talk to me about that! I'm content with my fate and I'm happy in this garden, with these plants. They are my only family! And yet sometimes I would like to hold a rose and smell it; lace my hair with jasmine; or pick a daisy's petals without them catching fire in my hands.

RAPPACCINI. Roses, daisies, violets, carnations: a frost wilts such plants, a breeze strips them bare. Ours are immortal.

BEATRICE. Fragile! That is why they are adorable! Gardens buzzing with blue flies and yellow bees; grass singing with crickets and cicadas . . . In our garden there are no birds, or insects or baby lizards sunning on the fences, no chameleons, no pigeons . . .

RAPPACCINI. Enough, enough. You can't have everything. And our plants are better. Their unexpected shapes have the beauty of feverish visions; their growth is as sure and fatal as the slow progress of a mysterious illness. Flowers and fruits shining like jewels. But emeralds, diamonds, and rubies are all inert matter, dead stones. Our jewels are alive. Fire flows through their veins and changes colour like the light in underwater caverns. Garden of fire! Garden where life and death embrace and exchange their secrets!

BEATRICE. Yes, all that is true . . . but I would like to have a cat and stroke his back until he turns into a soft electric ball. I would like to have a chameleon and put him on my skirt and watch him change colour. A cat, a chameleon, a green and yellow parrot who jumps on my shoulder and shouts: 'Who's a pretty girl then?' A little bird that I can hide between my breasts. I would like . . . (*Sobs.*)

RAPPACCINI. Don't cry, child. I'm too sensitive and I can't bear to see suffering in others. I would drink your tears . . .

BEATRICE (*angrily*). You can't, you know you can't. They would burn you like aqua regia. (*To the tree.*) Only you, my brother, only you can soak up my tears. (*Hugs the tree.*) Take my weeping, take a long draught of my life and give me a little of yours. (*Picks a fruit and eats it.*) Sorry for eating you; it's as if I were eating a piece of myself. (*Laughs.*)

RAPPACCINI (*to himself*). There, that's got that over with! (*Shrugs his shoulders and exits.*)

BEATRICE (*to the tree*). I'm ashamed, brother. How can I complain? No other girl in the city can wander through a garden like this one, or breathe in these perfumes or eat the fruit that I eat. When I come here, I feel as if I'm entering into myself. The air envelops me like a vast impalpable body, the vapour of the plants is as warm as the smell of a pure mouth, the moisture strokes me. I suffocate over there in the house, my head starts to pound, I get dizzy. If you could walk you would sleep with me: your breath would dissolve all my nightmares. If you could walk, we could stroll together through the garden; if you could talk, we could tell each other things and laugh together. (*Strokes the tree.*) You would be tall and handsome. You would have white teeth. The hair on your chest would be a handful of herbs. Tall and serious. And there would be no danger of you liking anyone else: you couldn't. And neither could I. (*To herself.*) I'm condemned to wandering in this garden, alone, talking to myself. (*To the tree.*) Talk to me, say something, even just 'good afternoon'.

GIOVANNI (*appearing on the balcony*). Good afternoon!

BEATRICE (*runs away, stifling a scream, but then returns and curtsies*). Good afternoon!

GIOVANNI (*throwing her down the bouquet*). They are freshly cut roses. If you smell them, they will tell you my name.

BEATRICE. Thank you, sir. My name is Beatrice.

GIOVANNI: And my name is Giovanni, I come from Naples
    and these roses . . .

> BEATRICE *picks up the roses, hides them in her breast,*
> *and exits running, leaving* GIOVANNI *in mid-sentence.*
> *The lights fade to black.*

Scene IV

The stage is in shadows. GIOVANNI'*s room is dimly lit. He*
mimes the words of THE MESSENGER.

THE MESSENGER. Let him sleep, and while he sleeps, let
    him battle with himself. Has he noticed that the bouquet of
    roses turned black the moment Beatrice took them in her
    arms, as if they had been struck by lightning? In the
    trembling twilight, and with his head spinning from the
    scents of the garden, it is not easy to distinguish a dry rose
    from one freshly cut. Let him sleep! Sleep! Dream of the sea
    covered by the sun's red and purple streaks, dream of green
    hills, run along the beach . . . No, every time you dream, you
    move further away from familiar landscapes. You wander
    through a city carved out of rock crystal. You are thirsty and
    thirst breeds patterned hallucinations. Lost in transparent
    corridors, you cross circular squares, terraces where
    melancholy obelisks watch over mercury fountains, streets
    that lead into the same street. Walls of glass close in and
    imprison you; your image is reflected a thousand times in a
    thousand mirrors which are themselves reflected a thousand
    times in another thousand mirrors. You are condemned
    never to leave yourself, condemned to search for yourself in
    glass-fronted galleries, always in view, never attainable:
    whatever is there before you, whoever looks at you with
    eyes pleading for a signal, a sign of brotherhood and
    recognition, that is not you, but your image. Condemned to
    sleep with your eyes open. Close them, go back, back to the
    darkness, beyond your infancy, further back, back to the
    source! Waves of time crashing against your soul! Row
    against them, row back, ride through the current, close your
    eyes, go down towards the seed. Someone has closed your
    eyelids. The transparent prison shatters, the crystal walls lie
    at your feet, transformed into a pool of still water. Drink

without fear, sleep, sail, let yourself be guided by the river of closed eyes. Morning will be born at your side.

Scene V

ISABELA. Sir, Doctor Baglioni wants to see you.

GIOVANNI. What, Doctor Baglioni, my father's friend?

ISABELA. The great doctor, sir, the star of the university.

GIOVANNI. Show him in, show him in! Or rather, ask him to wait a moment. I'll tidy myself up a bit and then meet him in the sitting room.

BAGLIONI (*entering*). No need, dear boy. Your father was my room-mate and study partner in this very city. His son is my son.

ISABELA *curtsies and leaves without speaking.*

GIOVANNI. Your visit has caught me off guard, sir. Please forgive the emptiness of this poor student room. Circumstances . . .

BAGLIONI. I understand everything and I forgive everything. At last, my friend, you are in Padua and the spitting image of your father.

GIOVANNI. I am touched by your kindness, doctor. I will tell you the reason for my trip: I came with the intention of studying law; I arrived yesterday and couldn't afford anywhere to stay apart from this poor room which you now honour with your presence . . .

BAGLIONI. It looks like a beautiful view: there is a garden next door.

GIOVANNI. A unique garden. I have never seen anything like it. It belongs to the famous Rappaccini.

BAGLIONI. Rappaccini?

GIOVANNI. I'm told he is a wise man, the master of marvellous natural secrets.

BAGLIONI. I see you know a lot about our luminaries, even those who don't deserve that description. In fact, Rappaccini is a genuine man of science. Nobody at the university can rival him . . . with just one exception.

GIOVANNI. You clearly know him then. Living together in the same city and sharing a love of science, you must be very good friends.

BAGLIONI. Steady on, impetuous boy. Rappaccini loves science, I grant you. But the very violence of that love, or some monstruous amorality, I don't know which, has overshadowed his soul. Men are instruments to him, opportunities for dubious experiments which, I have to say, are almost always unsuccessful.

GIOVANNI. He must be a dangerous man.

BAGLIONI. He is.

GIOVANNI. But what an amazing way to love science!

BAGLIONI. My dear boy, science was made for man, not man for science.

GIOVANNI. Which doesn't stop Rappaccini discovering some surprising cures.

BAGLIONI. He has been lucky at times. On the other hand, I know of some instances . . . But why are you so interested in your mysterious neighbour? You're not feeling ill, I hope?

GIOVANNI. I have never felt better. Last night, for example, I left the door to the balcony open and slept like a log.

BAGLIONI. The air in Padua is very pure . . . As for Rappaccini . . .

GIOVANNI. It is natural that since I have just arrived in this city his personality should have aroused my curiosity. He is my neighbour. And people talk so much about his extraordinary love for science.

BAGLIONI. I wish people would talk more about the consequences of that foolish love.

GIOVANNI (*violently*). There is an object on earth more precious to Rappaccini than all his science, and for it he would sacrifice all his knowledge.

BAGLIONI. What's that?

GIOVANNI. His daughter.

BAGLIONI. At last, my dear boy, I have discovered your secret! So, the beautiful Beatrice is the real reason behind all these questions!

GIOVANNI. I have hardly spoken to her, only yesterday afternoon.

BAGLIONI. No, no need to apologise. I don't know the girl. I've been told that several young men of Padua would kill for her . . . even though they've never met her. I've also been told that she is not just a paragon of beauty, but also a fountain of knowledge, capable in spite of her years of holding a professorship at the university. (*Laughs.*) Mine maybe . . . But that's enough idle gossip. (*Walks to the balcony.*) What a gloomy garden.

GIOVANNI. It may seem wrong to us, but you cannot deny that this garden displays a love – how can I put it – a wild love for truth, a passion for the infinite. That's why it makes your head spin.

BAGLIONI. Shh! Rappaccini just walked into his garden.

RAPPACCINI *comes out and examines the plants. Feeling himself watched, he raises his head and fixes his eyes on the balcony.* BAGLIONI *greets him coldly, but receives no reply. For a moment,* RAPPACCINI *stares at* GIOVANNI, *ignoring* BAGLIONI. *Then he exits.*

BAGLIONI. He saw us and didn't even condescend to return my greeting. He can't have recognised me; he just saw you. Does he know you?

GIOVANNI. How could he know me if I have just arrived.

BAGLIONI. I don't know, but I'll swear he is interested in you. A . . . scientific interest. And what role does Beatrice have in this conspiracy?

GIOVANNI. Professor, don't you think you're taking this a bit far? Neither father nor daughter know that I exist.

BAGLIONI. You never know with Rappaccini. I will reflect on what I have just seen. I don't want anything to happen to the son of an old friend.

GIOVANNI. What do you mean, sir?

BAGLIONI. Nothing, for the moment. Just a suspicion . . . and yet, almost a certainty. But it must be getting late and I'm expected at the university. Will I have the pleasure of seeing you at my home soon?

GIOVANNI. I would be honoured, Doctor Baglioni.

BAGLIONI. Then goodbye for now.

BAGLIONI *exits.* GIOVANNI *goes over to the balcony. Before he gets there* BAGLIONI *returns.*

BAGLIONI. The net that holds you is invisible but it can strangle you. If you help me, I will tear it apart!

BAGLIONI *exits.*

Scene VI

GIOVANNI *remains pensive. He waves aside his thoughts, walks out on to the balcony, goes back inside, paces about, goes back to the balcony and, his mind made up, jumps down into the garden. He examines the plants with curiosity and suspicion. All of his movements are those of an intruder and, at the same time, of a man who is wary of unseen dangers. He leans over to look at a flower. At this moment* BEATRICE *appears.*

BEATRICE. Good morning! I see our neighbour is also interested in flowers and plants.

GIOVANNI. I can't apologise enough for my impudence. I'm not a troublemaker; the truth is I was fascinated by this unusual vegetation; I couldn't resist the temptation. Almost without thinking I jumped down . . . And here I am!

BEATRICE. Don't apologise. I understand your curiosity and I am sure that my father wouldn't mind either. For him, curiosity is the mother of all science.

GIOVANNI. I don't want to lie to you. I'm not interested in botany and the mysteries of nature do not keep me awake at night. I came to Padua to study law. Fate has made us neighbours and yesterday I saw you – do you remember – strolling among all these plants. It was then I discovered my true vocation.

BEATRICE. I have to admit I don't quite understand you. Just one look at the garden and you discovered your vocation? Well, my father will be very proud . . .

GIOVANNI. No, not the garden. I recognised you, among so many unknown plants. You were as familiar to me as a flower, and yet also remote. Life budding between the rocks of a desert, with the simplicity with which spring surprises us every year. My whole being blossomed. My head, so long a sad engine of confused thoughts, melted into a lake. Since then, I have not thought: I reflect. Eyes open or eyes closed, I see only your image.

BEATRICE. I am not familiar with the customs of the world. I have lived on my own since I was a little girl, and I don't know how to reply. I don't know how to lie either. And even if I did know how, I would never lie. Your words have confused me, but they have not surprised me. I was expecting them, I knew that you had to say them . . . today or tomorrow.

GIOVANNI. Beatrice!

BEATRICE. How strange my name sounds on your lips! Nobody has ever pronounced it like that.

GIOVANNI. It's a bird. I say: Beatrice, and it opens its wings and starts to fly. Where to I don't know. Away from here . . .

BEATRICE. When I saw you, it was as if many doors were opening. I was surrounded, walled in. Suddenly, a gust of wind blew the doors and windows open, and they made me want to jump and dance. Last night I felt I was flying. But I landed here, in the garden. I felt that the scents of all these plants had been woven together into a net of invisible threads, which softly, smoothly enveloped me. I am tied to the ground. I am one of these plants. If I am picked, I will die. Go away, leave me here!

GIOVANNI (*drawing aside the imaginary net of perfumes*). I will cut a path through this thicket of perfumes. I will tear down the tangled branches of the invisible wood. With my nails and teeth I will dig a tunnel beneath the wall. I will become a sword and with one slash will cut the curtain in two. I will untie the knot. I will show you the world. We will go south. The sea will swell up from her bed to greet you and will wave her plume of salt. The pine trees on my street will bow down at your footfall . . .

BEATRICE. No, I don't know the world. The open air would suffocate me. (*Points to the garden.*) Its scent gives me life. If I shine, it is because of its light. I am made from its essence. Stay here!

GIOVANNI. To surround you as a river embraces an island, to drink the light that your mouth drinks. You look at me and your eyes weave me a fresh armour of reflections. To travel endlessly over your body, sleep between your breasts, dawn in your throat, sail up the canal of your back, lose myself around your neck, glide down to your belly. Lose myself in you, only to find myself waiting on the other shore. Be born in you, die in you.

BEATRICE. Spin tirelessly around you, me the planet and you the sun

GIOVANNI. Facing each other always, like two trees

BEATRICE. Growing, bearing fruit, ripening

GIOVANNI. Entwining our roots

BEATRICE. Entwining our branches

GIOVANNI. One tree

BEATRICE. The sunlight settles in our cup and sings

GIOVANNI. His song is a fan which unfurls itself slowly

BEATRICE. We are made of sun

GIOVANNI. We walk and the world opens up at our footsteps

BEATRICE (*waking up*). No, not that. The world begins in you and ends in you. And this garden is our whole horizon.

GIOVANNI. The world is infinite. It begins at your toenails and ends at the tips of your hair. You have no end.

BEATRICE. When I saw you, I also remembered. I remembered something which had been lost for a long time. But its mark is indelible, like a secret wound; something which suddenly appeared in front of me and said: look at me, remember me, you forgot me at birth, I am here.

GIOVANNI (*staring intently at her*). I would like to breach the wall of your brow and lose myself among your thoughts, get through to you, to your centre. Who are you?

BEATRICE. In my brow you can read all your own thoughts. My brow is a mirror which never tires of reflecting you. Your desire lives inside me. Before knowing you I knew nobody, not even myself. I didn't know that there was a sun, a moon, water, lips. I was one of these plants. I talked to this tree sometimes. He was the only friend I had. Yesterday you gave me some roses . . . What can I give you in return?

GIOVANNI. A bouquet of flowers from this tree. Having them next to my pillow tonight will be like having you there.

Goes up to the tree and reaches out his hand to pick a flower.

BEATRICE. No, don't touch it! It will kill you!

As she says these words, she brushes GIOVANNI's *hand.*
As if she had received an electric shock, she draws back
sharply. BEATRICE *hides her head in her hands, terrified.*
GIOVANNI *tries to approach her. She gestures him away*
and runs to the house. GIOVANNI *tries to follow her, but*
RAPPACCINI *appears in the doorway.*

GIOVANNI. Sorry . . . for being here . . . I'm too confused to
make excuses . . .

RAPPACCINI (*smiling*). You don't have to say sorry to a
neighbour.

GIOVANNI. I came into your garden without thinking,
attracted by these plants. The garden was stronger than my
will. And then I spent too long . . . Maybe I should go.

RAPPACCINI. As you wish. But I warn you, it will be difficult
to go back the way you came. Better if I show you the way
out.

GIOVANNI. Thank you, thank you.

RAPPACCINI (*showing him the way*). This way.

They both exit. Lights fade slowly to black.

Scene VII

A dim light comes up. GIOVANNI *and* BEATRICE *are*
upstage. While THE MESSENGER *speaks, the couple use*
movements and gestures to imitate the actions indicated by
the words.

THE MESSENGER. Distanced from the world, they wander
among the mysterious flowers and breathe in their strange
fumes which unfold like the cloak of delirium and then
evaporate without a trace, as the images of a dream dissolve
in the water of dawn. And in the same way, within a few
hours, there appeared and disappeared on Giovanni's hand –
the same hand that Beatrice had brushed the day before –
five small red blotches, which looked like five tiny flowers.
But they don't ask questions, they don't doubt, they don't
even dream: they contemplate each other, they breathe each
other. Are they breathing death or life? Neither Giovanni nor

Beatrice thinks about death or life, about God or the Devil.
They don't care about saving their souls or gaining wealth or
power, being happy or making others happy. Just looking in
each other's eyes is enough for them. He whirls around her,
and she spins around herself; the circles that he draws get
smaller and smaller; she falls silent and starts to close up
like a flower of the night, petal by petal, until she is
impenetrable. Hesitant, he wavers between desire and
horror, until at last he leans over her; and his helpless gaze
opens her up again and she unfolds and spins around her
beloved, who stays quiet, fascinated. But they never touch,
condemned to spin endlessly, propelled by two enemy
powers, which separate and unite them. No kiss, no caress.
Just eyes devouring eyes.

Scene VIII

The garden is empty. GIOVANNI *and* BAGLIONI *are in the
room.*

BAGLIONI. I hope this isn't a bad time. One of my patients
lives nearby and I thought I might drop round for a few
minutes on my way.

GIOVANNI. Doctor, you will always be welcome here.

BAGLIONI. No, I'm not fooling myself. The young are almost
always bored by the old. We try to encourage them but end
up annoying them. There is no solution. That is life. (*Pause.*)
I have been waiting for you in vain.

GIOVANNI. Doctor, I promise my absence over the last few
days doesn't mean that I have forgotten, it's just that I have
been studying. I spend the whole day studying.

BAGLIONI. Law, history or . . . botany?

GIOVANNI. Languages, doctor, foreign languages.

BAGLIONI. Greek, Latin, Hebrew or . . . the language of
birds? Goodness, what strange and lovely perfume!

GIOVANNI. Perfume?

BAGLIONI. Yes, a perfume, very light but very powerful. It
comes and goes, appears and disappears, it penetrates deep
into the lungs and dissolves in the blood like pure air . . .

GIOVANNI. Sometimes the imagination makes us see things, even smell things . . .

BAGLIONI (*interrupting him*). No, dear boy. This perfume is not a fancy of my spirit but a reality of my nose. I'm serious: the aroma which floods in to your room so intriguingly comes from there! It rises from that garden! And it comes out of your mouth: you exhale it every time you open your lips. Rappaccini and his daughter, the astute Beatrice, administer death to their patients, and it is wrapped in a perfumed mantle!

GIOVANNI. Say what you like about Rappaccini but don't mention Beatrice.

BAGLIONI. Rappaccini is a poisoner and his fatal obsession has led him to a wicked deed: he has turned his own daughter into a phial of poison.

GIOVANNI. You're lying! Beatrice is innocent.

BAGLIONI. Innocent or guilty, that girl lives and breathes death.

GIOVANNI. Beatrice is pure.

BAGLIONI. Accomplice or victim, it makes no difference. What is clear is that Rappaccini has chosen you as the subject of a new and terrible experiment. His daughter is the bait.

GIOVANNI. You're making it up! It's too horrible to be true.

BAGLIONI. And if it were?

GIOVANNI. I would be lost. There would be no escape . . .

BAGLIONI. There is one. We will trick Rappaccini. Here. (*Takes out a phial from his pocket.*) This phial contains an antidote more powerful than the famous Bezoar stone, or the earth of Lemnos, or the syrup of Ipecac.[4] It is the fruit of many sleepless nights and many years of study. If Beatrice is innocent, give it to her to drink. In a short time she will be back to her original self. And now, good-bye! Your fate rests in your own hands.

GIOVANNI *tries to say something.* BAGLIONI *silences him with a finger, gives him the flask and exits.*

Scene IX

GIOVANNI. It's a fairy tale, a jealous fabrication . . . But the bouquet of roses, the marks on my hand? (*Stares at his hand.*) No, nothing. I am in perfect health. I am strong, I love life, life loves me. And if it's true..? How can I find out . . . ? (*Paces around indecisively. Suddenly he shouts.*) Isabela! Madam! Come quickly, I need you!

VOICE OF ISABELA. Coming, coming! (*While* ISABELA *is coming upstairs,* GIOVANNI *looks at himself in the mirror and feels himself.*)

ISABELA: What can I do for you, sir?

GIOVANNI. Nothing, a small thing. Would you get me a rose? Like the ones you gave me the day I arrived.

ISABELA. A rose?

GIOVANNI. Yes, a red rose, a rose with dewdrops on it . . .

ISABELA. Goodness me! The gentleman is in love.

GIOVANNI. A freshly cut rose!

ISABELA. Right away, sir. (*Exits.*)

GIOVANNI. Even if Baglioni is right and Beatrice is fed on poison, I am fit and strong. The air of Naples protects me . . . And if it all turns out to be lies, I will cut out your distinguished tongue, Doctor Baglioni . . .

ISABELA (*holding the rose*). I couldn't find a prettier rose than this. Look at it, it's almost alive!

GIOVANNI (*interrupting her*). Thank you, Isabela. (*Gives her some coins.*) And now leave me, I want to be alone.

ISABELA. My goodness, you're moody! Young men are mad! (*Exits.*)

GIOVANNI (*holding the rose in his hand*). Red rose, little heart trembling in my hands. Thirsty rose. (*Blows on it.*) Revive, breathe in life! (*The rose turns black. Horrified, he drops it.*) It's true, it's true! My breath kills, I'm carrying death in my blood! I'm cursed, cut off from life! A wall of poison separates me from the world . . . and unites me with a monster.

BEATRICE (*from the garden*). Giovanni, Giovanni! The sun is up and the plants are calling us.

GIOVANNI (*dubious, then resolved*). Wait, I'll be there in a moment. (*Jumps down.*)

BEATRICE. I've been counting the hours to see you since dawn. The garden doesn't seem mine any more without you. I talk to you in my dreams and you don't answer: you speak in the language of trees, and instead of speaking words, you bear fruit.

GIOVANNI (*worried*). What kind of fruit?

BEATRICE. Big, golden fruit, dream-fruit. Didn't I tell you I dreamt it? (*Seeing a plant.*) Look, it's changed colour. And just smell it! Its aroma makes the whole garden sleepy.

GIOVANNI (*angrily*). It must be a very powerful drug.

BEATRICE (*simply*). I don't know. I don't know much about the properties of the plants. And my father doesn't know all of their secrets either, even if he says he does. Of course, they are new.

GIOVANNI. New? What do you mean?

BEATRICE. What a question? Don't you know? They are plants which didn't exist before, species invented by my father. He corrects nature, makes it richer, as if he were giving life to life.

GIOVANNI. Or rather he is making death richer. This garden is an arsenal. Every leaf, every flower, every root is a lethal weapon, an instrument of torture. We wander calmly through the executioner's home and are touched by his creations . . .

BEATRICE. Stop it! What you're saying is horrible!

GIOVANNI. Is there anything more horrible than this garden? Anything more horrible than us? Listen to me, poor Beatrice. Don't you realise who you are and how you live? The plague, typhoid, leprosy, mysterious illnesses which cover the body with scarlet jewels, lianas of fever, spiders of madness, rotten eyes which burst at midday, green slime . . . they're all here. This garden is a tumour in the heart of the city . . .

BEATRICE. Listen to me! You can't condemn me without listening to me . . .

GIOVANNI. Get back! Don't touch me! Rotten apple, poison apple. Dead, and dressed up in the shape of life.

BEATRICE. I was alone . . .

GIOVANNI. Like a cursed island! So you chose me. Now you have an accomplice. You can rejoice: our breaths are linked and they will wither the crops and poison the fountains. (*Pause*). Speak, say something!

BEATRICE (*calmly*). I expected all of this. I knew what you were going to say to me. But I was crazy and believed in a miracle. I've lived alone since I was a little girl and I've been happy with my fate. Sometimes the buzz of the world shook the walls of the house and those calls upset me . . . my blood pulsed to another rhythm. Then I looked at the garden, I was drugged by its deadly scent and I forgot that cats, horses, roses, carnations, men exist. Why should apples, pomegranates or pears matter to me if I had the fruit of this tree, which is like the tree of Paradise? My father told me that in this tree death has become life.

GIOVANNI. What you call life breeds sickness, madness, and death. Your breath kills.

BEATRICE. My breath kills, not my thoughts. I belong to my father, to his infinite dream. Like these plants, I am a replica and a challenge to nature: the most powerful poisons flow in my veins without hurting me. I am one of my father's creations: the most daring, the most reckless, the most . . .

GIOVANNI. Disastrous.

BEATRICE. Disastrous.

GIOVANNI. The most guilty . . .

BEATRICE. I'm not guilty. I have had nothing alive around me, I haven't hurt anyone, except myself. I haven't had a cat, or a dog, or a canary. No-one ever taught me how to sing, no-one played with me, no-one trembled with me in a dark room. My life has been made up of growing, breathing, ripening. Ahh, ripening!

GIOVANNI. Ripening like an infinitely desirable fruit, infinitely untouchable.

BEATRICE. I have lived the life of a seed, alone, sheltered within myself, planted in the centre of my being. Isolated.

GIOVANNI. An island that no human foot will ever stand on, a secluded island, lost in the immensity of time, condemned never to leave yourself.

BEATRICE. Sleeping, without memories or desires, firmly rooted in the ground, planted in myself. The world has split in two. You have picked me like a blade of grass, you have cut my roots, you have thrown me into the air. Hanging from your eyes, I have swung through the void. From that moment I have had nowhere. I would throw myself at your feet, but I won't because it would poison your shadow.

GIOVANNI. Condemned to look at each other but never to touch!

BEATRICE. Gazing at you is enough. Your gaze is enough for me. I do not own myself, I don't have my own existence, or my own body, or my own soul. Your thoughts have penetrated me and there is no cave or hiding place where you cannot enter. There is no room in me for me. But I want to be inside you, not inside me. Let me be one of your thoughts, the most insignificant! And then forget me.

RAPPACCINI'S VOICE (*unseen, lost in the garden*). Child, you are no longer condemned to solitude. Cut one of the flowers from our tree and give it to your beloved. He can touch it without fear. And he can touch you. Thanks to my science – and to the secret solidarity of your blood – your opposing natures have been reconciled. The two of you can now be one. Bound together you will travel the world, feared by all, invincible, like gods.

GIOVANNI. Surrounded by hatred, surrounded by death. Like two vipers hidden in the cracks of the earth.

RAPPACCINI'S VOICE. Fool! Surrounded by awe and reverent fear, life's victors, impenetrable, grand donors of death.

GIOVANNI. You're crazy! Your arrogance won't beat us. You won't catch us in your trap. There is a way out. I hold the key to our freedom. Beatrice, take this antidote and drink it without fear: it will give you back your true nature. (*Hands her the phial.*)

RAPPACCINI'S VOICE. Don't drink it, child, don't drink it. The antidote will poison you. You will die.

GIOVANNI. Drink it. The old man is trying to trick you again. Drink it without fear and disown this monster. You will be free.

RAPPACCINI. You're so ignorant! The elements in her blood have assimilated my poisons in such a way that any antidote will cause instant death. Child, don't drink it!

BEATRICE. Father, if you wanted to condemn me to solitude, why didn't you pluck out my eyes? That way I wouldn't have seen him. Why didn't you make me deaf and dumb? Why didn't you plant me in the ground like this tree? That way I would not have run after his shadow. (*To* GIOVANNI.) Ahh, blind, deaf, dumb, tied to the ground with irons, I would still have run to you. My thoughts embrace your image like a vine. I am bound to the wall by thorns and claws, I tear myself away and fall at your feet.

GIOVANNI. I opened my eyes and saw myself planted in this garden like a cursed tree, cut off from the flow of life . . .

BEATRICE. To get there, to true life, we wandered under the arches of death with our eyes closed. But you opened yours, you lost heart . . .

GIOVANNI. I got dizzy! I stepped back . . . Open your eyes, look at me, look at life!

BEATRICE. No, I'm going back to myself. At last I am travelling through myself and I possess myself. In the darkness I feel myself, in the darkness I penetrate my being and I go right down to my root and I touch the place of my birth. I begin in myself and I end in myself. A river of knives surrounds me, I am untouchable.

RAPPACCINI'S VOICE. Listen to me crying. I beg you not to drink it! I will withdraw. I will make nature change its course. I wanted to make you stronger than life: now I will humiliate death.

BEATRICE (*drinks*). I have now made the final leap, I am now on the other shore. Garden of my infancy, poisoned paradise, tree, my brother, my son, my only lover, my only husband, cover me, embrace me, burn me, dissolve my bones, dissolve my memory! I am falling, falling inwards, never to reach the bottom of my soul!

RAPPACCINI (*appearing*). Child, why have you abandoned me?

Epilogue

THE MESSENGER. One after the other the figures pass by – the Minstrel, the Hermit, the Lady. One after another they appear and disappear, they meet and part. Guided by the stars and by the wordless will of blood, they walk away, always further away, towards the discovery of themselves. They cross and merge for an instant and then scatter and are lost in time. Like the methodical movement of the suns and planets, they repeat the dance tirelessly, condemned to search for themselves, condemned to find themselves and lose themselves and search for themselves without rest through infinite corridors. Peace to those who search! Peace to those who are alone, spinning in the void! Because yesterday and tomorrow do not exist: everything is today, everything is here, present. What has passed, is still passing.

Curtain.

Endnotes

1. The characters in the original have both Spanish and Italian names. I suggest that Beatrice is pronounced in the English way, although Giovanni may choose to woo her using the Italian pronunciation, a playful gesture that leads to her remark: 'How strange my name sounds on your lips!'

2. When rehearsing the play, the best equivalents we found between the Tarot characters in the text and those in a pack of Tarot of the Witches cards matched the Minstrel with the Fool; the Queen of the Night or Lady with the Queen of Cups; the King with the Emperor; the Hermit and the Lovers with their direct namesakes; Death with the Moon; and Life with the Sun. These equivalents will depend, of course, on any particular production's interpretation of this scene, and on which set of Tarot cards is used.

3. Many of the names of the poisons and antidotes are not easily translatable into English. Paz told me: 'I took the names from different dictionaries. Many of the words I use do not have an equivalent in English or have another meaning. I tried, wrily, to list the poisons and herbs which might have interested a doctor in the 17th century. Strange names. So you have the freedom not just to translate but to adapt these passages.' I have tried to find direct equivalents where possible, Satan's boletus, for example. Otherwise, I have taken associations with the original word as the basis for choosing an English translation: for instance, I have translated *el bálano impúdico*,

which literally means 'the lewd tip of the penis' as 'the lecherous mandrake' in order to keep the phallic associations.

4. I have used different antidotes to translate *el estalión* and *la triaca romana*, although I have used the direct translation of *la piedra bezoar*.

INTERVIEW WITH OCTAVIO PAZ

SD: How did you come to write *Rappaccini's Daughter*?

OP: I wrote *Rappaccini's Daughter* in 1956 for the program of a
Mexican university theatre company called *Poetry in a Loud Voice*.
The painter Leonora Carrington immediately offered to take charge of
the costumes and set. This was one of the reasons which encouraged
me to write the play. In the production, we sought to achieve a union
between the text, the actor and the director.

SD: What are the literary sources of the play?

OP: It is adapted from a short story by Nathaniel Hawthorne. My play
follows its plot, not its text or its meaning: I use other words and have
another notion of evil and the body. Hawthorne's source – or the
source of his sources – lies in India. *Mudra Rakshasa*, or *The Seal
on Rakshasa's Ring*, by the poet Vishakadatta, who lived in the ninth
century, is a political drama about the rivalry between two ministers.
Among the strategies which one of them uses to beat his rival is the
gift of a desirable girl who is fed on poison. This theme of the lady
who is turned into a living phial of venom is popular in Indian
literature and appears in the *Puranas*. From India the story passed to
the West and, Christianized, it features in the *Gesta Romanorum* and
other texts. In the seventeenth century Burton picked up the tale in
The Anatomy of Melancholy and gave it an historical character: Porus
sends Alexander a girl brimming with poison. Thomas Browne repeats
the story: 'An Indian King sent Alexander a beautiful girl who was fed
on monkshood and other poisons, intending to destroy him, either
through copulation or through some other physical contact.' Browne
was Hawthorne's source.

SD: How would you define the genre of this play?

OP: I judge it to be a dramatic poem. You might think about Yeats'
theatre.

SD: What are the specifically theatrical traditions behind the play?

OP: It seems to me that the play combines two traditions which are
both very different and at the same time have points of contact: the
Japanese Noh theatre and the Spanish *auto sacramental*, written by
Calderón and others.

SD: How have you seen the play staged?

OP: I have seen two different productions of the play and both
surprised me. I didn't imagine them the way I saw them. I liked the
first one, at *Poetry in a Loud Voice*, very much.

SD: Did you intend the danger of scientific experimentation to be the principal theme of the play?

OP: This play does show a clear distrust of certain scientific experiments. I think that the reality of our times has given me the reason: biological manipulations, the nuclear danger etc.

SD: This is the only play you have ever written. Why?

OP: I have not written other plays because in my wandering life I have not found the opportunity to collaborate with a company which might have been interested in the rather experimental theatre which has always seduced me. I regret that.

SD: Can you imagine writing for the stage again?

OP: Yes, although it is a little late.

This was a faxed interview conducted in Spanish in November 1995.

NIGHT OF THE ASSASSINS

by José Triana

Oh so much! Oh so little! Oh the others!
Cesar Vallejo

. . . we are all dream monsters to ourselves.
André Malraux

. . . this human world penetrates us, participates in
the dance of the gods, without looking back, on pain
of being turned into our selves: into pillars of salt.
Antonin Artaud

Can we only love
Something created by our own imagination?
Are we all in fact unloving and unlovable?
Then one is alone, and if one is alone
Then lover and beloved are equally unreal
And the dreamer is no more real than his dreams.

T.S. Eliot

Characters

LALO
CUCA
BEBA

Setting

The 1950s. A basement or an attic. A table, three chairs, rolled-up carpets, dirty curtains with large floral-patterned patches on them, vases, a judge's gavel, a knife and various objects discarded in the corner next to a broom and a duster.

Acting Note

While these characters play other characters, they must do so with the utmost simplicity and spontaneity. They must not use characterising devices. They are capable of representing the world without any artifice. Bear this in mind for the production's staging and set. These characters are adults, but exhibit a fading adolescent grace. They are figures in a ruined museum.

For María Angélica Alvarez
For José Rodríguez Feo

La Noche de los Asesinos was written in 1965 and first staged on 4 November 1966 in the Teatro Estudio, Havana, Cuba, with the following cast:

LALO	Vicente Revuelta
CUCA	Miriam Acevedo
BEBA	Ada Nocetti

Director Vicente Revuelta

Designer Raúl Oliva

This translation of *Night of the Assassins* was first staged on 22 August 1994 in the Demarco European Art Foundation, Edinburgh, by the Southern Development Trust, with the following cast:

CUCA	Gabrielle Jourdan
LALO	Tighe Twomey
BEBA	Gemma Moses

Director Sebastian Doggart

Designer Line Loen

Producer Tanya Stephan

Act One

LALO. Shut the door. (*Beats his chest. Exalted, wide-eyed.*)
An assassin. An assassin. (*Falls to his knees.*)

CUCA (*to* BEBA). What's all this?

BEBA (*indifferently, watching* LALO). The performance has
begun.

CUCA. Again?

BEBA (*annoyed*). Of course! It's not the first time.

CUCA. Please don't get upset.

BEBA. Grow up.

CUCA. Mum and Dad haven't gone out yet.

BEBA. So?

LALO. I killed them. (*Laughs. Stretches his arms solemnly out
to the audience.*) Can't you see the two coffins? Look:
candles, flowers . . . We've filled the room with gladioli.
Mum's favourite. (*Pause.*) They can't complain. Now
they're dead we've made them happy. I myself dressed their
stiff, sticky bodies . . . And with these hands I dug a deep,
deep hole. Earth, more earth. (*Gets up quickly.*) They still
haven't discovered the crime. (*Smiles. To* CUCA.) What are
you thinking about? (*Caressing her chin as if she were a
child.*) I understand: you're scared. (*She moves away.*) Oh,
you're impossible.

CUCA (*dusting the furniture*). I can't stand all this nonsense.

LALO. Nonsense? You think a crime is nonsense? How cold
you are, little sister! Nonsense? Do you really think that?

CUCA (*firmly*). Yes.

LALO. Then what *is* important to you?

CUCA. I want you to help me. We have to tidy up this house.
This room is a pit. Cockroaches, rats, moths, caterpillars . . .
the whole bloody lot. (*Takes an ashtray from the chair and
puts it on the table.*)

LALO. How far do you think you're going to get with that duster?

CUCA. It's a start.

LALO (*authoritatively*). Put the ashtray back in its place.

CUCA. The ashtray belongs on the table, not on the chair.

LALO. Do what I tell you.

CUCA. Don't start, Lalo.

LALO (*picks up the ashtray and puts it back on the chair*). I know what I'm doing. (*Picks up the vase and puts it on the floor.*) In this house the ashtray belongs on the chair and the vase on the floor.

CUCA. And the chairs?

LALO. On the table.

CUCA. And what about us?

LALO. We float with our feet in the air and our heads hanging down.

CUCA (*annoyed*). Fantastic! Why don't we try it? What would people say if they heard you now? (*In a harder tone of voice.*) Look, Lalo, if you keep being pushy, we're going to have problems. Leave me alone. I'll do what I can.

LALO (*purposefully*). Don't you want me to help you?

CUCA. Don't mess things up.

LALO. Then don't mess with my things. I want the ashtray there. The vase there. Leave them where they are. It's you who's being pushy, not me.

CUCA. Oh right! Now it's me who's being pushy? Darling, that is priceless! Now it's me . . . ? Look, Lalo, please shut up. Order is order.

LALO. There is none so deaf as she that won't hear.

CUCA. What?

LALO. You heard.

CUCA. Well, darling, I don't understand. That's the honest truth. I don't know what you're on about. It all sounds crazy. It gets me into an utter state. I can't say or do anything. And if it's what I think it is, then it's sick.

LALO. Scared again? Get something into your tiny little head. If you want to live in this world you have to do many things, and one of them is to forget fear.

CUCA. Doesn't that sound easy!

LALO. Well, do it then.

CUCA. Stop hassling me. And don't preach, it doesn't suit you. (*Dusting a chair.*) Look at this chair, Lalo. How long since it was last cleaned? There are cobwebs even. Ugh!

LALO. Shocking! (*Approaching cautiously, purposefully.*) The other day I said to myself: 'We must clean up'; but then we got sidetracked into some nonsense and . . . Look, look at it. (*Pause. Purposefully.*) Why don't you help?

CUCA (*almost on her knees next to the chair, cleaning it*). Leave me out of it.

LALO. Go on.

CUCA. Don't push.

LALO. Just for a bit.

CUCA. I'm no use.

BEBA, *who has been upstage cleaning some old furniture and pots and pans with a rag, moves downstage. She smiles. Her movements are slightly reminiscent of* LALO's.

BEBA. Those corpses are unreal. Spectacular! They give me goose pimples. I don't want to think any more. I've never felt so happy. Look at them. They're flying, they're breaking up.

LALO (*grandly*). Have the guests arrived?

BEBA. I heard them coming up the stairs.

LALO. Who?

BEBA. Margaret and old Pantaleón.

CUCA *doesn't stop her work, although occasionally she pauses to look at them.*

LALO (*contemptuously*). I don't like those two. (*In another tone of voice. Violently.*) Who told them?

BEBA. I don't know! No, don't look at me like that. I swear it wasn't me.

LALO. Then it was her. (*Points to* CUCA.) Her.

CUCA (*still cleaning the furniture*). Me?

LALO. Yes, you. As if butter wouldn't melt in your mouth.

BEBA. Perhaps no-one told them. Perhaps they decided to come themselves.

LALO (*to* BEBA). Don't try and cover for her. (*To* CUCA, *who gets up and mops her brow with her right arm.*) You! You are always spying on us. (*Starts walking around* CUCA.) You watch our every step, every word we say, everything we think. You hide behind curtains, doors, windows . . . (*With a sly smile.*) Ha! The spoilt brat plays detective. (*Roars with laughter.*) Two and two make four. Elementary, my dear Watson. (*Suddenly.*) Ugh! (*Softly, like a cat watching its prey.*) You're never satisfied. What do you want to know?

CUCA (*fearful, not knowing what to do*). Nothing, Lalo, nothing . . . honestly . . . (*Sharply.*) Don't get at me.

LALO. Then, why do you watch us? And why do you mix with such dreadful people?

CUCA (*her eyes filling with tears*). I didn't mean to . . .

LALO. *That's* what I can't forgive.

CUCA. They're my friends.

LALO (*with furious contempt*). Your friends. You're pathetic. (*With a triumphant smile.*) Don't think you can fool me. You're being ridiculous. You resist, but you really want to run away . . . little Miss Muffet. I already know you haven't got the guts to call things by their real names. (*Pause.*) If you're against us, show us your teeth. Bite! Rebel!

CUCA. Stop it.

LALO. Come on!

CUCA. You're getting on my nerves.

LALO. You can do it.

CUCA (*choking*). I'm sorry, I'm really sorry.

LALO. Come on, get up.

BEBA (*to* LALO). Don't torment her.

LALO (*to* CUCA). Look at me.

CUCA. My head hurts.

LALO. Look at me.

CUCA. I can't.

BEBA (*to* LALO). Give her a few moments.

CUCA (*sobbing*). It's not my fault. It's just how I am. I can't change. I wish I could.

LALO (*irritated*). What a dunce you are.

BEBA (*to* CUCA). Come on then. (*Takes her aside and walks her over to a chair.*) Dry your tears. Aren't you embarrassed? He is right you know. You're being difficult. (*Pause. She strokes her hair.*) There, there. (*In an affectionate tone of voice.*) Don't look so sad. Give us a smile. (*In a maternal tone of voice.*) You shouldn't have done it; but if you've started, you might as well finish. (*Joking.*) Your nose has gone all red, just like a baby tomato. (*Tapping her nose with the index finger of her right hand.*) What a silly-billy you are! (*Smiles.*)

CUCA (*staying close to* BEBA). I don't want to see him.

BEBA. Calm down.

CUCA. I don't want to hear him.

BEBA. He won't eat you.

CUCA. My heart . . . Listen to it, it sounds like it's going to explode.

BEBA. Don't be a cry-baby.

CUCA. I swear, I swear.

BEBA. Well, get used to it.

CUCA. I want to run away.

BEBA. It will pass.

CUCA. I can't stand it.

BEBA. It gets easier.

CUCA. I feel terrible.

LALO (*holding a cauldron in his hand, making an invocation*). Oh, Aphrodite, illuminate this night of infamy.

CUCA (*to* BEBA, *distressed*). He's starting again.

BEBA (*to* CUCA, *soothingly*). Sshh. Don't pay any attention to him.

CUCA. I want to spit on him.

BEBA. Don't go near him. He bites.

LALO (*as Roman emperor*). Come to my aid; I'm dying of boredom.

CUCA, *incapable of putting herself on the same level as* LALO, *reproaches him in a mocking tone of voice.*

CUCA. What a performance! He's just like your uncle Chicho, don't you think, Sis? (*In disgust.*) You're a monster.

LALO (*as important gentleman*). When the gods are silent, the people shout. (*He throws the cauldron downstage.*)

CUCA (*as mother. Sarcastically*). That's right, smash the place up, you don't have to pay for it.

LALO (*smiling, facing the door*). What a delightful surprise!

BEBA (*to CUCA*). Are you feeling better? (CUCA *nods.*)

LALO (*greeting imaginary people*). Do come in . . . (*As if he were shaking their hands.*) Oh, how *are* you? Hello!

BEBA (*to CUCA*). Sure? (CUCA *nods.*)

LALO (*to BEBA*). They've arrived.

BEBA (*to LALO*). Keep them at a distance so they will go away.

LALO (*to BEBA*). They've come to get us.

CUCA (*to the imaginary people*). Good evening, Margaret.

LALO (*to CUCA*). They've come to sniff out the blood.

BEBA (*to the imaginary people*). How *are* you both?

CUCA (*to LALO*). You and your suspicious mind.

BEBA (*to CUCA, as mother*). Don't make things worse. (*To the imaginary people.*) Asthma is such a pyrotechnic illness. It must still be wreaking havoc among the masses.

LALO (*to CUCA*). I won't forgive you for this.

CUCA (*as if she were paying attention to what the imaginary people are saying. With a wicked smile to* LALO. *Between her teeth*). An eye for an eye . . .

BEBA (*as mother. To* LALO, *between her teeth*). Pretend you didn't hear, son.

LALO (*to BEBA*). How rude. (*In another tone of voice. With a hypocritical smile at the imaginary people.*) And how *are* you, Pantaleón? It's been so long since I last saw you. Have you been lost?

BEBA (*pestering the imaginary people*). How's your urine? They told me the other day . . .

CUCA (*pestering the imaginary people*). Is your bladder working OK?

BEBA (*amazed*). What? They *still* haven't operated on your sphincter?

CUCA (*scandalized*). Really? And what about the old hernia?

LALO (*with a hypocritical smile*). Margaret, you're looking *terrific*. Is that cancerous growth of yours still growing? (*To* BEBA.) You deal with them.

BEBA (*to* LALO). I've run out of things to say.

LALO (*aside. Pushing her*). Say anything. It doesn't matter.

Goes upstage.

BEBA (*looks at* LALO, *distressed. Pause. Immediately afterwards she throws herself into the fun of make-believing*). How *lovely* you are . . . It must be spring which gives you . . . I don't know . . . a special aura, a power . . . Oh, I don't know . . . Oh, isn't it hot? I'm sweating absolute *buckets*. (*She laughs.*) Ohhh, Pantaleón! Panties Pantaleón! You are a one! An absolute cad. Oh yes, you are. You can't play the fool with me. And that wart really has increased your pulling power.

LALO (*as* PANTALEON). Oh stop it, I don't believe a word of it. The years, my child, the passing years wither a man away and turn him into an old dish-cloth. (*He laughs mischievously.*) But if you'd seen me in my prime, in the good old days . . . Oh, if only I could have them again . . . But what's the point? That's asking for the impossible. (*In a special tone of voice.*) Today I have a little pain right here. (*Points to his abdomen.*) It's like a pin-prick . . . (*Sighs.*) I'm old, a rusting wreck of a man. And it gets worse every day. Our children don't respect us, and they don't forgive us either.

BEBA (*as* MARGARET, *annoyed*). Don't say that. It's not fair. (*Aside.*) There's a time and a place for everything. (*Smiling.*) What will these kind, lovely children think? (*To* CUCA.) Come here, pumpkin. Why are you hiding? Who are you afraid of? Who's the bogeyman? (CUCA *doesn't move.*) Come on, what's the matter, am I an ugly old woman? Come here, don't be silly, my sweet. Tell me something: how are your mummy and daddy? Where's your mummy?

LALO (*leaping up from his chair. Violently, to the audience*). You see? What did I tell you. That's what they came for. I know them. I'm right. (*To* CUCA. *Accusingly.*) They're *your* friends. Get them out of here. They're trying to find out . . . (*Shouting.*) Tell them to go to hell. Do you hear me? It's all over.

CUCA *doesn't know what to do. She moves, gesticulates, tries to say something but is neither able nor dares to do so.*

BEBA (*as* MARGARET. *To* CUCA). I don't want to leave just yet. We've come round for our regular visit. We've been meaning to come for weeks. And anyway, I'm feeling a bit woozy. Your mother should have some herbal tea.

LALO (*frantically*). Tell them to go, Cuca. Tell them to fuck off. (*As if he were holding a whip and were threatening them.*) Out. Get out of here. Into the street.

CUCA (*to* LALO). Don't be so rude.

BEBA (*as* MARGARET. *Crying in outrage*). I can't believe it. They're just throwing us out. It's outrageous. What beastly children.

CUCA (*to* LALO. *In control of the situation*). You have a terrible temper.

BEBA (*to the imaginary visitors*). I beg you to forgive him.

CUCA (*to* LALO). They haven't done anything to you.

BEBA (*to the imaginary people*). He has a terrible temper.

CUCA (*to* LALO). You just don't *think*.

BEBA (*to the imaginary people*). The doctor says he needs plenty of rest.

CUCA (*to* LALO). So tactless, so ill-mannered, so . . .

BEBA (*to the imaginary people*). Such an uncalled-for attack.

CUCA (*to* LALO, *who is laughing slyly*). God will never forgive you for this.

BEBA (*to the imaginary people*). Good-bye Margaret. Good-night Pantaleón. Don't forget, Mum and Dad went away to the country and we're not sure when . . . Oh, they'll be back pretty soon, I expect. Bye! Bye-bye! (*Blows them a kiss with feigned tenderness. Pause. To* LALO.) You made that really hard for me! (*She sits down upstage and starts to polish some shoes.*)

CUCA (*subtly threatening*). When Mum finds out . . .

LALO (*angrily*). Go on, then, tell her. (*Calling.*) Mum, Dad. (*Laughs.*) Mum, Dad. (*Defiantly.*) Don't wait. Go on. Run along and tell them. I'm sure they'll be grateful. Come on. Run, run. (*Takes* CUCA *by the arm and leads her to the door. He returns downstage centre.*) You're a disaster. You can never make up your mind. You want to and you don't want to. You are and you aren't. Do you think that is enough? If you really want to live, you always have to take risks. It doesn't matter if you win or lose. (*Sarcastically.*) But you want safety. The easy way out. (*Pause.*) That's where the danger lies. Because that's where you hang around, dithering, not knowing what to do, not knowing what you are and, worst of all, not knowing what you want.

CUCA (*sure of herself*). Don't puff yourself up too far.

LALO. You'll never save yourself, however hard you try.

CUCA. Nor will you.

LALO. It won't be you who stops me.

CUCA. Every day you will grow older . . . Here, here, here, shut up with the cobwebs and the dust. I know it, I can see it, I can breathe it. (*She smiles wickedly.*)

LALO. So?

CUCA. You're going down, down.

LALO. That's what you'd like to see.

CUCA. Don't make me laugh.

LALO. It's the truth.

CUCA. I'll do what I like.

LALO. At last you're using your claws.

CUCA. I'm just speaking my mind.

LALO. You don't realise that what I am proposing is simply the only solution we have. (*Takes the chair and moves it about in the air.*) I want this chair to be here. (*He suddenly puts the chair down in a particular place.*) And not there. (*He suddenly moves the same chair to another particular place.*) Because here . . . (*Quickly returning it to the first place.*) . . . it's more useful to me. I can sit down more comfortably and more quickly. And here . . . (*Places the chair in the second position.*) . . . It's useless, just a silly whim . . . (*Puts the chair back to the first position.*) Dad and Mum don't allow such things. They think that what I think and what I want to do are completely illogical. They want everything to stay where it is. Nothing must move from its proper place. And that's impossible. Because you and I and Beba . . . (*With a scream.*) It's intolerable. And they think I'm just doing these things to contradict them, to fight them, to upset them . . .

CUCA. In a house, the furniture . . .

LALO (*rapidly, energetically*). That's just an excuse. Who cares about this house, who cares about this furniture if we ourselves are nothing, if we simply pass through the house and between the furniture, just like an ashtray, a vase, or a floating knife? (*To* CUCA.) You could be a vase. Would you like to discover one day that's all you are? Or that you've been treated like a vase for most of your life? I could be a knife, couldn't I? And Beba, are you happy being an ashtray? No, no. That's stupid. (*In a mechanical rhythm.*) Come over here. Go over there. Do this. Do that. Do the other. (*In another tone of voice.*) I want my life. Every day of it, every hour, every minute. I want to do what I want and feel what I want. But my hands are tied. My feet are tied. My eyes are blinkered. This house is my world. And this house is getting old and dirty and smelly. Mum and Dad are to blame. I'm sorry but that's how it is. And the worst thing is that they don't stop a moment to consider whether things shouldn't be different. Nor do you. And Beba's even worse. If Beba plays our game, it's only because she has nothing else to do.

CUCA. Why do you blame Mum and Dad for everything?

LALO. Because they made me into a useless thing.

CUCA. That's not true.

LALO. Why should I lie?

CUCA. You're trying to cover yourself.

LALO. I'm trying to be as sincere as possible.

CUCA. That doesn't give you the right to demand so much. You're terrible as well. Do you remember the games you made up? You destroyed all our dolls. You invented crazy games. You wanted us to live in your shadow – or worse, you wanted us to be just like you.

LALO. That was the only way to free myself from the burden they placed on me.

CUCA. You can't deny they've always taken care of you, that they've always loved you.

LALO. I don't want them to love me like that. I've been everything to them, except a human being.

From upstage, still polishing the shoes, BEBA *imitates her father.*

BEBA *(as father).* Lalo, from now on you will scrub the floors. You will mend my clothes and you will do so with great care. Your mother is not well and somebody has to do these things. *(She continues polishing the shoes.)*

CUCA. Mum and Dad have given you everything . . .

LALO *(to* CUCA). At what cost . . . ?

CUCA. But what did you expect? Remember, Lalo, what Dad earned. Next to nothing. What more could he have given you?

LALO. Why have they always told me: 'Don't walk to school with so-and-so'; 'don't go out with what's-her-name'; 'so-and-so is a bad influence.' Why did they make me believe I was better than anyone else? Mum and Dad think that if we have a room, a bed and food, that's enough, that we should be grateful. They told us a thousand times that very few parents did as much, that only rich children enjoyed the kind of life we had.

CUCA. Try and understand them. That's the way they are . . . But sooner or later you were bound to try to get rid of them.

LALO. I couldn't. I believed in them too much. *(Pause.)* And what happened to my desires? My dreams?

CUCA. Since you were a kid, you always wanted your own way.

LALO. Since I was a kid, since I was that tall, they've been telling me: 'Do this.' And if I did it badly: 'You're useless.' And then came the beatings and the punishment.

CUCA. That's what all parents do. It doesn't mean you have to turn the whole house upside down.

LALO. I want things to have a real meaning, so that you, Beba, and I can say: 'We'll do this,' and we'll do it. And if it doesn't work, we can say: 'Too bad. Let's try again.' And if it does work, we can say: 'Great! Let's move on to the next thing.' Haven't you ever thought what it means to be able to think, to decide and to do things on your own?

CUCA. You know we can't just . . .

LALO (*violently*). We can't. We can't.

CUCA. Mum and Dad are right.

LALO. I'm right, too. Just as right as they are.

CUCA. Are you rebelling?

LALO. Yes.

CUCA. Against them?

LALO. Against everything.

At this moment BEBA *repeats the imitation of her father.*

BEBA (*as father*). Lalo, you will wash and iron. Your mother and I have agreed on this. There are the sheets, the curtains, the table-cloths and my office trousers . . . You will clean the toilets. You will eat in a corner in the kitchen. You will learn. I swear you will learn. Do you hear me? (*She goes upstage.*)

CUCA. Why don't you leave home then?

LALO. Where the hell would I go?

CUCA. Try.

LALO. I already have. Don't you remember? I always come home with my tail between my legs.

CUCA. Try again.

LALO. No . . . I know I can't live on the streets. I get confused . . . lost. I don't know what's wrong with me. I seem to fade away. They didn't teach me. No, they just mixed me up.

CUCA. How can you be a leader if you yourself admit . . . ?

LALO. This house is what I know. I'm resigned to it.

CUCA. Are you ready to start again then?

LALO. As many times as it takes.

CUCA. And see it right through?

LALO. It's my only escape.

CUCA. But don't you think the police will find out?

LALO. I don't know. Maybe . . .

CUCA. How can you win?

LALO. Wait and see.

CUCA. Well, I won't help you. Understand? I'll defend them
tooth and nail if I have to. I'm not interested in any of this. I
accept what Mum and Dad say. They don't interfere with
me. They give me everything I need . . . You're the
pigheaded one, not me. Dad's right when he says you're like
a cat: you close your eyes so you can't see the food they're
giving you. (*Steps forward.*) Go away. I won't play your
game. (*To* BEBA.) Don't you count on me either. (*In
another tone of voice.*) Oh, God, get me out of this mess.
(*Pause.*) They're older than us. They know more about life.
They've struggled, made sacrifices. They deserve our
respect at the very least. If something goes wrong in this
house, it's because it was bound to . . . No, no, I won't fight
them.

LALO (*amused. Clapping*). Bravo. A fine performance.

BEBA (*amused. Clapping*). You deserve an award.

LALO. We'll have to invent one.

BEBA. She's one to watch.

LALO. She's an imbecile.

BEBA. She's sensational.

LALO. She's an idiot.

BEBA. She's a saint. (*They applaud furiously and mockingly.*)

CUCA. Go on, laugh. My time will come. And then I'll show
no mercy.

LALO. What do you mean?

CUCA. I'll do what I feel like.

LALO. You just try.

CUCA. You can't order me about. (*She walks back a few steps,
moving away from them.*)

LALO (*sarcastically*). You're getting scared. (*Laughs.*)

CUCA (*furiously*). I've got hands, nails, teeth.

LALO (*aggressively, defiantly*). I'm in charge now.

CUCA. Don't come near me.

LALO. You'll do what I tell you. (*Seizes her arm and they begin to fight.*)

CUCA (*furiously*). Let go.

LALO. Will you obey me?

CUCA. Bully.

LALO. You'll do anything I tell you.

CUCA. You're hurting me.

LALO. Yes or no?

CUCA. It's not fair . . . (*Totally defeated.*) All right, I'll do anything you tell me.

LALO. Quick. Get up.

CUCA (*to* BEBA). Help me.

BEBA *walks towards* CUCA. LALO *stops her with one movement.* CUCA *pretends that she cannot get up.*

LALO. Let her get up on her own.

BEBA (*to* LALO). Forgive her.

LALO (*shouting*). Keep out of this.

BEBA (*desperately*). Oh, you're always shouting! I can't stand it. I came here to help you or to have fun. Because I don't know what else to do . . . Round and round we go . . . We get shouted at for anything: for a glass of water, a bar of soap on the floor, a dirty towel, a broken ashtray . . . Aren't there more important things to live for? I wonder sometimes what the clouds, the trees, the rain, and the animals are all for. Shouldn't we stop and think about these things? And I run to the window and stick my head out . . . But Mum and Dad start shouting again: 'What are you thinking of, child? Look at the dust and soot on the window. Get inside, or you'll catch a cold.' If I go to the living room and turn on the radio, they say: 'You're wasting electricity. Last month and the month before that we used so much and we can't go on like this. Turn it off. That noise is driving me crazy.' Or if I start singing that song you made up recently, 'The living room's not the living room,' the whole house explodes like an upturned ants' nest, and they start shouting again: Mum and Dad shout at Lalo, Lalo shouts at Mum, Mum shouts at Lalo, Lalo shouts at Dad, Dad shouts at Lalo, and I'm left in the middle. In the end I come and hide here . . . But you don't even notice and carry on arguing, as if this house's problems could be solved with words. And now you two end up rowing as well. Oh, I can't bear it any more. (*Determined.*) I'm getting out. (LALO *grabs her arm.*) Let me go. I don't want to hear any more about it. Deaf, blind. Dead, dead.

LALO (*tenderly but firmly*). Don't say that.

BEBA. That's what I want.

LALO. If you helped me, perhaps we can save ourselves.

BEBA (*looking up at him suddenly amazed*). What do you mean? (*She holds on to his arms.*) All right, we can do it. Today.

LALO *quickly picks up two knives. He examines their edges and starts scraping them against each other.*

BEBA (*to* LALO). Are you going to tell the story again?

CUCA (*to* BEBA). Quiet, please.

BEBA *moves about the stage. Each character takes up a distinctive position.*

BEBA (*as gossiping neighbour*). Shall I tell you something, Cacha? It was in all the papers. Yes, dear, yes. But you know old Margaret who lives at the corner, and Pantaleón, who's only got one eye? Well, they saw everything, and I mean everything. And they told me all about it.

LALO (*scraping the two knives quite firmly*). Ric-rac, ric-rac, ric-rac, ric-rac, ric-rac, ric-rac.

BEBA (*as drunk shop-keeper*). Old Pantaleón and Margaret know everything . . . Bloody hell! Some mothers do 'ave em, I tell you. What is the world coming to . . . ? Have you seen the photo on the front page?

LALO (*scraping the two knives violently*). Ric-rac, ric-rac, ric-rac, ric-rac, ric-rac, ric-rac, ric-rac.

BEBA (*as* MARGARET *speaking to her friends*). We dropped round there about half-past nine . . . The usual time. Well dear, the moment I walked in I said to myself: 'Goodness gracious me. Something's funny here.' You know me, I have a nose for these things, and sure enough. What a sight, dearie! (*Horrified.*) Blood all over the place. It was frightful. Look at my hair, it's still standing on end. Oh, it makes me shiver all over. I can't describe it properly, you should have

seen the . . . Ugh! It's horrible even thinking about it.
A stream, incredible . . . I think there were some syringes.
Isn't that right, Pantaleón? And pills and ampoules . . .
Those children are wicked, and it's in their family. Oh,
Consolación, ask Angelita what she saw a few days ago . . .
Awful! And such sweet parents, so self-sacrificing. It's
that Lalo, he's the ring-leader. No doubt about it. It was
him, him and no-one else . . . Ah! you should have seen his
knife . . . Dear Lord, what a butchers knife!

LALO (*in his own world*). Ric-rac, ric-rac, ric-rac, ric-rac, ric-
rac, ric-rac, ric-rac, ric-rac, ric-rac, ric-rac.

BEBA (*as* PANTALEON). I said to Maggie: 'Hold your horses,
woman.' But she immediately started blathering on about
the youth of today, and how awful they all are . . . You know
what a blabber she is. They . . . No, I tell a lie. *He,* Lalo . . .
Although at times I can't help thinking that . . . Well,
goodness knows who did it . . . But I could almost swear on
it. Because the girls . . . I can't see it. If you had seen Lalo's
face . . . It was incredible. He looked possessed . . . Yes, yes,
the devil in person. He almost tried to beat us up . . . And me
with my arthritis . . . I won't stand for it. I don't care what
he does; that's his problem. But insulting us . . . Well, God
may forgive him, but I won't! He's a nasty piece of work, a
right bastard . . . Ah, if you had seen that bloodbath . . . And
smelt the stench . . . It's all so weird, isn't it! (*With an
hysterical giggle.*) You're lucky you didn't see it . . . It was
grisly . . . Grisly, yes . . . Grisly is the word . . . We must do
something. (*Grandiosely.*) We would like to make a formal
complaint against this inhuman child. (*In another tone of
voice.*) What do you think?

LALO (*still playing his bizarre game*). Ric-rac, ric-rac, ric-rac,
ric-rac, ric-rac, ric-rac, ric-rac, ric-rac, ric-rac, ric-rac.

LALO *continues scraping the knives together. This simple
action, combined with the sounds that he makes, builds up to
a delirious climax.* CUCA *becomes a newspaper boy,* BEBA
goes upstage.

CUCA (*yelling*). Morning news! Latest news! Murder on
Church Street! Buy a copy, lady. Don't miss it, sweetheart.
Thirty-year-old son butchers his parents! See how the blood
ran . . . Full-colour supplement. (*In a sing-song voice.*) Forty
times he stabbed his wrinklies! Forty times! Photos of the
innocent parents! Buy it! It'll really shock you, sir!

Frightening, folks! Morning news! (*To back. Drifting off.*)
Latest news.

LALO (*continuing to play his game*). Ric-rac, ric-rac, ric-rac,
ric-rac, ric-rac, ric-rac, ric-rac, ric- rac, ric-rac, ric-rac, ric-
rac, ric-rac, ric-rac, ric-rac, ric-rac.

Pause. BEBA *walks downstage centre.*

BEBA (*as father*). Lalo, what have you been up to? What are
you staring at? Take that look off your face. Who have you
been with? Tell me. Knives? What do you think you're
doing with those knives? Answer me. Have you lost your
tongue? Why are you home so late?

LALO (*as teenager*). I bumped into some friends, Dad . . .

BEBA (*as father*). Give those to me. (*Taking the knives away
violently.*) Always messing about. (*Checking the sharpness
of a knife.*) That is sharp. Are you planning to kill someone?
Tell me, I want an answer. Don't just stand there, you idiot.
Who do you think you are? Why didn't you ask my permission? If I've told you once, I've told you a thousand times:
this is no time to come home. (*She slaps him around.*) When
will you learn some respect? How do you think your mother
feels? Eh? You're breaking her heart! Is that what you want?
Do you want us both to die of broken hearts? You just don't
think! And take that look off your face. (*She pushes him towards the chair.*) Sit down. Do you want me to ground you
again? (LALO *makes a gesture.*) Don't answer back. Such
insolence. I've given you everything. You brat, you wicked,
ungrateful brat. It's me who makes all the sacrifices . . . Yes,
your mother gets at me for going out with my friends and
the girls from the office. Well, more than one business deal
has fallen through because of you and the rest of my family.
Can't you see the sacrifices I've made? Thirty years . . .
Thirty years behind a desk getting ulcers from being pushed
around by my bosses, doing without . . . I don't even have a
proper suit, or a decent pair of shoes. And this is how you
pay me back! Thirty years is no joke. Thirty years working
for my son, and today he turns out to be a good-for-nothing,
a slob who doesn't want to work or study . . . Well, tell me,
what *do* you want? And what have you been up to?

LALO (*trembling*). We were reading . . .

BEBA (*as father*). Reading? Reading what? What do you
mean, reading . . . ?

LALO (*thoughtfully*). An adventure magazine, Dad.

CUCA *walks downstage centre confidently, with mischievous intent.* BEBA *goes upstage.*

CUCA (*as mother*). Magazines. Magazines. Magazines. That's a lie. Tell us another. Tell us the truth. (BEBA, *as father, approaches* LALO *aggressively.*) No, Albert, don't hit him. (*To* LALO.) Where is the money I hid in the sideboard? Did you take it? Have you spent it? Have you lost it? (*With hatred.*) Thief. You little swine. You bastard. (*Tears welling in her eyes.*) I'll tell your father. No, don't say anything. You're a disgrace. He'll kill you if he finds out. Holy Mary, mother of God, what have I done to deserve this? (*Furiously, to* LALO.) Come on, give me back the money. Give it back or I'll call the police . . . (*Rifles through* LALO's *pockets. He submits completely. She screams.*) Thief. You bloody thief. I *will* tell your father. I ought to beat you. Whip you. Put you in reform school. (LALO *has his back to the audience.*)

BEBA (*from upstage, like a little child*). Mum, mum, is this an elephant?

LALO (*as father*). Beba, come here. Show me your hands. (BEBA *walks downstage centre. Shows him her hands.*) Those nails must be cut. They make you look like a . . . (*To* CUCA.) Give me some scissors, woman. (CUCA *goes up to* LALO *and whispers in his ear.*) What? What's that? Really? And Lalo? Where's he gone? (CUCA *and* LALO *look at* BEBA *with evil intent.*) Is it true what your mother says? Come on, own up. Own up, or I'll . . . So you lifted your skirt and showed your knickers off to a bunch of perverts? Can this be true? (BEBA *gesticulates silently.*) You filthy creature. (CUCA, *as mother, smiles.*) I'm going to . . . (LALO *and* CUCA *corner* BEBA.) Do you want to become a whore, is that it? Huh? (*Shaking* BEBA *by the shoulders.*) Well, not while I'm alive, do you hear? If I catch you doing anything sluttish, I'll kill you. Is that clear? (*Pause.*) Where is your brother. (*Calling.*) Lalo, Lalo! (*To* CUCA.) You say he's stolen some money from you?

BEBA (*coming out of part*). I can't. My head's exploding.

LALO (*ordering*). Go on, you can't stop.

CUCA (*sarcastically*). Do what your master says.

BEBA (*agonized*). Air, I need some air.

LALO (*To* BEBA.) The doorbell's ringing.

BEBA *collapses on to a chair.*

CUCA (*as mother*). Have you heard, Albert?

BEBA (*desperately*). Please, I think I'm going to be sick.

LALO (*annoyed*). She ruins everything, she does.

CUCA (*as mother*). Sshh! Wait a second, children. There goes the doorbell again.

BEBA (*as father. Greeting an imaginary person who comes through the door*). Come in, Angelita. How lovely to see you.

CUCA (*as mother. To* BEBA). Tell me, poppet. Go on, you can tell me. What's wrong? (*Feigning self-denial and concern.*)

LALO (*as father. To the imaginary person*). Don't stand on ceremony, Angelita. (*His tone of voice is convincingly cordial and spontaneous.*) Make yourself at home. Please sit down.

CUCA (*as mother. To* BEBA). Make yourself comfortable, honey. Do you want a cushion? (*Her words are heavy with sincerity.*) Why don't you just lean back and relax?

LALO (*as father*). And Lalo? Where's he hiding? Oh, Angelita, you have no idea what those kids are like. Only three of them, but it's still like living in a war zone.

CUCA (*as mother. To* LALO). Albert, I think . . . (*To the imaginary person.*) I'm so sorry, Angelita, I'm not looking after you very well, but I think my little girl might be sick; she's got a tummy ache . . .

LALO (*as father*). Have you taken her temperature? (CUCA *nods.*)

CUCA (*as mother*). How very embarrassing.

LALO (*as father, to the imaginary person*). You see what I mean? They're little devils. But I don't let them get away with anything. I rule them with a rod of iron, although not literally of course.

CUCA (*as mother. Anxious. To* LALO). What can we do?

LALO (*as father*). Does she have a temperature? (CUCA *shakes her head.*) Have you given her some camomile tea?

CUCA (*as mother*). She doesn't want anything.

LALO (*as father*). Well, make her then.

CUCA (*as mother*). She'll be sick.

LALO (*as father*). Give her some normal tea then.

CUCA (*as mother*). Oh, Angelita, you can't imagine the suffering, the grief . . . Why did we ever have children?

LALO (*as father. Forcing her to drink from a teacup*). Drink. (BEBA *rejects it.*) Do what I say. Drink it all up.

BEBA (*screams; out of part*). Just leave me alone. (*Gets up furiously. Centre stage.*) You're monsters. You're both the same. (*Shouting upstage.*) I want to go. Let me go. (CUCA *and* LALO *try to stop her, but she gets to the door. Screaming.*) Mum, Dad, get me out of here. (*Falls beside the door, crying.*) Get me out of here.

LALO (*as father*). What's going on?

CUCA. Nice performance. (*Going up to* BEBA.) You, it had to be you . . . You always push me into it: 'Go on, don't be wet. It'll be a laugh.' I can't believe it. Come on, up you get. (*Helps her to get up. As mother.*) Remember we've got a visitor. (*To the imaginary visitor.*) They're so spoiled, it's exhausting . . . (*To* BEBA. *Taking her back to the chair where she had been sitting.*) That's a girl, aren't you a good girl, well done . . .

BEBA (*as little girl*). I want to go.

CUCA (*as mother*). Where do you want to go, pet?

LALO (*out of part; violently*). This isn't right. There's no point.

CUCA (*as mother*). Don't lose your temper, Albert.

LALO (*out of part*). I feel like strangling her.

CUCA (*as mother*). Patience.

BEBA (*crying*). I'm scared.

LALO (*out of part*). Scared of what? Why is she crying?

CUCA (*as mother*). Ignore it. That's the best way, Albert.

LALO (*as father. Awkwardly*). It's just that sometimes . . . (*Slapping his right knee.*) You don't understand, woman.

CUCA (*as mother*). What do you mean I don't understand? (*Sighs.*) Oh, Albert, what a baby you are. Isn't he, Angelita?

BEBA (*furiously. Gets up*). I want to do something. I'm going to crack up. I want to go. I can't stand being shut up. I'm suffocating. I'm going to die and I don't want to be crushed, buried in this room. Anything but that. I don't want any more of this. Please, please, please, let me go.

CUCA *goes up to* BEBA *and puts her arm around her. She feigns great tenderness with her expression and gestures.*)

CUCA (*as mother*). Go if you must, my darling. You are a little worked up. (BEBA *stays in the dark, upstage.* CUCA *returns with a smile that gives way to laughter.*) Have you ever seen anything like it? It was as if we were torturing her. What imaginations these children have . . . ! (*Sits down and arranges her hair.*) Look at me. I must look like a dog's dinner. I haven't had time to catch my breath all day. What an ordeal, Angelita, what an ordeal! I'm so sorry I've not been looking after you better . . . (*Listens to the imaginary person.*) But you're like one of the family. (*Smiles hypocritically.*) All the same, I do like to do things properly. Don't I, Albert? Don't lose your cool so easily, dear. We must stay perfectly calm and collected. (LALO *gets up.*) Where are you going? Think carefully before you do anything. (LALO *looks at her pointedly.*) Ah yes, I understand. (LALO *walks to the dark side of the stage.*) He's gone to keep an eye on what those little terrors are up to. You need eyes in the back of your head, or rather everywhere . . . You have to keep your ear to the ground. You always have to be on the watch, on the lookout, because they can be very, very naughty.

At this moment LALO *enters with an old and dirty bridal veil.* LALO *imitates his mother in her youth, on her wedding day in church. In the background,* BEBA *hums the wedding march.* LALO's *movements should not be exaggerated. A certain ambiguity prevails on this occasion.*

LALO (*as mother*). Oh, Albert, I'm scared. The smell of the flowers, the music . . . So many people have come, haven't they? Your sister Rose didn't come, nor did your cousin Lola . . . They don't like me! I know they don't, Albert! I know it! They've been saying horrible things about me, and about my mother too. Oh, I don't know! Do you really love me, Albert? Do I look pretty? Ah, my tummy hurts. Smile. There's that creep Dr. Nuñez and his wife . . . Do you think people are counting the months? If they find out, I'll die of embarrassment. Look, Espinosa's daughters are smiling at you, those sluts, whoops, did I say that word . . . ? Ah, Albert, I feel dizzy, my tummy hurts, hold me, don't tread on my train or I'll fall over . . . Oh, honey, I want to get rid of this baby . . . I know you're determined to have it, but I don't want it . . . Oh, I'm going to faint . . . Albert, Albert, this is ridiculous . . . We didn't have to get married today, another day would have been better . . . Oh, that music and the smell of those flowers, ugh! And there's your mother, that bitch, whoops, did I say that word . . . ? Ah, I don't know . . . Albert, I can't breathe . . . This damned brat! I'd like to rip it out myself . . .

CUCA (*as mother. Hatefully, biting the words*). You make me sick. (*Wrenching the veil off him.*) I don't know how I gave birth to such an abortion. I'm ashamed of you, ashamed of your whole life. And now you want to save yourself? No way; forget about salvation . . . Drown yourself. Die. Do you think I'm going to let you, you of all people, criticise me, in front of visitors? Don't you see what you are? You're a cretin! (*To the imaginary person.*) I'm so sorry, Angelita. Please don't go. (*In her previous harsh and firm tone of voice.*) I've been asking you to help me for ages. There are loads of things to clean in this house: the dishes, the fridge, the dust, and those marks on the mirrors. So much to be done: mending, darning, sewing. (LALO *goes up to* CUCA.) Get out. You want to turn this house upside down and I won't allow it. Not over my dead body. The ashtray goes on the table. (*Puts the ashtray on the table.*) The vase goes on the table. (*Puts the vase on the table.*) Who do you think you are? I'll tell your father right now . . . (*With disgust and rancour.*) You wretch, what would you do without us? What have you got to moan about? Do you think we are stupid? Yes? Well, I'll tell you, we're no better or worse than anyone else. But if you think we'll let you order us around, you're very wrong. Do you know what I've sacrificed to keep this house running smoothly? Do you think we'll just give it up like that? If you want to go, go. I'll pack your bags myself. There's the door.

CUCA *stands with her back to the audience.* LALO *approaches the table and contemplates the knife with indifference. He picks it up and caresses it. He stabs it into the centre of the table.*

LALO. How much longer? How much longer?

BEBA. Don't get impatient.

LALO. If only we could do it today.

BEBA. You're being stupid.

LALO. Right now.

> LALO *grabs the knife from the table. He looks at his two sisters and rushes upstage.*

BEBA. Don't do it.

CUCA. You'll be sorry.

BEBA. Be careful.

CUCA (*sings weakly*). The living room is not the living room.

> *The two sisters are in position,* BEBA *stage right,* CUCA *stage left. They have their backs to the audience. Simultaneously, they utter a frightful, shattering scream.* LALO *enters. The two sisters fall to their knees.*

LALO (*holding the knife*). Silence.

BEBA and CUCA (*start singing quietly*). The living room is not the living room, the living room is the kitchen. The bedroom is not the bedroom, the bedroom is the bathroom.

LALO. Now I feel calm. I'd like to sleep, sleep, sleep forever . . . But I'll do that tomorrow. Today I have a lot to do. (*The knife slips from his hands and falls to the ground.*) How easy it all is . . . ! You just walk into the room. Slowly, on tiptoes. The slightest noise would mean disaster. And you move forward, hanging in mid-air. The knife doesn't tremble. Nor does your hand. You know what you're doing. The wardrobes, the bed, the curtains, the vases, the carpets, the ashtrays, the chairs: they all push you towards the naked, wheezing, sweating bodies. (*Pause. Determined.*) And now we must clean up the blood. Wash them. Dress them. And fill the house with flowers. Later on, we'll dig a deep, deep hole and wait until morning . . . (*Pensively.*) So easy . . . so terrible.

> *The two sisters have stopped singing.* CUCA *picks up the knife and starts cleaning it on her apron. Long pause.*

CUCA (*to* BEBA). How do you feel?

BEBA (*to* CUCA). All right.

CUCA (*to* BEBA). It's tiring.

BEBA (*to* CUCA). The worst thing is, you get used to it.

CUCA (*to* BEBA). But some day . . .

BEBA (*to* CUCA). It's like everything.

LALO. Open the door. (*Beats his chest. Exalted, wide-eyed.*) An assassin. An assassin. (*Falls to his knees.*)

CUCA (*to* BEBA). What's all this?

BEBA. The first part has ended.

Blackout.

Act Two

As the curtain rises, LALO *is on his knees, his back to the audience, his head hanging low.* CUCA *is standing up, looking at him and laughing.* BEBA *impassively takes the knife which is lying on the table.*

CUCA (*to* BEBA). Look at him. (*To* LALO.) That's how I like to see you. (*Laughing.*) Now it's my turn. (*Laughs long and hard.*)

LALO (*imperiously*). Shut the door.

CUCA (*to* LALO, *closing the door*). I can't stand you!

BEBA (*to* CUCA, *looking at* LALO *disdainfully*). You're pathetic.

CUCA (*to* LALO). What's wrong with you? Listen, little one: we've got to carry on. We're not going to do things by half this time. I'm fed up with leaving the job unfinished.

LALO (*crestfallen*). We always have to begin again.

CUCA. Fine. I agree. But I still say that today . . .

LALO (*annoyed*). Yes, yes . . . Whatever you say.

CUCA. Whatever I say, no. Whatever must be. Or am I now the inventor of all this? That's a good one!

BEBA (*annoyed. To* CUCA). But you love . . .

CUCA (*offended*). And what do *you* want me to do, little girl?

BEBA. Anything but that.

CUCA. No, my sweet, the time has come and I have to see it through to the end.

BEBA. You know I'm right.

CUCA. I don't care.

BEBA. Then I'm going.

CUCA. You're staying.

BEBA. You're trying my patience.

CUCA. Don't threaten me.

BEBA. I can scratch and kick.

LALO. That's enough arguing.

CUCA (*to* BEBA). That's right: pipe down.

BEBA. Hah! I don't believe it. I am not going to let myself rot
away behind these walls. I hate this place. You two like all
this rubbish. But I'm young, and one of these days I'm
going to get out of here and not come back and then I'll be
able to do what I like. What do you think of that? (*Pause.*)
You didn't want to do it at the beginning, did you? But now
you're capable of killing to get what you want. It's as if
the salvation of your souls were at stake . . . Yes, your salvation . . . Don't look at me like that. Salvation from what?
Maybe you just want to save your own skin? (*Deliberately.*)
That's why you called the police. That's why you're about
to start the investigation and the interrogation. Did you do
this? No, no. You didn't do it? Hey, officer, how could I
have done it? But we've found a clue. There are the fingerprints. One of you committed the crime. Do you think you
can fuck with us, eh? Do you think you can take us for a
ride? I don't want to get involved in that.

CUCA. You have to see it through to the end.

BEBA. It never ends.

CUCA. Don't give up.

BEBA. I'm tired. It's always the same. Do this. Do that. Why
do we go round and round like this . . . ? (*More intimate.*)
Anyway, I don't want to get mixed up . . . (*Changes her
tone of voice.*) It's no fun.

CUCA. Everything you're saying is complete crap. (*Like her
mother.*) A right little gem you've turned out to be! Do you
think I'm just going to sit back and watch after what *he* has
done? I will defend Mum and Dad's memory. I will defend
them against anything.

BEBA. Don't touch me.

CUCA (*as mother, with authority*). Put that knife back where
you found it. (BEBA *obeys and drops the knife on the floor.*)
Not like that.

BEBA (*furiously*). You do it then.

CUCA (*slyly, with a smirk*). Control yourself. Come on, let's
　　have everything back in its proper place. (*Changes her tone
　　of voice.*) The best is yet to come. (BEBA *replaces the knife
　　in a satisfactory way.*) We must be very careful.

BEBA (*furiously*). Count me out.

CUCA (*mentally arranging the room*). The lamps, the curtains
　　. . . It's a mathematical question.

BEBA (*furiously*). Go and find someone else. Or do it all
　　yourself.

CUCA. You've been in on it from the start. You can't pull out
　　now.

BEBA. We'll see about that.

CUCA (*authoritarian, as mother.*) Nobody can foul up.

BEBA. Let's hope the unexpected happens.

CUCA. I'm depending on that as well. (*To* LALO.) Get up.
　　(LALO *doesn't reply.*)

BEBA (*furiously*). Leave him alone. Can't you see he's
　　suffering?

CUCA. Keep out of this.

BEBA. You should have waited. Maybe . . . Just a moment.

CUCA. I know what I'm doing.

BEBA (*with subtle sarcasm*). It's all right by me. But
　　remember I'm on my guard. Ready, at any moment . . .

CUCA (*rapidly, furiously*). To do what?

BEBA. To break out.

CUCA. Really? So you are against it . . . ? Well, listen very care-
　　fully to what I'm going to say: don't even think I'm going to
　　let you interfere. You're just a tool, a cog, a screw . . . You
　　should be happy about that. (*Pause.*) Don't make that face.
　　(*In a threatening tone of voice.*) All right, but you'll have to
　　take the consequences. In this house, everything is part of
　　the game. (*She moves around, trying to arrange things, and
　　listing them.*) Vase, knife, curtains, glasses . . . water, pills.
　　The police will be here in a minute . . . Syringe, ampoules . . .
　　All we have to do is disappear . . . vanish. (BEBA *makes as
　　if to leave.* CUCA *stops her.*) No, my sweet. Don't be silly.
　　You understand? (CUCA*'s sarcastic tone of voice makes
　　BEBA *flinch.*) What? You don't like what we're doing? Do

you want to throw a spanner in the works . . . ? We'll be invisible. Do you have anything to add? We are innocent. Do you want to take sides? (*To* LALO.) Get up. It's late. (*To* BEBA.) Are you going to defend the indefensible? Perhaps he's not an assassin? (*To* LALO.) Tidy yourself up a bit. You look like a corpse. (LALO *gets up clumsily.* BEBA *puts a pack of cards on the table and then spreads them out. To* BEBA.) That would never have crossed my mind.

LALO (*his back still to the audience. To* BEBA). Bring me some water.

CUCA (*imperiously*). No, that's not allowed. (*Approaching* LALO, *straightening out his clothes. Quite tenderly.*) You have to wait. (*As mother.*) That collar is a scandal . . . You look like a tramp.

LALO. My throat is dry.

BEBA (*as mother, quite tenderly*). Did you not sleep well?

LALO. I need to go outside for a while.

CUCA (*violently*). You're not going anywhere.

LALO. Just for a minute.

CUCA. Absolutely not. Everything is ready. What are you trying to . . . ? Are you playing with me? Well, I won't let you.

CUCA *tries to stop* LALO, *who moves to escape. She grabs him by his shirt collar. They struggle violently. For a moment,* BEBA *just watches them in amazement. Then she becomes morbidly interested in the fight and starts to walk around* CUCA *and* LALO.

LALO. Let go of me.

CUCA. No way.

LALO. Who do you think you are?

CUCA. Who do you think *you* are?.

LALO. You're scratching me.

CUCA. All part of the game. This is life or death. And you can't escape. I'll do anything to see you put away.

BEBA *runs to the dark side of the stage where the door is.*

BEBA (*screaming*). The police, the police.

The two siblings stop fighting. LALO *falls into a chair, beaten.* BEBA *stands beside the closed door.* CUCA *stands on the other side of the door, also upstage.*

CUCA (*in her previous tone of voice, furiously*). I'll never forgive you. It's your fault. All your fault. If you want to die, go ahead and die.

BEBA. Sshh! Be quiet.

Long pause. BEBA and CUCA start to move slowly, almost in slow motion. They are now the two policemen who discover the crime.

CUCA (*as policeman 1*). Very dark in here.

BEBA (*as policeman 2*). Smells horrible.

CUCA (*as policeman 1*). Bloodstains everywhere.

BEBA (*as policeman 2*). Looks like they've killed a couple of pigs.

CUCA (*as policeman 1*). It was pigs what did it.

BEBA (*as policeman 2*). Swine.

The two sisters walk as if in a darkened gallery. LALO remains in the chair. The sisters stop in front of him and pretend to shine a torch on him.

BEBA (*as policeman 2*). Got him.

CUCA (*as policeman 1*). What a fight he put up. (*To LALO, violently.*) Get up. Come on, move it, move it. (LALO *tries to shield himself from the torch's glare.*)

BEBA (*as policeman 2*). Hey, boy . . . One move and I'll blow your head off.

CUCA (*as policeman 1*). Come on, get up.

BEBA (*as policeman 2*). It's curtains for you, boy. (LALO *gets up and puts his hands up.*) We'd better be quick.

CUCA (*as policeman 1*). Frisk 'im.

BEBA (*as policeman 2*). This guy is dangerous. (*Frisks* LALO's *clothes and body.*) Where are your papers? What's your name? (LALO *makes no reply.*) Can't you see you're under arrest? If an officer of the law asks you a question, you answer him. Now who screamed?

CUCA (*as policeman 1*). Have you killed someone?

BEBA (*as policeman 2*). Where's all the blood from?

CUCA.(*as policeman 1*). Do you live with your parents?

BEBA (*as policeman 2*). Do you have any sisters and brothers? Answer.

CUCA (*as policeman 1*). You did 'em in, didn't you? Answer. It's in your own interest.

LALO (*very vaguely*). Don't know.

BEBA (*as policeman 2*). What do you mean, 'don't know'? Do you live on your own?

CUCA (*as policeman 1*). And all these clothes . . . ? Let him be. (*Smiles.*) He'll talk in the end.

BEBA (*as policeman 2*). Nobody can save him now, mate. (*Smiles. Crudely.*) He's a hard bastard. He probably started by robbing them. But that wasn't enough, so he decided to kill them. (*To* LALO.) Your own parents? I can hardly believe it. Did you poison them? (*Holds up the box of pills and puts it back on the table.*) How many pills . . . ? (LALO *doesn't reply. He occasionally smiles.*) Come on, out with it . . . If you talk, it'll be easier for you. (*To* CUCA, *showing her the syringe.*) Look. He probably . . .

CUCA (*as policeman 1*). It looks like this crime's a real whopper. (*To* LALO.) Where are the bodies? (*To* BEBA.) No sign of them.

BEBA (*as policeman 2*). Where did you hide them? Did you bury them?

CUCA (*as policeman 1*). We'll have to search the house from top to bottom. Comb it, every inch of it.

BEBA (*as policeman 2*). Why did you kill them? Answer. Did they abuse you?

LALO (*dryly*). No.

CUCA (*as policeman 1*). Time's up, sonny. Why did you kill them?

LALO (*confidently*). I didn't do it.

CUCA (*as policeman 1*). You've got a nerve!

BEBA (*as policeman 2*). Were they asleep?

CUCA (*as policeman 1*). Don't play tough-guy with me. So you didn't kill anyone? Not your parents? Not your brothers? None of your relations? (LALO *shrugs his shoulders.*) Then what have you done?

BEBA (*as policeman 2*). Did you smother them with their pillows?

CUCA (*as policeman 1*). How many times did you stab them?

BEBA (*as policeman 2*). Five? Ten? Fifteen?

CUCA (*as policeman 1*). You're not going to tell me this is all a game. There's blood all over the shop. Look, you're covered in it yourself. How can you deny it? I've never seen such a crime. (*Suddenly.*) Where are your parents? Stuffed in a trunk? (*Pause. Reconstructing the scene.*) You walked slowly, on tiptoes, so as not to make a noise . . . Your parents were snoring. You were holding your breath and the knife in your hand didn't even tremble . . .

LALO (*proudly*). Wrong. You're lying.

CUCA (*as policeman 1*). Then what did happen? (*Exhausted.*) Ah, this house is a labyrinth.

BEBA (*as policeman 2. He has been examining the room*). Here's the proof. (*Points to the knife.*) We're getting there. (*Stoops to pick it up.*)

CUCA (*as policeman 1, shouting*). Don't touch it.

BEBA. (*as policeman 2*). We have to check it for fingerprints. (*Picks the knife up with a handkerchief and puts it on the table.*)

CUCA (*as policeman 1*). If he continues refusing to . . .

BEBA (*as policeman 2*). I'll sort him out in a moment. (*To LALO.*) Come here. You better talk or else I'll . . . Look. I don't want to have to resort to violence. But who do you think we are? We're not just here for decoration. (*In a tone of voice which is both threatening and persuasive.*) Talk, it's in your own interest. You've had plenty of time to think. (*In a friendlier tone of voice.*) Talk, come on, it's for your own good. (*Looking at* CUCA.) It'll all be taken into account, don't worry. (CUCA *goes to the side of the stage, searching for clues.*) You'll feel much better once you've told us all about it. It's very easy, very, very easy. (*In an almost familiar tone of voice.*) How did you do it? Why did you do it? Did they abuse you verbally or . . . ? Was there some kind of robbery? What really happened? Perhaps you've forgotten? Try and remember . . . Let's see, take your time.

LALO (*very haughtily*). None of you could understand.

BEBA (*as policeman 2, persuasively, smiling*). Why do you say that? (*More intimately.*) Come on, boy, own up.

CUCA (*as policeman 1, offstage*). Don't worry. I've found it. (*Comes on stage, rubbing his hands together.*) Just take a look! It's a disgusting sight! Horrible! It'd make anyone's hair stand on end. (*Reconstructing the scene.*) There's a pick and a shovel. He's dug this massive hole. I don't know how he did it on his own . . . And there, at the bottom are two bodies with a little earth on them. (*Going up to* LALO *and slapping him on the back.*) So this young gentleman did nothing, did he? (BEBA *goes over to the place from where* CUCA *has come.*) Yes, yes, I understand. (*With a smile of satisfaction.*) The young gentleman is innocent. Well, well, well . . . (*Stares at him disdainfully.*) This young gentleman's days are numbered. (*In a vulgar tone of voice.*) You've signed your own death warrant, Sonny-Jim.

BEBA (*coming on set, no longer as policeman 2*). It's awful.

CUCA (*as policeman 1, in a vulgar tone of voice*). Don't get melodramatic.

BEBA. It made me go weak at the knees.

CUCA (*as policeman 1*). This kid is quite something.

BEBA. It was bloodcurdling.

CUCA (*as policeman 1*). Come on, pull yourself together. (*To* LALO, *disdainfully.*) You're a . . . You make me want to . . . (*To* BEBA.) Let's draw up the charges.

BEBA. What? But he hasn't confessed yet.

CUCA (*as policeman 1*). It's not necessary.

BEBA. I think it will be.

CUCA (*as policeman 1*). We've got enough evidence.

BEBA. We should at least try . . . (*Going up to* LALO.) Lalo, you must tell us. You must talk. Why? Why, Lalo?

CUCA (*as policeman 1*). Don't let up on him now.

BEBA. (*To* LALO, *almost begging.*) Don't you understand, it's a formality. We need a confession. Say whatever you like, whatever comes into your head, even if it's illogical or absurd. Please say something. (LALO *remains impenetrable.*)

CUCA (*as policeman 1*). Let's get back to the station. The charges. The report.

BEBA *walks gravely over to the table and sits down. From this moment on, the stage should take on a new dimension, an eerie strangeness. The elements used are vocal sounds, beating on the table, and rhythmic foot-tapping, first by* BEBA *and then by both* BEBA *and* CUCA.

CUCA (*dictating, automatically*). In the neighbourhood of this police station, and being the fifth day . . .

BEBA (*moving her hands over the table, automatically*). Tac-tac-tac-tac. Tac-tac-tac-tac. Tac- tac-tac-tac.

CUCA. . . . in the presence of the duty officer, we the undersigned, Officer 421 Cuco and Officer 842 Bebo, brought in for questioning an individual claiming to be called . . .

BEBA. Tac-tac-tac-tac. Tac-tac-tac-tac. Tac-tac-tac-tac. (CUCA *moves her lips as if she were still dictating.*)

CUCA. The officers affirm that finding themselves in the area corresponding to their assigned patrol . . .

BEBA (*beating her hands on the table with great sense of rhythm*). Tac-tac-tac-tac. Tac-tac-tac- tac. Tac-tac-tac-tac.

CUCA. . . . heard raised voices and a public disturbance . . .

BEBA. Tac-tac-tac-tac. Tac-tac-tac-tac.

CUCA. . . . arguing and fighting . . .

BEBA. Tac-tac-tac-tac. Tac-tac-tac-tac.

CUCA. . . . and having heard a cry for help . . .

BEBA. (*Beating her hands on the table and tapping her feet rhythmically and automatically.*) Tac-tac-tac-tac. Tac-tac-tac. Tac-tac-tac-tac.

CUCA. . . . and upon entering the aforementioned house . . .

BEBA. Tac-tac-tac-tac. Tac-tac-tac-tac.

CUCA. . . . discovered two bodies . . .

BEBA. Tac-tac-tac-tac.

CUCA. . . . with contusions and first-degree injuries . . .

BEBA. Tac-tac-tac-tac. Tac-tac-tac-tac.

CUCA *starts to beat on the table and to tap her feet like* BEBA. *The scene reaches a delirious climax which lasts a moment. Pause.* BEBA *and* CUCA *seem to return to normality.* CUCA *shows a piece of paper to* LALO.

CUCA (*authoritatively*). Sign here.

Pause. LALO looks at the piece of paper. Looks at CUCA. Takes the paper with contempt and studies it closely.

LALO (*furiously, firmly, defiantly*). I don't accept. Do you understand? This is all rubbish. It's disgraceful. (*Pause. Almost mockingly.*) I think it's splendid, terrific, that you should try and interrogate me using these appalling techniques. It's so logical. Almost . . . normal, natural. But what do you want? Do you think I'm going to sign this shitty piece of paper? You call this the law? You call this justice? (*Shouting. Tears up the piece of paper.*) Crap, crap, crap. This is the dignified thing to do. This is the exemplary thing to do. This is the respectable thing to do. (*Angrily stamps on the torn-up paper. Pause. Smiling bitterly, almost crying.*) How nice, how dignified, how exemplary it would be if you were just to say: guilty. And be done with it. Next case, please. But to do what you're doing now . . . (*To CUCA.*) Are you not satisfied with what has happened? Why are you trying to feed me with a pile of fictions? Do you think I'm a moron? (*Mockingly.*) Or do you think I'm trembling with fear. Well, let me say it loud and clear: no. I am not afraid. (BEBA *hits the table with the gavel.*) I'm guilty. Yes, guilty. So judge me. Do what you like. I'm entirely in your hands. (BEBA *bangs the gavel again.* LALO'*s tone of voice becomes less violent, although he still acts arrogantly.*) If your Honour will allow me . . .

BEBA (*as judge*). The public will remain silent, or the court will be cleared and this hearing will proceed *in camera*. (*To CUCA.*) Prosecution may proceed.

CUCA (*to BEBA*). Thank you very much, your Honour. (*To LALO.*) The accused is aware of the difficulties we have encountered in our attempts to clarify the circumstances surrounding the events which took place on that ill-fated morning . . . of . . . (BEBA *bangs the gavel.*)

BEBA (*as judge*). I must ask the prosecution to be more specific and clear in the formulation of his questions.

CUCA (*as public prosecutor*). Excuse me, your Honour, but . . .

BEBA (*moving her gavel*). I must ask the prosecution to attend exclusively to his cross-examination.

CUCA (*as public prosecutor. To* BEBA). Your Honour, throughout all previous questioning, the accused has been exceptionally evasive, which has made it impossible to reach any . . .

BEBA (*as judge. To* CUCA. *Bangs the table hard*). Keep to the point.

CUCA (*as public prosecutor. Solemnly*). Your Honour, let me repeat that the accused has systematically obstructed all attempts to arrive at the truth. For this reason, I submit for the consideration of the court the following questions: is he permitted to make fun of the Law? Should he make fun of the Law? Is not the Law, the Law? If we are *permitted* to make fun of the Law, does the Law stop being the Law? If we *should* make fun of the Law, is the Law something other than the Law? In short, ladies and gentlemen of the jury, do we all have to become mind readers?

BEBA (*as judge. Implacable, hammering the table*). I insist that the prosecution does not stray beyond its remit.

CUCA (*as public prosecutor, showing off her theatrical abilities*). Ah, ladies and gentlemen, the accused, like every guilty man, fears the weight of Justice . . .

LALO (*furiously, but containing himself*). You're trying to trap me. I can see you coming. You're trying to destroy me, I won't let you.

CUCA (*as public prosecutor. Solemnly and furiously. To* BEBA). Your Honour, the accused is behaving in contempt of court. In the name of the Law, I request that correct procedure be followed. What is the accused trying to do? Is he trying to disrupt proceedings? If that is his objective, we have to rule him publicly out of court. The processes of Law and Justice must remain logical. Nobody can complain about their methods. They were made to suit mankind. But it appears that the accused either does not understand, or does not want to understand, or perhaps he suffers from mental disorder . . . Or maybe he prefers to hide himself, to take cover behind a smokescreen of stupidity and aggression. I must ask every single member of this jury and the court in general to examine his attitude carefully and, at the appropriate time, to deliver a verdict which is both balanced and implacable. Ladies and gentlemen, on the one hand, the accused openly declares his guilt, that is, he admits that he

has killed. This regrettable deed lies beyond the limits of
normal behaviour and represents an intolerable threat to
everyone who walks the streets of this city. On the other
hand, the accused denies everything, in an indirect way of
course, and seeks to muddle up the chain of events through
a cunning combination of sophistries, contradictions,
banalities, and absurdities. Phrases like: 'I don't know';
'possibly'; 'maybe'; 'yes' and 'no'. Are these answers?
Note also the frequent resort to: if I had a clear memory
of events . . . Ladies and gentlemen of the jury, this is all
inadmissible. (*Comes forward until he is centre-stage, with
great theatrical effect.*) The Law cannot stand idly by in the
face of such a case, where degradation, malice, and cruelty
are combined so horrifically. Standing before you, ladies
and gentleman, you see the most repulsive assassin in all of
history. Look at him. Could anyone fail to feel revulsion at
this scum, this nauseating rat, this pool of phlegm? Doesn't
he make you want to be sick, to curse him? Can the Law just
stand by and watch? Ladies and gentlemen of the jury,
ladies and gentlemen of the court, can we allow such an
individual to share our hopes and ideals at a time when
humanity, or rather our society is marching on the resplendent path of progress, heading towards a golden dawn?
(LALO *tries to say something, but the torrent of* CUCA's
oratory blocks any act, gesture or word from him.) Look at
him. Indifferent. Relaxed. Immune to any feeling of tenderness, understanding, or pity. Look at that face. (*Loudly.*)
The cool face of a killer. An assassin. The accused denies
committing the murder for money, either in order to steal or
to inherit his parents' meagre pension. Why did he kill then?
We cannot be certain about any of his motives. May we
conclude that he did it out of hatred? Revenge? Or was it
simple sadism? (*Pause.* LALO *moves impatiently in his
chair.* CUCA *continues in a measured tone of voice.*) Can
the Law allow a son to kill his parents?

LALO (*to* BEBA). Your Honour . . . I want . . . I should
like . . .

CUCA (*as public prosecutor*). No, ladies and gentlemen of the
jury. No, ladies and gentlemen of the court. A thousand
times no. The Law cannot accept such contempt. The Law
has created order. The Law is eternally vigilant. The Law
demands good manners. The Law protects man from
primitive and corrupt instincts. Can we have pity on a

creature who violates the principles of natural law? I ask the ladies and gentlemen of the jury, I ask the ladies and gentlemen of the court: can we allow ourselves the indulgence of pity? (*Pause.*) Our entire city rises up in anger. A city of proud and silent men comes forward determined to claim for Justice the body of this monster . . . demanding that he be exposed to the fury of true human beings whose only desires are for peace and harmony. (*Grandly.*) And so, I demand that the accused help us establish the true course of events. (*To* LALO.) Why did you kill your parents?

LALO. I wanted a life.

CUCA (*as public prosecutor, violently*). That's not an answer. (*Rapidly.*) How did you do it? Did you give them some concoction, some poison? Or did you smother them with their pillows as they lay helplessly in bed? Where do the syringes and pills come in? Or are they just red herrings? Explain, prisoner at the bar. (*Pause.*) Did you kill them in cold blood? Was it planned step by step? Or was it a crime of passion? *You* tell us. Did you only use this knife? (*Exhausted.*) And finally, prisoner at the bar, why did you kill them?

LALO. I felt they were persecuting me, harassing me.

CUCA (*as public prosecutor*). Persecuting you? How? Harassing you? How?

LALO. They never let me alone.

CUCA (*as public prosecutor*). But the witnesses testify that . . .

LALO. The witnesses are lying . . .

CUCA (*as public prosecutor*). Are you contesting the statements made by the witnesses?

LALO (*Firmly*). There was nobody there that night.

BEBA (*as judge. To* LALO). The accused must be more precise in his answers. This is absolutely necessary. Are you sure you mean what you've just said? The Court demands both truth and precision. The Court expects the accused to observe, without prejudice, these articles of procedure . . . The prosecution may proceed.

CUCA (*as public prosecutor*). Let us now turn to your close relatives. Your grandmother, for example, your aunts and uncles, all your nearest and dearest. Did you see each other often? What kind of relationship did you have with them?

LALO. None.

CUCA (*as public prosecutor*). Why?

LALO. Mum hated Dad's family and Dad didn't get along with Mum's family.

CUCA (*as public prosecutor*). Aren't you exaggerating?

LALO. None of our relations visited us . . . Mum didn't want them to come round. She said they were jealous and hypocritical. Dad said the same thing about Mum's relations. And they wouldn't let us visit them either . . .

CUCA (*as public prosecutor*). This doesn't seem to have much basis in fact to me. Why . . . ?

LALO. They kept on telling us that we were better people, that they were all common, that they had no class . . .

CUCA (*as public prosecutor*). And you never tried to make contact with them?

LALO. I tried once, but it didn't work.

CUCA (*as public prosecutor*). Do you know the witness Mrs. Angelita . . . ? (*To the audience.*) Her surname, please. Thank you. The witness Angela Martínez.

LALO. Yes.

CUCA (*as public prosecutor*). Did she go to your house, either before or after the incident in question?

LALO. She did. Before. (*Pause.*) At around 6pm.

CUCA (*as public prosecutor*). In her statement, she insists that you were all playing a strange game. What was the game that you played at home? (*Pause.*) Wasn't it a bit . . . unhealthy? (*Pause.*) Answer. Wasn't it a deviant game?

LALO (*firmly*). I don't know.

CUCA (*as public prosecutor*). Your parents, according to my understanding, complained about you.

LALO. All my life, as long as I can remember, I've been hearing the same complaints, the same sermons, the same nagging.

CUCA (*as public prosecutor*). They must have had some reason for complaining.

LALO. Sometimes they did, sometimes they didn't . . . When a reason is hammered home over and over again, it stops being reasonable.

CUCA (*as public prosecutor*). Were your parents really so demanding?

LALO. I don't understand.

CUCA (*as public prosecutor*). The question is this: what kind of relationship did you have with your parents?

LALO. I'm sure I've told you already. They questioned me. They made demands on me. They spied on me.

CUCA (*as public prosecutor*). What questions did they ask? What demands did they make? Why were they spying?

LALO (*desperate*). I don't know. I don't know. (*Repeating in a mechanical voice.*) Wash the dishes, wash the tablecloths, wash the shirts. Clean the vase, clean the bathroom, clean the floors. Don't sleep, don't dream, don't read. You're useless.

CUCA (*as public prosecutor*). Ladies and gentlemen of the jury, ladies and gentlemen of the court, do you believe these are motives strong enough to drive an individual to commit a murder?

LALO (*stammering*). I wanted . . .

CUCA (*as public prosecutor*). What did you want? (*Pause.*) Answer.

LALO (*sincerely*). A life.

CUCA (*as public prosecutor. Sarcastically*). And did your parents take your life away from you? (*To the audience.*) Objection, m'lud, the accused is evading the question.

LALO (*passionately*). I wanted, I longed, I desperately longed to do things for myself.

CUCA (*as public prosecutor*). And did your parents stop you?

LALO (*confidently*). Yes.

CUCA (*as public prosecutor*). How?

LALO. They said I was a fool, a slob, a no-hoper.

CUCA (*as public prosecutor. With great patience*). And what were the things you wanted to do? Would the accused care to elaborate?

LALO (*tormented, making a great effort, a little confused*). It's very hard . . . I don't know. Things. You know? Things. How can I put it? I know they exist, that they're out there . . .

I just can't at the moment. (CUCA *smiles maliciously*.)
Look . . . I know it's something else, it's just that . . . (*Confidently*.) I tried every way I could to please them . . . I caught
pneumonia once and I . . . No, I can't tell you about that . . .
I just . . . Things always went wrong for me. I didn't want it
to be that way but I couldn't do anything else; and then . . .

CUCA (*as public prosecutor*). Then what?

LALO. They shouted at me, they hit me, they punished me,
endless hours locked in my room. They told me a thousand
and one times I was better off dead, that they wanted to see
me leave home to see how I coped and whether I would die
of starvation.

CUCA (*with a cynical smile*). Are you sure about what you're
saying?

LALO. Yes.

CUCA (*as public prosecutor*). Go on, go on.

LALO. I was very unhappy.

CUCA (*as public prosecutor*). Why?

LALO. It felt like the house was caving in on me.

CUCA (*as public prosecutor*). I don't understand? Exactly
what do you mean?

LALO. The walls, the carpets, the curtains, the lamps, the sofa
where Dad took his siesta, and the bed, and the wardrobes,
and the sheets . . . the whole lot, I hated them, I wanted them
to go away.

CUCA (*as public prosecutor*). You hated the whole lot. And
your parents? You hated your parents as well, didn't you?

LALO (*distracted*). Maybe I should have just run away. Gone
anywhere: to hell or Timbuktu.

CUCA (*as public prosecutor*). Ladies and gentlemen of the
jury, ladies and gentlemen of the court . . .

LALO (*continuing, as if hypnotised*). One day, when I was
playing with my sisters, I suddenly discovered . . . (*Pause*.)

CUCA (*as public prosecutor*). What did you discover?

LALO (*in the same tone of voice as before*). We were in the
living room; no, I lie . . . We were in the back room. We
were playing . . . Or rather, we were acting . . . (*Smiles
foolishly*.) You might think it silly but . . . I was the father.

No, that's not true. I think at that moment I was the mother. It was just a game . . . But there, right at that moment, I had this idea . . . (*Smiles foolishly again.*)

CUCA (*as public prosecutor*). What idea?

LALO (*smiling as before*). It's very simple, but it gets complicated. You never know whether you're saying what you feel. I . . . (*Moves his hands as if he were trying to explain things with this movement.*) I knew what my folks were offering me wasn't life, and could never be life. So I said to myself: 'If you want to live you have to . . . ' (*Stops and makes a stabbing gesture or clenches his fists as if tearing something apart.*)

CUCA (*as public prosecutor*). What did you feel at that moment?

LALO. I don't know. You tell me.

CUCA (*as public prosecutor*). Were you afraid?

LALO. I think I was, just for a second.

CUCA (*as public prosecutor*). And then?

LALO. Then I wasn't.

CUCA (*as public prosecutor*). You got used to the idea?

LALO. I got used to it.

CUCA (*as public prosecutor*). What? (*Banging the table.*) Ladies and gentlemen, this is unprecedented.

LALO. It's true. I got used to it. (*As* LALO *progresses through the monologue, he becomes transformed*). It sounds terrible, but . . . It's not how I wanted it, but the idea kept on buzzing around in my head. At first, I wanted it to go away. Do you know what I mean? But it kept on telling me: 'Kill your parents. Kill your parents.' I thought I was going crazy, I swear. I jumped into bed. I started getting the shivers . . . I had a temperature. I thought I would pop like a balloon. I thought the devil was beckoning to me. I lay trembling under the blankets . . . You should have seen me . . . I couldn't sleep. Not a wink night after night. It was dreadful. I saw death creeping up on me from behind the bed, from between the curtains, from inside the wardrobe. It became my shadow and whispered to me from inside the pillows: 'Assassin.' And then, as if by magic, it disappeared. And I sat in front of the mirror and saw my mother lying dead in her coffin and my father hanging by his neck laughing and shouting at me. And at night I felt my mother's hands in the pillows, scratching my face. (*Pause.*) Every morning I woke up in pain. It was as if I were rising from the dead, clasped by two corpses which had been chasing me in my dreams. There were moments when I was tempted . . . but no . . . no . . . Leave home? No way! I knew what I was up against . . . I would always come back and then I would promise never to do it again. By then I was determined never again to embark on that crazy adventure. Anything but that! Then I had the idea of arranging the house in my own way, of running things myself . . . The living room is not the living room, I said to myself. The living room is the kitchen. The bedroom is not the bedroom. The bedroom is the bathroom. (*Short pause.*) What else could I do? If I didn't do that, I would end up destroying everything. Everything. Because everything was complicit, everything was plotting against me; everything knew my every thought. If I sat down in a chair, the chair wasn't the chair but my father's corpse. If I picked up a glass of water, I felt that what I had in my hands was my dead mother's damp neck. If I played with a vase, an enormous knife would suddenly fall out of it. If I cleaned the carpets, I could never finish the job because they turned into an enormous clot of blood. (*Pause.*) Haven't you ever felt like that? I was suffocating, suffocating. I didn't know where I was or what it was all about. And who could I talk to? Was there anyone I could trust? I was stuck in a deep hole and there was no way out . . . (*Pause.*) But I had a strange idea that I could save myself . . . I don't know what from . . . Anyway, it's just an expression . . . You try to explain the whole thing and you almost . . . usually you can't . . . Perhaps I wanted to save myself from the suffocating, from being shut in . . . Soon after, without knowing why, things began to change. I heard a voice one day, but I didn't know where it was coming from . . . And then I heard my sisters laughing and joking all round the house. And mixed in with their laughter I heard thousands of voices repeating in unison: 'Kill them. Kill them.' No, I'm not just making it up. I swear it's true. (*As if inspired.*) From then on I knew what I had to do. Gradually I realised that everything, the carpets, the bed, the wardrobes, the mirror, the vases, the glasses, the spoons and my own shadow, they were all murmuring, telling me: 'Kill your parents.' (*He says it in an almost musical ecstasy.*) 'Kill your parents.' The whole house, everything, everything was pushing me towards this heroic act. (*Pause.*)

CUCA (*violently*). I'm leaving. You're cheating.

LALO. We've got to see it through to the end.

CUCA. I can't let you . . .

LALO. You've tried to make it go your way as well.

CUCA. I can't believe you're doing this. We each have a part; we agreed.

LALO. Is that so? All right then . . .

BEBA (*as judge, banging her gavel*). Order! Silence in court!

CUCA (*as mother. To* BEBA). Officer, forgive my interruption; but I must ask for a thorough investigation of this case, right from the beginning. I demand a retrial. That's why I'm here. I want to make a statement. My son is making himself out to be a victim, but that's the complete opposite of the truth. I demand that justice be done. (BEBA *starts to repeat the tac-tac of the typewriter. Exaggerating.*) If you knew what this beast has done to our lives. It's so dreadful, so . . .

BEBA (*as officer. To* CUCA). Go on . . .

LALO (*almost out of part*). But Mum, I . . . (LALO *feels cornered.*) I . . . I swear . . .

CUCA (*as mother*). Don't you swear at me. You want to come across as a fool, but I know your tricks, your games. I know them because I gave birth to you. Nine months of dizziness, vomiting, aches, and pains. And they were just the warnings of your arrival. Are you trying to confuse me? Why are you swearing these things to me? Do you think you've won over your audience? Do you think you can save yourself? Well tell me, save yourself from what? (*Roars with laughter.*) What planet are you living on, sonny? (*Mockingly.*) Oh, my little angel, I'm so sorry for you. You really are, well, I won't say what you are . . . (*To* BEBA.) Do you know something, officer? One day he got it into his head that we should rearrange the whole house the way he wanted it . . . As soon as I heard this ridiculous idea, I refused to listen to another word on the subject. His father hit the roof. You can't imagine what it looked like . . . The ashtray on the chair. The vase lying on the floor. Awful! And then he started singing at the top of his voice, running all round the house: 'The living room is not the living room. The living room is the kitchen.' When that happened I pretended not to hear, as if I were listening to the rain. (*To* LALO.) You've only told the bits which interest you. Why don't you tell the rest of the story? (*Mockingly.*) You've told them about your martyrdom, now tell them about ours, your father's and mine. Let me refresh your memory. (*To* BEBA, *transformed.*) Your Honour, if you knew the tears I have shed, the humiliation I have suffered, the hours of anguish, the sacrifices . . . Just look at these hands . . . It makes me sick to look at them. (*On the verge of tears.*) My hands . . . If you had seen them before I got married . . . Now I've lost everything: my youth, my happiness, all my little pleasures. I've sacrificed everything for this animal. (*To* LALO.) Aren't you ashamed? Do you still think you've done something heroic? (*Disgusted.*) You wretch. I don't know how I could have carried you for so long in my belly. I don't know why I didn't drown you at birth. (BEBA *bangs her gavel.*)

LALO. Mum, I . . .

CUCA (*as mother*). Shut up. Just shut up. You're not worth the bread we put on your plate. You're not worth one of the contractions I had giving birth to you. Because you, you are the guilty one. And no-one else.

LALO (*Violently*). Leave me alone. Just leave me alone.

CUCA (*as mother. Violently*). I'm getting old. Think about that and make some sacrifices. Do you think I don't have a right to live? Do you think I'm going to spend my whole life in perpetual agony? Your father doesn't care about me and neither do you. Where will I end up? Yes, I know you're waiting for me to die, but I won't give you that satisfaction. I'll shout to the neighbours, to everyone in the street. You'll see. That will be my revenge. (*Shouting.*) Help! Help! They're killing me. (*Bursts into tears.*) I'm a poor old woman dying of loneliness. (BEBA *bangs her gavel.*) Yes, your Honour, I'm imprisoned by these four dirty walls. I never see the light of day. My children don't care. I'm withered, wilting . . . (*As if she were looking at herself in a mirror. Starts stroking her face and ends up slapping it.*) Look at this skin. Look at these wrinkles. (*Pointing to her wrinkles with rancour and disgust. To* LALO.) You'll get them one day. All I want is for you to go through the same as I have. (*Haughtily.*) Your Honour, I have always been an honest woman.

LALO (*slightly mockingly*). Are you sure? Think carefully, Mum.

CUCA (*as mother*). What do you mean? What are you suggesting?

LALO (*sarcastically*). I mean, I know you're lying. I mean, you once accused me of . . .

CUCA (*as mother. Indignantly, interrupting him with a cry.*) Lalo! (*Pause. Gently.*) Lalo, are you trying to say . . . ? (*Pause. Takes a few steps. She looks annoyed again.*) This is just the limit! Your Honour . . . (*Almost sobbing.*) Oh, Lalo . . . (*Wiping her tears away.*) You say I . . . ? (*With obvious doubt.*) Is that possible? (*With a faint smile.*) Oh, I'm sorry, your Honour . . . I could have done it . . . But it was just a silly mistake. (*Laughs crudely.*) I got completely hooked on this red taffeta dress I saw in the window of the New Bazaar. It was so divine. My husband was earning a pittance. You can't imagine . . . I had to perform miracles every month just to make ends meet. So, as I was saying, your Honour, I was mad about that dress. I had to have it. I had dreams about it. I even saw it in my soup. At last, one day I decided to buy the dress with the housekeeping money. So I made up a story.

BEBA (*as judge*). What kind of story?

CUCA (*as mother. With great self-confidence*). When Albert got home, drunk as usual, I said to him: look, dear, will you have a word with your son . . . (*Goes up to* BEBA *to whisper in her ear.*) Because I think he's stolen some money from us.

BEBA (*as judge*). Why did you do it?

CUCA (*as mother. Vulgarly*). I don't know . . . It was easier that way . . . (*She finishes the story with a flourish.*) So Albert took off his belt and beat poor little Lalo . . . Oh, I hate to think how many times he beat him . . . In fact, he was completely innocent, but . . . I wanted that red dress so much! (*Going up to* LALO.) Do you forgive me, my son?

LALO (*hard*). There's nothing to forgive.

CUCA (*as mother. Slightly hysterical*). Have some respect, Lalo. (*In a dramatic tone of voice.*) I've changed. I'm fat and ugly now . . . Ah, this body!

LALO. Don't think about it.

CUCA (*as mother. With authority*). Show some respect, I said.

LALO. I was only playing around.

CUCA (*as mother. Hard and imperious*). Well, don't play with me. Your father is an old fool who's chasing something which doesn't exist. So are you. Let him be a lesson to you ... He thinks he's Superman, but actually he's a nobody. He's always been a failure. He's always been all talk, and he thinks he can carry on like that. Sometimes I wish he'd lie down and die. Why did I have to get hitched to a man who couldn't offer me a better life than this? (*Pause.*) Come on. (*Pause.*) If it wasn't for me, your Honour, this house wouldn't even be standing ... It was all me ...

LALO (*as father. In an assured, almost frightening voice*). She's lying, your Honour.

CUCA (*as mother. To* LALO). How dare you?

LALO (*as father. To* BEBA). It's true. She's trying to paint everything black. She sees only the motes in the eyes of others, not the beam in her own. I have been at fault at times as a parent. And so has she. (*In a more assured tone of voice.*) Like all parents we've done some things which have been unfair and other things which have been unforgivable.

CUCA (*as mother*). You used to come home with lipstick on your collar.

LALO (*as father*). Shut up. You don't want me to tell the truth.

CUCA (*as mother*). Your honour, he was always drinking, he used to bring his friends over at all hours of the night ...

LALO (*as father*). Who wears the trousers in our house?

CUCA (*as mother*). I'm in charge of the house.

LALO (*as father*). There. 'I'm in charge of the house.' Yes, you, you're in charge all right. That's all your life comes down to. You've made fun of me. You've humiliated me. That's the truth. Domination. (*Short pause.*) I've been an idiot, a complete asshole, if you'll excuse my French.

CUCA (*as mother*). Well done. At least you admit it.

LALO (*as father*). What's the point of denying it? (*Pause. Ordering his thoughts.*) I went into marriage with few illusions. If I said I was pinning all my hopes on marriage, I'd be both exaggerating and lying. I went into it like most people, thinking that it would sort out a few problems: clothes, food, stability . . . some company and . . . well . . . a few little liberties. (*Kicking himself inside.*) Idiot! You idiot! (*Pause.*) I never thought it would turn out like it did.

CUCA (*as mother*). You never thought, full stop. 'You take the low road and I'll take the high road.' That's what a lot of people think. But I was different.

LALO (*as father*). She's right there. She certainly was very different. The problems started a few days before the wedding: the church wasn't smart enough, the train on your dress wasn't long enough. And your sisters said this, and your mother said that, and your cousin said the other, and your aunt said something else, and your friends didn't agree at all, and your granny thought we should have invited the so-and-sos, and that the cake should have been ten rather than nine tiers high, and that your friends should come from better backgrounds . . .

CUCA (*as mother*). Go on, go on. Spit it all out, get it all out of your system. At last I can see that you hate me.

LALO (*as father*). Yes, I do. And I don't know why. But I know I do. When we were just going out you went to bed with me because you knew that was the only way you could catch me. And that's the truth.

CUCA (*as mother*). Carry on, carry on. Don't stop.

LALO (*as father*). You didn't want kids. You hated them. But no way could you stay single. No way. You had to catch a husband. It didn't matter who. Having one was all that mattered.

CUCA (*as mother. Going up to him furiously*). I hate you, I hate you, I hate you.

LALO (*as father*). A husband made you feel secure. A husband made you respectable. (*Ironically.*) Respectable . . . (*Pause.*) I can't quite explain . . . Anyway, life is like that, so if you want to . . .

CUCA (*as mother*). Lies, lies, lies.

LALO (*as father*). Will you let me finish?

CUCA (*out of part*). You're cheating again.

LALO (*as father*). You don't want people to know the truth.

CUCA (*out of part*). I'm talking about something else.

LALO (*as father*). You're scared of seeing it through to the end.

CUCA (*out of part*). You're trying to crush me.

LALO (*as father*). And you? What have you been doing? Tell me. What have you done to me? And to them? (*Mocking.*) 'I'm growing ugly, Albert. I'm in the family way. We can't bring them up on your salary.' (*Pause.*) And I didn't know the reasons, the real reasons. And today, I say to you: 'Put your hand on your heart and answer this question: Did you ever love me?' (*Pause.*) Oh well, don't say anything. I can see clearly now. It's taken years to sink in. 'Albert, those children . . . I can't handle them. You take care of them.' As time passed, your demands grew greater, and your selfishness grew with them. (*Pause.*) And me, in the office, with my figures, and the gossip and the friends who came up to me and said: 'How long are you going to put up with this, mate?'

CUCA *starts singing: 'The living room is not the living room, the living room is the kitchen. The bedroom is not the bedroom, the bedroom is the bathroom.' CUCA's singing and LALO's words should proceed in counterpoint. BEBA starts singing, first as a growl and then gradually becoming a sweet, simple, almost naive song.*

LALO (*continues, mockingly*). And you? 'Your sister called today. She's so nosey. Oh, these children. Look at my hands: the washing up did this. I'm losing my mind, Albert, I wish I were dead.' And then came your tears and the children started screaming and I thought I was going mad and everything started spinning . . . I used to escape from the house, sometimes at midnight, and go for a few drinks, and I felt like I was drowning, drowning. (*Pause. Without taking a breath.*) And other women were there and I didn't dare think about them . . . And I felt a terrible urge to leave, to fly away, to break with everything. (*Pause.*) But I was afraid, and fear paralysed me and I couldn't make up my mind and I got stuck between two stools. I thought one thing and I did another. It's terrible to have to admit it. And only to realise at the end. (*Pause.*) I couldn't do it. (*To the audience.*) Lalo, if you want to do it, you can. (*Pause.*) Now I ask myself why I didn't live out all my thoughts, all my desires. And I have to reply: because I was afraid, afraid, afraid.

CUCA (*as mother. Sarcastically*). Well, honey, you can't blame me for that. (*Pause, defiantly.*) And what did you want me to do? Those children were a nightmare. They turned my house into a pigsty. Lalo ripped the curtains and smashed the crockery. Beba wasn't content with tearing apart the pillows . . . And you expected to come home and find everything tickety-boo. Do you remember when Lalo peed all over the living room? You threw a fit and said. 'That never happened in *my* home.' Was that my fault as well? Eh? I used to put a chair here. (*Moves a chair.*) And I would find it over here. (*Moves the chair to another place.*) What was I supposed to do?

LALO (*as father. Beaten*). The house had to be cleaned. (BEBA *stops singing.*) Yes . . . The furniture had to be changed . . . (*Pause. With great melancholy.*) We really should have found a new house. (*Pause. Slowly.*) But we're old now and we can't. We are dead. (*Long pause. Violently.*) You always thought you were better than me.

CUCA (*as mother*). I've wasted my life away on you.

LALO (*as father. Vengefully*). You can't escape, love. Carry on. Carry on. Carry on.

CUCA (*as mother. Sobbing*). You pathetic pen-pusher. I wish you were dead.

BEBA (*as* LALO. *Shouting and moving in circles around the stage*). Throw out the carpets. Pull down the curtains. The living room is not the living room. The living room is the kitchen. The bedroom is not the bedroom. The bedroom is the bathroom. (BEBA *and* LALO *are at opposite ends of the stage with their backs to the audience.* LALO *doubles up slowly with a piercing scream.*) Ayyyyyy! (*Sobbing.*) I can see my dead mother. I can see my father with his throat cut. Tear this house down.

Long pause.

LALO. Open the door.

LALO *falls to his knees.* CUCA *slowly gets up, walks over to the door upstage and opens it. Pause. Goes over to the table and picks up the knife.*

BEBA (*in a normal tone of voice*). How do you feel?

CUCA (*in a normal tone of voice*). Stronger.

BEBA. Satisfied?

CUCA. Yes.

BEBA. Really?

CUCA. Really.

BEBA. Are you ready to do it again?

CUCA. You know the answer to that.

BEBA. One day we'll do it for real.

CUCA (*interrupting*). Without anything going wrong.

BEBA. Were you surprised you managed to do it?

CUCA. Everything's surprising.

LALO (*sobbing*). Oh, Beba, Cuca, if only love could do it . . .
   If only love . . . Because in spite of everything, I love them.

CUCA (*playing with the knife*). That's ridiculous.

BEBA (*to CUCA*). Poor little thing, let him be.

CUCA (*to BEBA. Laughing mockingly*). Look at him. (*To*
   LALO.) That's how I like to see you.

BEBA (*serious again*). All right. Now it's my turn.

   Curtain.

INTERVIEW WITH JOSÉ TRIANA

SD: What was the initial stimulus for *Night of the Assassins*?

JT: My two younger sisters and I used to shut ourselves up to invent games in which we acted out scenes from adult life. We dressed up and acted out thousands of strange things. My father earned enough to support us, but we were a poor family. I was always passionate about the games I played with my sisters. Sometimes we did dangerous things. When I was eight, I accidentaly tore off my sister's fingernail. That engraved itself on my mind. Growing up, I realised that theatre was the game turned into a ritual. When I started writing *Night of the Assassins*, it had characteristics of the 'enter Mother, enter Father' kind of theatre, with lots of characters. But then I turned it into something much more synthetic, and cut it down to a game played by three siblings. There is nothing autobiographical about it because in our house we never tried to kill our parents, who were very sweet. But I recognise it does contain the suggestion that we must all separate ourselves from our parents. We must do what our parents have not done.

SD: How would you summarise the play in one sentence?

JT: Let us live without fear. All our acts are weighed down by the terrible weight of fear, but I still want to live without it. I want people to live life as they dream it.

SD: Isn't the play as much about love as it is about fear?

JT: It's about desperate love, about people who don't know where to place their love. They talk about hatred, but it is love that lies behind their words. They are ashamed to say the words 'I love you.' Like many people, they are not used to saying those words, because they feel they are not allowed to.

SD: How important is the theme of power?

JT: I have tried to use family power relations and family games as a way of confronting the theme of power. So there are two games: the generational game, and the game of power. Many people look for someone to resolve their problems, but they should be seeking to be more humble. We all think we're very important, but we should see ourselves more as leaves in the wind. We should each search to realise the dream of being an averagely perfect man.

SD: You wrote the play six years after the Cuban Revolution. Does it comment on it at all?

JT: Yes. I told the Cuban revolution in the play: 'There are evils in our house. It is getting old and dirty and smelly. We have to tidy it up.'

SD: What does the play say about the nuclear family?

JT: It asks whether there are foundations other than the nuclear family on which we can build contemporary society. Why does Lalo want to play the game and then decide not to play any more? Once he has committed the hypothetical crime, he realises that he has failed. He says that it's not possible any more. But the others insist. They keep acting like their parents. Their game is transformed into the terrible game of their mother and father.

SD: Do you think that there are aspects of the play which are uniquely Cuban or Latin American?

JT: The play is definitely Cuban.

SD: In what way?

JT: In every way. The characters, how they move, all their gibberish – it is all Cuban. I am a man from the tropics, who gesticulates, who externalises things in a very different way to someone English or French. An actor needs to understand this to seduce the audience. The actor needs to be physically free.

SD: How would you advise a European performer to understand Cuban physicality?

JT: He needs to know Cuban music: the *danzón*, which is the classic Cuban dance music, or the *son*. He must know Cuban gestures as well. There may be universal themes in the play, but the behaviour of the characters is somehow dislocated, extravagant. The actors' movement should come from the solar plexus.

SD: What is the physical relationship between the three performers?

JT: They seduce each other, they repel each other, as always happens.

SD: By seduction, do you mean that there is a sexual love between the siblings?

JT: Sometimes yes, sometimes no. They take hold of each others' faces and bodies, they caress each other sometimes, protect each other. Because they are alone.

SD: Is that dangerous?

JT: Naturally. But incest is also a fundamental thing. Who is not incestuous? What mother, what father, what child is not incestuous? They must be, because love lies between them. If the director manages to give the performers rhythm and grace, the audience will accept that.

SD: What are the things you have liked and disliked about the productions you have seen of the play?

JT: I have seen seven different productions. I saw the premiere in Cuba. I saw a scandalous one in England where the acting was extraordinary, but I didn't like how they transposed a Nazi world into the play. Then I saw one in New York in which the actors were good, but the director did not understand the play. He wanted to turn it into a mass murder. The actors opposed this, as did I. Then I saw something the critic Diana Taylor did with the play. I have also seen two productions from Miami. The most recent one suffered from the most common defect, which is the vulgarisation of the text. There was one scene in which the actress took out her breasts to act out the mother feeding her child. That was not necessary. But it also achieved a mobility which seduced both European and Latin American people in the audience. The silly game of the chair took on a magical dimension on the stage. They were living in an enchanted world in which they really could kill their parents. They set very funny traps for the audience, like the sound of the doorbell made by the actress. All these productions were very different, and I think the play is wide open to interpretation.

SD: How would you advise a designer to investigate the play?

JT: Investigate all the artistic associations suggested by the text. Let out the little child inside you. Fill it with all the images you have of when you were a child: hats, a little moon, clay, a feather duster, a flower. They must all become magical when they are in contact with the actors, and that must be communicated to the audience. Nothing repressive, no coarse realism. Everything should be light. The knives can be two sticks. Just things from children's games. Let the objects be a response to the invisible. All the time the audience should be going in and out of the invisible. Trapping the invisible is what art is all about.

SD: What kind of music do you associate with the play?

JT: Cuban music. A *batá* drum, for example. Or a bolero like *Te odio*. The actors could just start singing it, and dancing to it. European music could be there too, like some of Piaf's songs, or *Ne me quittes pas*, as sung by Nina Simone.

SD: Does the play have any roots in the Afro-Catholic religion of *santería* which is so important in Cuba?

JT: Yes. No one knows that. No one has discovered that before. They are in a room of mysteries, a secret world.

This was a verbal interview conducted in Spanish, in Paris in December 1993.

SAYING YES

by Griselda Gambaro

Decir Sí was written in 1974 and first performed at the Teatro del Picadero, Buenos Aires in July, 1981, with the following cast:

PELUQUERO   Leal Rey
HOMBRE   Jorge Petraglia

Director Jorge Petraglia

This translation of *Saying Yes* was first performed at the Gate Theatre, London on January 21, 1996, with the following cast:

HAIRDRESSER   Kevin Colson
MAN   Emilio Doorgasingh

Director Sebastian Doggart

Inside a hairdresser's. A window and a door. A hairdresser's swivel chair, a chair, a little table with scissors, a comb and shaving instruments on it. A big white cloth, and some dirty rags. Two bins on the floor, one big, one small, with lids. A dustpan and brush. A free-standing mirror. The ground around the chair is covered with cut hair. The HAIRDRESSER *is sitting on the chair. He leafs through a magazine, waiting for the last customer of the day. He is a big, silent man, who moves slowly. He looks troubled but inscrutable. It is disconcerting not to know what lies behind his look. He never raises his voice, which is sad and servile. The* MAN *enters. He looks very shy and insecure.*

MAN. Good afternoon.

HAIRDRESSER (*raises his eyes from the magazine, looks at him. After a moment*). . . . afternoon . . . (*Does not move.*)

The MAN *tries a smile, which is met with no reply. Looks at his watch furtively. Waits. The* HAIRDRESSER *throws the magazine down on the table, and gets up as though he were containing his fury. But instead of looking after his customer, he goes over and looks out the window, his back turned.*

MAN (*conciliatory*). It's clouded over. (*Waits. Pause.*) It's hot. (*No reply. Loosens the knot of his tie, slightly nervous. The* HAIRDRESSER *turns round and looks at him sternly. The* MAN *loses his confidence.*) Not that hot . . . (*Without going nearer, he cranes his neck towards the window.*) Not a cloud in the sky . . . Cc . . . cleared up. I was wrong. (*The* HAIRDRESSER *looks at him inscrutably, motionless.*) I wanted . . . (*Pause. Raises his hand to his head and gestures vaguely.*) If . . . if it's not too late . . . (*The* HAIRDRESSER *looks at him without replying. Then he turns his back on him again and looks out of the window. The* MAN *is anxious.*) Has it clouded over?

The HAIRDRESSER *is motionless for a moment. Then he turns round.*

HAIRDRESSER (*brusquely*). Shave?

MAN (*quickly*). Not, not a shave. (*Inscrutable look.*) Well . . .
I don't know. I . . . I shave myself. On my own. (*The
HAIRDRESSER is silent.*) I know it's not convenient,
but . . . Well, maybe you can give me a shave. Yes, yes,
a shave too. (*Goes over to the chair. Puts a foot on the
footrest. Looks at the HAIRDRESSER waiting for an
invitation, who gives him a faint, obscure gesture. The MAN
does not dare sit down. He takes his foot down. Touches the
chair timidly.*) This chair is strong, solid. Made . . . made of
wood. Antique. (*The HAIRDRESSER does not reply. He
nods and stares intently at the seat of the chair. The MAN
follows the HAIRDRESSER's gaze. He sees cut hair on the
seat. Impulsively, he picks it up. Looks at the ground.*)
May I? . . . (*Waits. Slowly, the HAIRDRESSER shakes his
head. The MAN is conciliatory.*) Sure, that would be filthy.
(*Realises that the floor is covered with cut hair. Smiles,
confused. Looks at the hair in his hand, then at the ground,
and finally decides to put the hair in his pocket. The
HAIRDRESSER smiles brusquely. The MAN is relieved.*)
Well . . . a haircut and . . . a shave, yes, a shave. (*The
HAIRDRESSER, who has stopped smiling suddenly,
scrutinises the chair. The MAN does the same. Impulsively,
the MAN takes one of the dirty rags and cleans the seat.
The HAIRDRESSER leans over and stares sternly at the
back of the chair. The MAN looks at him , then follows the
direction of his gaze. On another sudden impulse, he cleans
the back of the chair. Happy.*) There you are. It doesn't
bother me. (*The HAIRDRESSER looks at him inscrutably,
which disconcerts him.*) Lending a hand . . . Isn't that what
we are here for? You scratch my back, I'll scratch yours.
I don't mean that rudely! It's just a saying . . . silly people
have. (*Waits. The HAIRDRESSER is silent and motionless.*)
You . . . must be tired. Lots of customers?

HAIRDRESSER (*laconically*). Enough.

MAN (*timidly*). May . . . may I sit down? (*The HAIRDRESSER
looks at him inscrutably.*) Well, I don't have to. Perhaps
you're tired. When *I* am tired . . . I get in a bad mood . . .
But as you were open, I thought . . . You were open, weren't
you?

HAIRDRESSER. Open.

MAN (*more confidently*). May I sit down? (*The* HAIRDRESSER *slowly shakes his head.*) All in all, I don't . . . have to. Maybe you cut hair standing up. I like to eat steak standing up myself. It's not the same thing, I know, but you feel steadier. If you have good legs! (*Laughs. Interrupts himself.*) Not everyone has . . . You do!

The HAIRDRESSER *pays no attention to him. He stares at the ground. The* MAN *follows his gaze. The* HAIRDRESSER *looks at him as if he were expecting him to act in a particular way. The* MAN *quickly picks up the gist. He takes the brush and sweeps the cut hair into a pile. Looks at the* HAIR-DRESSER *happily. The* HAIRDRESSER *turns his head to the dustpan, and makes the slightest hint of a gesture. The* MAN *is quick to respond. He takes the dustpan and scoops up the hair from the ground, helping with his hands. He blows to sweep up the last of the hair, but scatters the hair already in the dustpan. Worried, he looks around him, sees the bins, opens the bigger one, and says happily.*

Shall I throw it in here? (*The* HAIRDRESSER *shakes his head. The* MAN *opens the smaller one.*) Here? (*The* HAIRDRESSER *nods. The* MAN *looks encouraged.*) There you are. (*Big smile.*) All done. Nice and clean. Because it's disgusting if you let that mess pile up. (*The* HAIRDRESSER *looks at him darkly. The* MAN *loses confidence.*) No . . . nooo. I didn't mean it was dirty. Lots of customers, lots of hair. Lots of cut hair, and bristles too, and then it gets mixed up and . . . Hair grows so fast, doesn't it? Better for you! (*Laughs stupidly.*) I say that because . . . If we were all bald, you could sit back and take it easy. (*Interrupts himself. Quickly.*) I didn't mean that. You'd find another job.

HAIRDRESSER (*neutrally*). I could be a doctor.

MAN (*relieved*). Ah! Would you like to be a doctor? Operating, curing people. Pity that we all die, isn't it? (*Cheerfully.*) People always die on doctors! Sooner or later. (*Laughs and stops with a gesture. The* HAIRDRESSER'*s face is very dark. The* MAN *is frightened.*) No, they wouldn't die on you! You would have customers, patients, who were very old. (*Inscrutable look.*) Ancient. (*The* HAIRDRESSER *continues staring.*) We'd live forever. If you were a doctor, we'd live forever.

HAIRDRESSER (*softly and sadly*). Nonsense.

Goes over to the mirror, looks at himself. Gets closer and then moves away, as if he cannot see himself clearly. Then he looks at the MAN, *as if he were to blame.*)

MAN. You can't see. (*Impulsively, he takes the rag with which he cleaned the chair and cleans the mirror. The* HAIRDRESSER *takes the rag out of his hands and gives him a smaller one.*) Thank you. (*Cleans the mirror diligently. Spits on it and rubs. Happy.*) Look yourself. The flies have crapped on it.

HAIRDRESSER (*mournfully*). Flies?

MAN. No, no. Dust.

HAIRDRESSER (*as before*). Dust?

MAN. No, no. Misted up. Misted up by breath. (*Quickly.*) Mine. (*Cleans.*) They're good mirrors. The ones they make today make us look like . . .

HAIRDRESSER (*weakly*) Marmots . . .

MAN (*confidently*). Yes, marmots! (*The* HAIRDRESSER, *as if he were carrying out a test, looks at himself in the mirror, and then looks at the* MAN. *The* MAN *corrects himself quickly.*) Not everyone! The ones who are marmots! Me! More of a marmot than me!

HAIRDRESSER (*sadly and weakly*). Impossible. (*Looks at himself in the mirror. Passes his hand over his cheeks, checking whether he has any stubble. Touches his long hair, pulls the forelocks.*)

MAN. And who cuts *your* hair? Do you do it yourself? What a problem. It's like being a dentist. Now that makes me laugh. (*The* HAIRDRESSER *looks at him. He loses confidence.*) Opening your mouth and taking your own tooth out . . . Impossible . . . Although a hairdresser could, if he had a mirror . . . (*Moves his fingers like scissors over his neck.*) Why should *I* want to stick my face in someone else's gob. It makes me feel sick. It's not like hair. Better to be a hairdresser than a dentist. It's more . . . hygienic. People nowadays don't have . . . lice. A bit of dandruff, grease. (*The* HAIRDRESSER *parts the hair on his scalp, looks as if he were checking something, then looks at the* MAN.) No, not you. No sirree! Me! (*Checks.*) Me neither . . . You don't have to worry about me. (*The* HAIRDRESSER *sits down on the chair. Indicates the shaving instruments. The* MAN

looks at the instruments and then at the HAIRDRESSER..
He understands the implication. Recoils.) I . . . I can't. I've
never . . .

HAIRDRESSER (*weakly*). Go on. (*Ties the white cloth under
his own chin, waits calmly.*)

MAN (*determined*). Tell me, do you do this to everyone?

HAIRDRESSER (*very sadly*). Do what? (*Leans right back in
the chair.*)

MAN. No, because you don't have enough faces! (*Laughs
without conviction.*) Once one person has shaved you,
anyone else would . . . What would they find? (*The*
HAIRDRESSER *indicates the utensils.*) Well, if you want,
why not? Once, when I was a boy, everyone jumped across
a puddle, a smelly, green puddle, and I didn't want to. 'I
won't!', I said. 'Let those idiots jump across if they want to'.

HAIRDRESSER (*sadly*). Did you fall in?

MAN. Me? No . . . They threw me in, because . . . (*shrugs his
shoulders*) It . . . annoyed them that I didn't want to . . . risk
it. (*Cheers up again.*) So . . . why not? Jump across the
puddle or . . . hey, give someone a shave? You don't need
any particular skill, do you? Even idiots can shave themselves! There's no special skill in it! Any old fool can be a
hairdre . . . ! (*Interrupts himself. The* HAIRDRESSER *looks
at him gloomily.*) But no. You have to have a good aim, a
steady hand, a sharp . . . eye to see . . . the hair . . . I pull out
the ingrowing ones with little tweezers. (*The* HAIRDRESSER
sighs deeply.) Alright, alright! Don't be impatient. (*He
lathers the* HAIRDRESSER*'s face.*) There. I've never met
anyone so impatient. It's exhausting. (*Realises what he
has said and corrects himself.*) No, you are dynamically
exhausting. Exhausting to other people. But not to me . . . it
doesn't affect me. I understand. Action is the spice of life
and life is action and . . . (*His hand trembles, he touches the*
HAIRDRESSER*'s mouth with the soapy brush. The*
HAIRDRESSER *slowly takes a corner of the cloth and
wipes himself. Looks at the* MAN.) Sorry. (*Brings the razor
up to the* HAIRDRESSER*'s face. He stops and looks at the
old and rusty razor. In a barely audible voice.*) It's jagged.

HAIRDRESSER (*mournfully*). Impeccable.

MAN. It's impeccable. (*On a desperate impulse.*) Old, rusty,
and blunt, but impeccable! (*Laughs hysterically.*) Don't say

anything! I believe you, and you wouldn't say one thing and mean another. Why would you do that? It's your face, isn't it? (*Brusquely.*) Don't you have a strop, a sharpening stone? (*The* HAIRDRESSER *snorts sadly, which discourages the* MAN.) A . . . knife? (*Makes a sharpening gesture.*) Well, I have my character and . . . on we go! I'm made that way! (*Makes a pushing gesture with his finger.*) I am what I am! I can fly! (*Shaves. Stops.*) Did I cut you? (*The* HAIRDRESSER *shakes his head mournfully. Encouraged, the* MAN *shaves.*) Aahh! (*Dries him hurriedly with the cloth.*) Don't panic. (*Exaggerated.*) Blood! No, a scratch! I'm . . . very nervous. I'll put a little onion skin on it. Do you have any . . . onions? (*The* HAIRDRESSER *looks at him darkly.*) Wait! (*Goes through his pockets anxiously. Pleased, he pulls out a sticking plaster.*) I . . . I always carry one with me. In case my feet hurt, I walk a lot, and it gets hot . . . a blister here, and another . . . there. (*Puts the plaster on him.*) Perfect! Anyone would have thought I was a professional! (*The* HAIRDRESSER *takes off the rest of the soap from his face, putting an end to the shave. Without getting up from the chair, he leans forward towards the mirror, looks at himself, pulls off the plaster, and throws it to the ground. The* MAN *picks it up, tries to straighten it out, and puts it in his pocket.*) I'll keep it . . . it's almost new . . . it might be useful for another . . . shave . . .

HAIRDRESSER (*points to a flask, weakly*). Cologne.

MAN. Oh, yes! Cologne. (*Opens the bottle, smells it.*) What a lovely smell! (*Gags at the nauseating smell. Disgusted, he pours some cologne into his hands and slaps it on to the* HAIRDRESSER's *face. Rubs his hands to get rid of the smell. Puts one hand to his nose to check whether the smell has disappeared, pulls it away quickly, on the verge of vomiting.*)

HAIRDRESSER (*sweeping his hair back with his hand. Weakly*). Haircut.

MAN. A haircut as well? I . . . I can't. I really can't do that.

HAIRDRESSER (*as before*). Haircut.

MAN. Look, sir. I came here to have my hair cut. I came to have *my* hair cut! I have never had to deal with a situation as . . . extraordinary as this. Unusual . . . but if you want . . . I . . . (*Takes the scissors, looks at them with disgust.*) I'm a determined man . . . in everything. Everything! Because my mother taught me that . . . and life . . .

HAIRDRESSER (*gloomily*). Chit-chat. (*Sighs.*) Why don't you concentrate?

MAN. What for? And who wants to stop me from chit-chatting? (*Waves the scissors.*) Who would dare? You see what happens to anyone who dares? (*Dark look from the* HAIRDRESSER.) Do you want me to shut up? As you like. You! You'll be the one responsible! Don't blame me if . . . Right now I could do anything I felt like!

HAIRDRESSER. Haircut.

MAN (*tenderly and persuasively*). Please no, not the hair, better not to mess around with your hair . . . what's the point? It really suits you long . . . it's modern. Hip . . .

HAIRDRESSER (*mournfully and inexorably*). Haircut.

MAN. Oh, yes? A haircut, is it? Come on then! You're hard-headed, aren't you? But mine is harder! (*Points to his head.*) I have a rock up here. (*Laughs like someone condemned to death.*) I'm not easily persuaded! No, sir! I won't tell you about those who've tried. There's no need! And when I like something, nobody gets in my way. Nobody! And I can assure you that . . . there is nothing I like more than . . . cutting hair! I . . . I'm crazy about it! (*Excitedly, brusquely.*) I have a blister on my hand! I can't cut your hair! (*Puts the scissors down. Happy.*) It hurts.

HAIRDRESSER. Hair – cut.

MAN (*takes hold of the scissors, beaten*). You're the boss.

HAIRDRESSER. Sing.

MAN. What me? Sing? (*Laughs stupidly.*) Not on your life . . . Never! (*The* HAIRDRESSER *half sits up in his chair, and looks at him. The* MAN *speaks very faintly.*) Sing what? (*The* HAIRDRESSER *replies by shrugging his shoulders sadly. He reclines again in his seat. The* MAN *sings in a barely audible voice.*) Fígaro! . . . Fígaro . . . qua, Fígaro là . . . ! (*Starts to cut.*)

HAIRDRESSER (*weakly, wearily*). Sing better. I don't like it.

MAN. Fígaro! (*Increases the volume.*) Fígaro, Fígaro! (*Lets out a terrible squeak.*)

HAIRDRESSER (*as before*). Shut up.

MAN. You're the boss. The customer is always right! Although
the customer . . . is me . . . (*The* HAIRDRESSER *stares at
him*) is you . . . (*Cuts his hair terribly. Tries to improve the
situation, but makes it worse, becoming more and more
nervous.*) If I don't sing, I can concentrate . . . better.
(*Clenching his teeth.*) I'll just think about this, about cutting,
(*cuts*) and . . . (*With hatred*) Take that! (*Cuts off a big
clump. Horrified at what he has done. Steps back, holding
the clump of hair in his hand. Then he tries to stick it back
on the* HAIRDRESSER's *head. He wets the clump of hair
with some saliva. Keeps trying. Cannot do it. Smiles falsely.*)
No, no, no. Don't panic. I cut off a long bit, but . . . no harm
done. Hair is my speciality. I take some off and then make it
all even. (*He surreptitiously drops the clump of hair and
kicks it away. Cuts.*) Very good! (*The* HAIRDRESSER *is
looking at himself in the mirror.*) Head down a bit! (*Tries to
lower his head, the* HAIRDRESSER *lifts it up.*) Don't you
want to? (*Tries again.*) Come on, come on, you're being
difficult . . . Isn't the mirror misty? (*Tries to mist it up with
his breath.*) It doesn't show you how you really are, you
know! (*Looks at the* HAIRDRESSER. *He is petrified by the
HAIRDRESSER's smiling face, but tries again.*) When the
girls see you . . . they'll say: 'Who cut that gentleman's
hair?' (*He hardly cuts, just snipping the top. Without
conviction.*) A hairdresser . . . from France . . . (*Desolate.*)
But no. It was me . . .

HAIRDRESSER (*raises his hand slowly. Sadly.*). Enough.
(*Goes up to the mirror, realises he looks a mess, but does
not reveal any obvious fury*).

MAN. I can carry on. (*The* HAIRDRESSER *continues looking
at himself.*) Give me another chance! I haven't finished. I'll
take a little off here, and the sideburns, I've still got the
sideburns to do! And the moustache. You don't have one.
Why don't you let your moustache grow? I can leave mine
to grow as well, and that way we can be like brothers!
(*Laughs anxiously. The* HAIRDRESSER *flattens the hair
over his temples. The* MAN *perks up.*) Yes, yes, it suits you
smoothed down like that. Just right. Oh, I like it. (*The*
HAIRDRESSER *gets up from the chair. The* MAN *recoils.*)
That was . . . an interesting experience. How much do I owe
you? No you should owe me, shouldn't you? I mean,
normally. But it's not an abnormal situation either. It's . . .
funny. That's it: funny. (*Exaggerated.*) Ha, ha, ha!

(*Humbly.*) No, it's not that funny. Do you . . . do you like how . . . (*The* HAIRDRESSER *looks at him inscrutably.*) . . . I cut it? Considering I'm a . . . beginner . . . (*The* HAIRDRESSER *pulls at the hair on the back of his neck.*) We could be partners . . . No, no! I don't want to interfere in your business! I know you have many customers, I don't want to take them away from you! They are all yours! They belong to you! Every little hair in here is yours! Don't get me wrong. I could work for free. Me! Please! (*Almost crying.*) I told you I didn't know how to! You made me! I can't say no when people ask me for something . . . so nicely! And what does it matter? I didn't cut your arm off! If you'd lost your arm, you could have complained. Or lost a leg! But to worry about your hair! What an idiot! No! Not, an idiot! Hair grows! In a week's time, you . . . Well! Down to the ground! (*The* HAIRDRESSER *points to the chair. The* MAN *reacts incredulously to the offer, and his eyes light up.*) Is it my turn? (*Looks behind him as if searching for someone.*) Good, good! At last, we understand each other! All things come to him who waits! (*Sits down, arranges himself happily.*) A haircut and a shave, please! (*The* HAIRDRESSER *ties the cloth under the* MAN's *chin. Swivels the chair round. Takes the razor and smiles. The* MAN *lifts his head.*) Cut well. Nice and even.

The HAIRDRESSER *plunges the razor into the* MAN. *A big scream. Swivels the chair again. The white cloth is drenched in blood which trickles to the floor. He takes the small cloth and dries it delicately. He lets out a deep, weary, good-natured sigh. He stops cleaning. Picks up the magazine and sits down. Lifts his hand to his head, and pulls off a wig. Throws it on to the* MAN's *head. Opens the magazine and starts to whistle sweetly.*

Curtain.

INTERVIEW WITH GRISELDA GAMBARO

SD: What led you to write *Saying Yes*?

GG: I wanted to express metaphorically an individual and social identity. Using humour and a specific medium, the theatre, I told a story of different types of conduct – passivity, indiscriminate assent, pusillanimity – which were taken to the limit, in order to stimulate reflection about daily behaviour.

SD. In what ways have you seen *Saying Yes* produced?

GG: I have only seen two productions of *Saying Yes*. As a principle, I only attend the premieres of my plays and some functions related to that premiere. From time to time I break this rule because of special circumstances, such as a director who particularly interests me, or the promise of an exceptional performance. I saw the premiere of *Saying Yes* in Buenos Aires in 1982, as part of a programme called Open Theatre (*Teatro Abierto*), made up of short plays by different writers produced in a spirit of solidarity by the best directors, actors and designers, as a protest to the military dictatorship. Then, years later, I saw a production in New Hampshire, USA, where the Man greatly resembled Woody Allen, both physically and in his acting. In that staging, *Saying Yes* took on a local character. Yet even in another language I saw that the situations retained the same resonance. It was a stimulating interpretation, both for its scenic effectiveness and for the reception it provoked from the audience, who reacted in an immediate way to the comedy of the text. I noticed that the audience did not place itself imaginatively in another country in order to understand the play, but did so in its own.

SD: How do you fit into the tradition of the 'grotesque' in Argentine theatre?

GG: The grotesque has been very important in Argentina, particularly as a result of the great playwright Armando Discépolo (1887-1971). Taking the model of Pirandello's grotesque he created an autonomous product with its own characteristics. In this way the grotesque had a great impact on the Argentine stage, and with distinct variations it influenced many Argentine playwrights for more than half a century. Although I do not consider myself to be a playwright belonging to that genre, its way of observing has influenced me, as has both its sudden alternations between humour and the dramatic, and its treatment of the ridiculous.

SD: What role does naturalism have in your work?

GG: I would not define my theatre as 'naturalistic' nor do I think that it contains elements of naturalism. I have not been interested in following that line. In my theatre there is a tension which breaks with the notion of 'the natural'. Situations and the use of language are accentuated in a way that does not correspond to naturalism.

SD: What relationship, if any, does your theatre have to Antonin Artaud's 'theatre of cruelty'?

GG: I have taken on the transgressive impulses of the 'theatre of cruelty', and I am grateful to Artaud for warning us about empty forms and the disadvantages of psychological and analytical theatre. I do not share Artaud's other views, or I use them selectively, since many of his hypotheses are reactions to a sophisticated society and the rational, discursive French theatre of his age. This has not been, nor is, the situation of Latin American society and theatre.

SD: In what ways do you think your theatre is specifically Argentine?

GG: My theatre is specifically Argentine, because it could not be anything else. I was born in Argentina; I use and recreate its language; and I feed off its historical, social and political reality. I work with the sediment and the resulting product is a culture which is *mestizo*, a hybrid of the little-known indigenous culture on one hand, and the immigrant culture on the other. I believe I carry forward the old indigenous gesture of putting the ear to the ground and writing and narrating, through the novel or the theatre, what the earth dictates to me.

SD: Which writers have influenced you as a playwright?

GG: I have been influenced by many playwrights, especially Shakespeare, Chekhov, Pirandello, O'Neill, Armando Discépolo, Francisco Defilippis Novoa (1892-1930) and Roberto Arlt (1900-1942). I have also been influenced by poets and novelists, who have broadened my horizons .

SD: What kind of theatre do you enjoy going to?

GG: The only thing which matters to me is the quality of each theatrical experience, and I have no preference for any particular genre or aesthetic trend. I do remember some magnificent productions: one I saw in Argentina in 1995 of Heiner Müller's *Hamlet Machine*, by a group called The Ring-Road of Objects (*El Periférico de Objetos*) who work with puppets in an entirely original approach. From Europe, I particularly remember the *Oresteia*, directed by Peter Stein; *Le Récit de la servante Zerline* by Klaus-Michel Grüber; and *Une femme douce* by Robert Wilson.

SD: Have you been able to earn a living by writing?

GG: Yes. I receive performance and publication royalties, both from novels and the theatre, and I earn fees from conferences and jury panels.

SD: How important to your writing and your identity as a writer is the fact that you are a woman?

GG: We write what we are, and I cannot write outside my gender, which has marked me biologically, socially and culturally. Writing, identity and gender for me make up one single package.

SD: Is there a feminist dimension to the plays you write?

GG: I am principally concerned about writing good plays and I absolutely do not force myself to include a feminist dimension in them. However, in plays like *Bad Blood* (*La Mala Sangre*, 1983), *From the Rising Sun* (*Del Sol Naciente*, 1984), and *Minor Concerns* (*Penas sin Importancia*, 1990), although I would not say there was a feminist dimension, the focus does centre more on the female. Their protagonists are women and those plays reveal a commitment to and an identification with women which is more explicit and obvious than in other works.

SD: Do you think your gender has helped or hindered your career as a playwright, both in Latin America and outside?

GG: The fact I am a woman may have helped, in some circumstances, to publicise my plays in Latin America, the USA and Europe. But this remains in the realm of speculation. I prefer to think that interest has been due to the fact that the plays were good.

SD: One of the most common explanations for the small number of women playwrights in Latin America is that male chauvinism has blocked women playwrights, not only from having their works staged, translated or published, but by discouraging them from writing or thinking about writing in the first place. Would you agree with this?

GG: I think that has been the case, although the situation has been reversed in recent times. The theatre has a direct connection with society, and as standards have changed in society and women have won over areas previously reserved for men, so women have also conquered the area of play writing. Of course, at the beginning of the century it was unthinkable for a woman to be given incentives to write drama – although some did. Today, not only are the incentives there, but there are also greater possibilities of production, translation and publication. Nevertheless, there are still areas which have not been conquered at all, and where the smaller presence of women is very evident, for example in every kind of anthology, and in the composition of jury panels. This has not been because there is a general lack of female playwrights and writers, but because if the events are organised by men, automatic discrimination persists in the selection process.

SD: As a leading female playwright, do you think you have any social or political role to encourage women to write plays?

GG: I do have an influence on young people, and I think that in my case, for ethical and political reasons, that influence goes beyond the purely theatrical. It reveals itself particularly strongly in women because of an obvious identification, although it is also acknowledged by male authors. In Argentina, there have always been isolated examples of female playwrights, but I am the first female playwright with an extensive body of work. My plays have now been performed regularly for thirty years, and have had a great impact, both with the critics and with the public. Inevitably, this has opened doors to the generations that follow me; and in Argentina today we see what can be called the first generation of female playwrights, a group of female authors born around 1960, who are still not translated but who do have a body of work that has been performed and published.

SD: How have audiences from different cultures varied in their reception of your plays?

GG: A play can have a multiplicity of meanings which change according to each audience. Naturally, my first audience is the Argentine public who share the same culture. But every play has at least two meanings: one for the here-and-now, and another for different geographies and different times. In Stuttgart, when *The Siamese Twins* premiered in 1993, the audience identified with the play through what was happening in Germany at that moment, principally xenophobia and a lack of solidarity. In Medellín, Colombia, a parable of excessive authority was seen in *Saying Yes*, which referred both to the power of women within the home, and to male chauvinism which, paradoxically, also exists in that society. As for the 1992 London production of *Bad Blood*, directed by Kate Rowland, I got the impression from reading the critics that the play's violence had a greater impact on the English spectator than it did in Argentina. Perhaps these situations were not so significant for us because we have lived through them. I also noticed that, owing to the lack of clear conventions, the critics were somewhat bewildered when they tried to determine the aesthetic of the play. On the other hand, the British production of *The Walls*, directed by Rachel Kavanaugh in 1993, seemed to have received a clearer reading, perhaps because it is a more 'classical' work in its structure and situations. But in general, European audiences come to see an Argentine play with certain preconceptions, which lead to a reductionist vision, still confined to the tango or to the sad folklore of torture and repression.

SD: Who are your favourite Latin American playwrights of the last 50 years?

GG: I couldn't make an exhaustive choice. For different reasons I would redeem an infinity of works, plays by the Mexicans Elena Garro, Vicente Leñero, Emilio Carballido; by the Cuban José Triana; by the Uruguayan Carlos Manuel Varela; by the Venezuelans Rodolfo Santana, Isaac Chocron, Elisa Lerer; by the young Costa Rican Ana Istarú; and by many Argentines: Roberto Arlt, Armando Discépolo, Roberto Cossa, Daniel Veronese and Patricia Zangaro.

SD: What, if anything, does the collective term 'Latin American theatre' mean to you?

GG: This term contains many differences and some fundamental similarities. Latin America is a continent which, apart from Brazil, has the same language, although every country has its own history and idiosyncrasies. This has been translated to theatrical activity, where important differences can be observed: some countries have a very strong theatrical tradition, like Mexico, Chile, Uruguay, Argentina, while in others, the development of the theatre is less notable, as in Bolivia or Paraguay. But what unites Latin American Theatre is that it belongs to countries which are up against tough economic conditions, acute social inequalities and subjugation to the international financial centres. This, then, conditions and characterises the themes, the type of investigation, the means of production, and even determines our aesthetic. Latin American theatre means a sense of belonging, wide thematic freedom, variety of forms, and search.

This was a faxed interview conducted in Spanish in January 1996.

ORCHIDS IN THE MOONLIGHT

by Carlos Fuentes

Production Notes

1) Both women are of an indefinite age, between thirty and sixty years old. At some moments they are closer to the first age; at others, to the second. Throughout the play, DOLORES dresses like a stylised Mexican *campesina*: plaits gathered round her head in a bun tied together by rose-coloured ribbons, bougainvilleas behind her ears, rustic clothes made of percale, ankle-length boots and a shawl. MARIA, on the other hand, changes costume several times. The physical characteristics of the women are not fixed. Ideally, the roles will be played by María Félix[1] and Dolores del Río.[2] Even more ideally, they will alternate in the roles. In their absence, they can be played by actresses who are like them: tall, slender, dark, with distinctively sculpted bones, especially in the face: high and shining cheekbones, sensual lips quick to laughter and anger, defiant chins and combative eyebrows. This does not prevent the perversion, if necessary, that the roles should be played by two rosy-cheeked, blond, plump women. As a last resort, and in the absence of all the above-mentioned possibilities, the protagonists can be two men.

2) The set is conceived as a territory shared and constantly disputed by the two women. MARIA identifies with the style of certain objects and decorations: white bear skins, a white satin divan, a wall of mirrors. DOLORES stresses her possession of rustic Mexican furniture, paper flowers and clay piggy banks. Each possesses, on opposite sides of the set, a small altar dedicated to herself on which are photographs, posters of old films, little statues and other prizes. The common territory is a vast wardrobe upstage, made up of mobile clothes rails like the ones found in hotels and receptions. Hanging there are all types of clothes imaginable, from crinoline to sarong, from the customary national dress of Mexico to Emmanuel Ungaro's latest collection. They are all costumes that the two actresses have used during their long screen careers. Downstage left is a metallic, prison-like door. Centre-stage, in front of the wardrobes, is a white toilet with a white telephone on the seat.   C.F., 1982

Orchids in the Moonlight was written in 1982. This translation
was first staged by the Southern Development Trust on
9 August 1992 in the Teatro Nacional, Havana, Cuba, and
then had its British premiere at the Richard Demarco Gallery
Theatre, Edinburgh on 17 August 1992.

MARIA	Tanya Stephan
DOLORES	Tami Hoffman
FAN	Simon Taylor

Director Sebastian Doggart

Designer Clare Brew

Producers Pippa Harris & Ian J. Clarke

Characters

MARIA

DOLORES

THE FAN

NUBIAN SLAVE GIRLS

MARIACHIS

Setting

Venice, the day Orson Welles died.[3]

The area lit is downstage centre. DOLORES *sits next to a walnut colonial table, covered by a worn paper tablecloth, earthenware crockery from Tlaquepaque, paper flowers and a jug of fresh water.* DOLORES *stares intently at the audience for thirty seconds, first quite challengingly, arching her eyebrows; but gradually losing her self-confidence, lowering her gaze and looking to her left and right as if she were expecting someone. Eventually, her hands trembling, she pours herself a cup of tea, raises it to drink, looks back at the audience, again first challengingly, then in terror. She drops the cup noisily and stifles a piercing scream, the theatricality of which is drowned out by real tears. She groans several times, throwing her head back against the chair, raising one hand to her brow, covering her mouth with the other, trembling. From between the clothes rails upstage* MARIA *appears, slowly, moving with the enormous contained tension of a panther. Her dark flowing hair falls over the fur collar of a gown of thick brocade, which looks copied from the czar's robes in* Boris Godunov. MARIA *walks towards* DOLORES, *adopting an air of pragmatism; she arranges her hair, puts on the gown and kisses* DOLORES *from behind.* DOLORES *responds to* MARIA*'s embrace by stroking her hands and trying to move her face closer towards her.*

MARIA. It's very early. What's wrong?

DOLORES. They didn't recognise me.

MARIA. Again?

DOLORES. I was sitting here having my breakfast, and they didn't recognise me.

> MARIA *sighs and kneels down to pick up* DOLORES' *cup and breakfast plate. The helpless trembling of* DOLORES' *voice is replaced by a very faint tone of supremacy.* MARIA*'s presence is enough to cause this.*

DOLORES. They recognised me before.

MARIA. Before?

DOLORES *looks scornfully at* MARIA *kneeling down.*

DOLORES. They asked for my autograph.

MARIA. Before.

DOLORES. I couldn't go out to a restaurant without a crowd gathering to look at me, undressing me with their eyes, asking for my autograph . . .

MARIA. We haven't gone out. (DOLORES *looks at* MARIA, *silently interrogating her.*) I mean we're alone.

DOLORES. Where?

MARIA. Here. In our apartment. Our apartment in Venice.

She pronounces the proper name in an atrocious imitation of an English accent: Ve-Nice, Vi- Nais.

DOLORES (*correcting her patiently*). Vé-nice, Vé-Niss. How do you say Niza in French?

MARIA. Nice.

DOLORES. Well, now you add a Ve. Ve-Nice.

MARIA. The point is, we're alone here and we haven't gone out. Don't confuse me.

Amazed, DOLORES *crouches down to get closer to* MARIA*'s face.*

DOLORES. Can't you see them in front there, sitting down looking at us?

MARIA. Who?

DOLORES stretches out her arm dramatically towards the audience. But her wounded and secretive voice seems out of tune with her choice of words.

DOLORES. Them. The audience. *Our* audience. Our faithful audience who have paid in ready money to see us and applaud us. Can't you see them sitting in front there?

MARIA laughs, checks herself so as not to offend DOLORES, tosses her head and starts to take off DOLORES' Indian sandals.

MARIA. Let's get dressed.

DOLORES. I'm ready now.

MARIA. No. I don't want you to go out barefoot. (*She puts her cheek next to* DOLORES' *naked foot.*) You hurt yourself last time.

DOLORES. A thorn. That's nothing. You took it out for me. I love it when you take care of me.

MARIA *kisses* DOLORES' *naked foot.* DOLORES *strokes* MARIA's *head.*

DOLORES. Where are you going to take me today?

MARIA. First promise me that you won't go out barefoot again. You're not a Xochimilco Indian. You're a respectable lady who can hurt her feet if she goes out into the streets with no shoes on. Promise?

DOLORES (*nodding*). Where are you going to take me today?

MARIA. Where would you like to go?

She starts to put some old-fashioned boots on DOLORES.

DOLORES. Not to the studios.

MARIA. To the film museum?

DOLORES. No, no. It's the same. They don't recognise us. They say we're not us.

MARIA. So what? We don't *have* to be announced.

DOLORES. They just don't treat us the way they did before, they don't reserve the best seats for us . . .

MARIA. So what? We sit in the darkness and we see ourselves on the screen. That's what matters.

DOLORES. But they don't see *us* now.

MARIA. That's better. That way we see ourselves like the others see us. Before we couldn't. Remember? Before we were divided, looking at ourselves on the screens like ourselves while the audience was divided, wondering: shall we watch them on the screen or shall we watch them watching themselves on the screen?

DOLORES. I think the most intelligent preferred to watch us while we were watching ourselves.

MARIA. Yes? Why?

DOLORES. Well, because they could see the film again many times, and many years after the opening night. On the other hand, they could only see *us* that night, the night of the première. Remember? Wilshire Boulevard . . .

MARIA. The Champs Elysées . . .

DOLORES. The spotlights, the photographers, the autograph hunters . . .

MARIA. Our cleavages, our pearls, our white foxfurs.

DOLORES. Our fans.

MARIA (*interrupted from her dream*). Our elephants?

DOLORES (*condescendingly*). Our admirers, our fanatics, f-a-n-s.

MARIA. Sorry. I don't speak gringo.

DOLORES. Ah, you're jealous of my Hollywood, it's always been like that.

MARIA. *Oye!* I've never had to dress up as a Comanche Indian and speak Tomahawk English like you did. God forbid! Anyway, how can I be jealous of you for something that doesn't exist? My success was in Paris, *señorita*, and that does exist. It's existed for two thousand years. Look out of the window and tell me where Hollywood is. We've spent twenty years here . . .

DOLORES (*urgently*). Shhhh, shhhh. Forget about Hollywood, forget about Paris, remember where we're living now, we have Venice . . .

MARIA (*stopping herself, closing her eyes*) We will always have Venice.[4]

DOLORES. If you put your head out of the window you can see the Grand Canal. Yes, the passing gondolas and motorboats, here from our apartment in the Palazzo Mocenigo which was Lord Byron's palace in Venice. Look, tell me if I'm right.

MARIA (*without opening her eyes*). Yes, you're right. We're in Venecia. We will always have Venecia.

DOLORES (*happily*). What more do you want? Do you want more?

MARIA (*without opening her eyes*). No. This is a good place to die. There are no more ripples on the water. The whole city is a ghost. Don't ask us for proof that we exist. Here we'll never know if we've died or not. Venecia.

DOLORES. Well, that's cleared up. Then no-one can see us. Yes? I'm right.

MARIA (*opening her eyes*). Today we see ourselves the way the others see us on the screen. We are sitting quietly amongst the others, very decent and well-behaved, *ya*?

MARIA *stops putting on* DOLORES' *shoes and gets up,
visibly irritated, takes a black cigar and lights it.*
DOLORES *watches her with curiosity.*

DOLORES. How upset you get by your own dreams.

MARIA. They're nightmares when I have them with you.

DOLORES. You'd better not close your eyes again. You look
so helpless, you poor thing.

MARIA (*laughs*). Behave yourself, woman, please. We can't
go on playing fickle vamps. We're not what we were. Now
we are decent and grown up. Don't forget that,

DOLORES *retreats and continues to put on her boots hastily
and precisely.* MARIA *drops her lit cigar into* DOLORES'
breakfast teapot without her noticing.

MARIA (*brashly*). It's the end of the orgy, Borgy.

*She heads upstage rapidly and picks out some trousers and
a jacket, both emerald green. While she dresses,* DOLORES
*finishes putting on her shoes. Then she takes a rococo
dressing mirror and tries to look at the reflection of her feet
the way other women look at their faces.*

DOLORES. You don't have to lecture me. I've always been
decent.

MARIA. Well I haven't and I don't regret it.

DOLORES. It's not a question of regrets. Nobody chooses her
cradle.

MARIA. Nor her bed either.

DOLORES. Do you think so?

MARIA (*laughs*). If I've slept in a hundred beds in my life, I
haven't chosen more than ten of them.

DOLORES. And the other ninety?

MARIA (*directly*). They were called hunger, ambition, or
violence.

*She appears dressed and gives a twirl like a professional
model.*

MARIA. What do you think?

DOLORES. Divine. You look like luxury asparagus.

MARIA (*laughs and turns towards her wall of mirrors*). I dress
in the colour of your envy, darling, to spare you from mental
exertion. Don't wither on me, bougainvillea.

She puts her jewelry on in front of the mirror. The serpent theme is predominant: bracelets, rings, a necklace like a cobra coiled around MARIA*'s neck.*

DOLORES. Who gave you those jewels? Your lover or your husband?

MARIA (*with supreme insolence*). Both.

DOLORES. You haven't told me where you're going to take me.

MARIA. Guess.

DOLORES (*suddenly frightened, she stops looking at her feet in the mirror*). No . . . again . . . again? . . . No . . . you don't . . .

MARIA. You're right. Unless you see me dressed in black, we're not going to a funeral.

DOLORES (*violently*). Give me the paper.

She stretches out her hand. She drops the mirror. The glass breaks. MARIA *reacts slowly, with repressed anger and caricatured resignation.*

MARIA. Seven years bad luck. It's good to know we won't live that long. Although that would be bad luck: to stay here together for seven more years.

DOLORES. Don't change the subject. Give me the paper.

MARIA. What for? You know his life by heart.

DOLORES. It's not that. It's Mamá.

MARIA. Mamá?

DOLORES. You're very careless. You leave the newspaper lying around anywhere, on the toilet; Mamá comes in to . . . Mamá comes in and reads it.

MARIA. So what?

DOLORES. You know Mamá can't stand finding out about somebody else's death. I've told you to . . .

MARIA. Somebody else? *Oye, chiquita*, there is no way she would read the paper to find out about her own death. It's tough to snuff Mamá, but not that tough.

DOLORES. I've told you to tear up the paper and flush it down the toilet. Mamá . . .

MARIA. I doubt if she will survive her own death.

DOLORES. No, it's even more painful than that. She may survive you and me, she may survive us.

MARIA (*continuing*). Although who knows; that sly old fox may even beat us at that: not surviving us, but surviving herself. There are mothers like that.

DOLORES. Shhhh, don't let her hear you, please. What if she . . . ?

MARIA. Don't worry, little one. The dead person is younger than Mamá.

DOLORES (*relieved*). Ah, then she will be happy.

MARIA. Sure. Let her find out. It's not she who should be unhappy, but you.

DOLORES (*naively*) Did I know him?

MARIA. How sure you are that he was a man.

DOLORES. Did I know *her* then?

MARIA. Right the first time, wrong the second.

DOLORES. I knew *him*. (*Upset*) Don't tell me. I don't want to know any more. Let me imagine. (*She stands up*) It depresses me to find out that an old lover has died before me. People will think that he was older than me. And I've never had a lover older than me. I won't be anyone's widow. I told all my men: Our life began the moment we met . . . (*Sings*) . . . *el mismo instante en que nos conocimos.*[5] (*She walks to the white divan*) Now I'm going to rest. Bring me some cotton wool for my eyes, please.

She reclines on the white divan. MARIA *offers her the cotton wool.* DOLORES *covers her closed eyelids with the cotton wool.*

DOLORES. Hey you, don't you want to rest before going out.

MARIA. I don't need to.

DOLORES. Sorry. I forgot. How many months did you spend at that rest cure in Switzerland?

MARIA. It wasn't rest, I've already told you. It was a nightmare. I had the nightmare of spending God knows how many years taking care of you, watching you spend Mondays, Wednesdays and Fridays with the blinds drawn, flat on your back with cotton wool on your peepers . . .

DOLORES. What a strange way of speaking. There is a bad education.

MARIA. Shut up. Watching you spend Tuesdays and
Thursdays in a tub full of ice cubes, taking care of you, you
taking care of yourself and me wasting away my life so that
on Saturdays and Sundays I could unleash you to run like a
gazelle through the meadows, and everyone could say: How
does she do it? If she had her début in 1925! She danced
with Don Porfirio![6] She learnt Spanish with La Malinche![7]
Sir Walter Raleigh was her godfather!

DOLORES (*coldly*). I get very tired. I only go out on Sundays
now, to lunches in the country. Never at night any more.
You know that, lovely Mariquita.

Pause.

They don't recognise you either.

MARIA *remains cold, statuesque, standing in front of her
mirrors.*

MARIA. Insult me. (*Silence from* DOLORES.) Go on. You
have my permission. Take revenge on me. (*Obstinate
silence from* DOLORES.) Call me what you like. Use those
sickly names that I hate so much. Call me lovely Mariquita,
Marucha, Marionette, Marujita, Mariposa, María Bonita,
Mary Mary Quite Contrary, call me . . .

DOLORES. María Félix.

MARIA *freezes, then trembles with gratitude. She turns
around. She stops looking at herself in the mirror. She looks
at* DOLORES, *lying down, her eyes covered. She goes over
to her.*

MARIA. Really? Do you believe that? (DOLORES *nods.*)
You're not kidding me? You're not flattering me?
(DOLORES *shakes her head.*) For you, am I . . . her?
(DOLORES *stands up, her eyes blinded like a female
Oedipus. She stretches her hands out in a gesture of
blessing.* MARIA *throws herself into her arms. The cotton
wool continues to blind* DOLORES.)

MARIA. The very beautiful María Félix?

DOLORES *strokes* MARIA's *face.*

DOLORES. The youngest and most beautiful dead bride in the
world, a dead bride on horseback, in the arms of her lover
the dashing, strong horseman, galloping towards the peak of
dead souls.

MARIA. Remember the terror of the open plain, the ravishing and awesome Doña Bárbara?

DOLORES. 'They say she's a terrible woman, captain of a band of bandits, ready to kill anyone who stands in her way.'

MARIA (*standing up, abandoning* DOLORES' *blind embrace*). I the man eater, I the bandit woman, I the warrior nun, I the old crock, I the devil's own cunt.

DOLORES. The soulless woman. You were a few pounds overweight then.

MARIA *approaches* DOLORES *and snatches away the cotton wool from her eyes.*

MARIA. Look. Look closely. A goddess does not get old.

DOLORES. Not even the kneeling goddess.

MARIA. No. When I'm ninety, I'll go out into the street dressed exactly the same as you see me now, very neat, all dressed up and serious. And when the children see me they'll say. 'It's her! It's her' and I'll scatter them like this, with my stick. You nasty little brats, you peeping Toms! What are you staring at?

She stops as if making a bold statement. DOLORES *takes advantage of the pause to say hurriedly:*

DOLORES. Tell me, tell me everything I was in Hollywood, bird of paradise, Carmen . . . (*Now it is* MARIA *who remains obstinately silent.*) Madame du Barry . . . (MARIA *returns to her mirror.*) Ramona.

MARIA. Ah yes, I saw that as a girl in Guadalajara.

She looks at herself in the mirror.

DOLORES. You saw me?

MARIA. I saw her. Yes. I saw her.

Long pause. She stops looking at herself in the mirror, with a sigh.

MARIA. I think after all I will get changed for the funeral of your ex-lover, if he can be called that.

DOLORES. Who? Who was he?

MARIA *disappears behind the folding screens again.*

MARIA. How should I know? All that happened before I was born. Mamá told me. Ask her.

DOLORES. Shhh! Don't let her hear you. You already know . . .

MARIA. Ha! She told me about it with pride, the big idiot.

DOLORES. María! She's our mother.

MARIA. She made an example of you. How has Lolita kept herself so well, so young, so appetising?

DOLORES. Our creator . . .

MARIA. Because no-one has touched her.

DOLORES. The author of our days.

MARIA. Not that she's a virgin, no . . . (DOLORES *hugs herself in anguish and continues imitating the acts being described by* MARIA, *who is dressing out of sight of the audience.*) . . . but nobody's ever touched her breasts, that's why they look like a fifteen year old's, all bouncy, with happy pink nipples. Nobody's groped her. Nobody has ever lain on top of her. She's never felt eighty kilos of *macho* on top of her. No. Everything always delicate. Always sideways like this . . .

MARIA *appears dressed totally in black, clothes which are exaggeratedly tragic and old-fashioned: a long skirt, a blouse buttoned to the ears and veils. She is adjusting a pearl necklace around her neck. On seeing her,* DOLORES *freezes.*

MARIA. *La Señora* has no children, she's never given birth. Her belly doesn't wobble like jelly and her buttocks aren't like Zamoran buns. *La Señora* is simply perfect, a dark, silky Venus, *la Señora* . . . *la Señora* made our eyes pop out of our heads. (*She points to herself.*) Like this.

DOLORES. What do you know about those things? You have no idea what Hollywood was, what it was like to be a Latina in Hollywood, fighting first against prejudice, then against advancing age. Why do you laugh about age? Age is the climbing vine, age is the actress' visible leprosy and an actress who had children had to hide or deny them and hated them and beat them. An actress betrayed by her children was like a goddess, not just a kneeling goddess, but humiliated, forced to run errands and come back loaded with tins, steaks, oranges and cauliflowers . . . I wanted to be weightless, winged, a dark flame.

MARIA. Nothing hurt Dolores.

DOLORES. I think a lot about her. She shone brighter than anyone. When her light goes out, the world shall be night.

MARIA *watches her scornfully.*

MARIA. You stole that from one of my movies.

DOLORES *(resigned)*. Probably. God wrote our destinies but not, unfortunately, our scripts.

MARIA. And the directors we had!

DOLORES. Apart from Buñuel and Welles.

MARIA. Who used us as furniture.

DOLORES. No. He used me as an animal. I was the leopard woman in *Journey into Fear.*

She snarls, amused.

MARIA. Darling, at least a panther has a history . . .

DOLORES. Leopard.

MARIA. Panther, leopard, they're both cats, aren't they? At least you know how to imitate them. But what about those directors who told me: 'Come on, María, give me lots of *Ummmm*, eh? Come on, lots of *Ummmm.*' 'What's that, señor?' 'What I said, *Ummmm.*'

DOLORES. *Ummmm.*

MARIA. *Ummmmmmm.*

They both start a parodic game of ummms, *improvising scenes and dramatic situations until, still* ummmming, *in crescendo, they embrace and kiss. From love they pass to hate. Pretending to claw at each other, they fall over and roll around on the floor, and the* ummms *no longer designate either fury or laughter, but a constant interplay between the two.* MARIA *is the first to stand up, shaking off the dust from her black clothes, replacing the veils over her face, composing herself in front of the mirror.*

MARIA. When I'm ninety, I'll go out into the street dressed exactly the same as you see me now, very neat, and I'll scatter the gaupers with my stick. What are you staring at? What are you staring at?

DOLORES. You repeat yourself, darling.

Angry and weeping, MARIA *starts to break down.*

MARIA. What are you staring at? Am I not desirable any
more? Am I no longer María Bonita, the piece of ass who
excited your parents and grandparents? Am I no longer the
cutest sex kitten you ever had the good fortune to lay your
sad eyes on? No longer? Is there no-one left to write boleros
for me, to send a hydroplane out to me on Lake Patzcuaro
with orchids and paté? Is there not a bullfighter who will
dedicate a bull to me, a cowboy who will ride me senseless?

From the floor, DOLORES *has been watching her with
growing scepticism, shaking her head.*

DOLORES. No, no, no. She'd never have said those things.

MARIA. You think so?

DOLORES. Of course not. It's like if I said: I'm no longer the
little girl who went to the Convent of the Sacred Bleeding
Heart and learnt to write in a spider's scrawl; I'm no longer
the adolescent who married a Mexican aristocrat at
seventeen and then scandalised my family by dumping him
at nineteen to become a moviestar.

MARIA. But it's true.

DOLORES. Ah, it's true. Then you admit *I am* Dolores del
Río?

MARIA. Don't put words into my mouth. I said it was true for
her life, not for yours, Lolita, because you're not her.

DOLORES. I don't like to insist, my love, but I want you to
understand that we both live only on the screen, in the image
of Doña Barbara and María Candelaria, not in anyone's
private biography.

MARIA. You said I was María. You admitted it.

DOLORES. And you didn't reciprocate. Sorry for my lie. I
praise your sincerity.

The two women watch each other for a moment.

MARIA. Have you read today's paper?

DOLORES. No. You beat me to it. That's how you found out
about his death before I did, remember?

MARIA. That was in yesterday's paper.

DOLORES. But his funeral . . .

MARIA. It's already been. Yesterday.

DOLORES. Then you lied to me.

MARIA. Why would I do that, sweetheart.

DOLORES. You're all dressed in black.

MARIA. Sorry. I thought we were going to the cemetery today to pay our respects to the deceased, who was buried yesterday. Do you want me to go dressed for a carnival like you?

DOLORES *now comes out of her languour on the floor, stands up and occupies the place in front of her mirror as if the news of the death had aroused something more than flirtatiousness.*

DOLORES. Dolores. My pains I carry in my heart, not in my clothes.

MARIA. Ah, Dolores is Dolores, Dolores is her pains, not her rags.

DOLORES *carelessly rearranges her hairdo and dress, singing softly.*

DOLORES. 'Son de la loma, cantan en llano.'[8]

MARIA (*singing softly*). 'Ya no estás más a mi lado, corazón.'

DOLORES (*singing softly*). 'Corazón, tu dirás lo que hacemos, lo que resolvemos.'

MARIA (*abruptly interrupting the stream of consciousness*). That's enough. We're talking about clothes, threads, rags.

DOLORES. Simplicity is the sign of a wealthy cradle.

MARIA. No, *señora*. If you're a fat cat, then you should dress as a fat cat and show the plebs you're a fat cat. And if not, why sweat if you're going to end up with all your millions dressed like a wild flower, a humble peasant girl.

DOLORES. You wouldn't understand.

MARIA. Why?

DOLORES. Because it cost you to make it. Because you desperately need to stand out from them.

MARIA. From whom?

DOLORES. From the herd, from the masses. Because in a word, darling, you lack breeding.

MARIA. So I should go around dressed like a little ranch hand, like you.

DOLORES. You could never understand. These are things you're born with.

MARIA. What? Sure, I understand you wanting to dress up as the most beautiful flower on the *hacienda*. That way they might forgive you. I understand that.

DOLORES. Nobody's threatening me.

MARIA. They're threatening us. And even if you doll yourself up, they'll still uncover you. Or do you think the Commies will hang the bankers and respect those of us who make more money than a banker?

DOLORES. We are national treasures.

MARIA. Tell that to your friend Madame du Barry.

DOLORES. Anyway, Mexico is a long way away. There's not going to be a revolution here.

MARIA. Here. In Venice? Did I say it right this time?

DOLORES. Here. In Venecia.

MARIA. Where we've retired with our sacks full of the gold we earnt in the Mexican cinema.

DOLORES. We brought money back to the country. We're evens. Anyway, Madame du Barry was like you, baby, not me.

MARIA. What? Are we living in life or the movies? You are Madame du Barry because your idol played her on the silver screen. Biographies don't count. What counts is La Belle Otero: who she is, who she is and who I am. And Madame du Barry counts. Who she is, who she is and who you are. *Ça va?*

DOLORES. Except that *I am* Dolores del Río.

MARIA. Have you read today's paper?

DOLORES (*Alarmed*). What does it say?

MARIA. Listen to this. There are reports that María Félix flew to France yesterday to attend the Grand Prix at Deauville where one of her horses is running.

DOLORES. That doesn't surprise me. It's well known that woman likes the sport of kings.

MARIA. Just a moment. It then says that Dolores del Río has accepted the part of an old Seminole Indian whose

grandson is being played by Marlon Brando, in a production
by Metro . . .

DOLORES. Me? Marlon Brando's grandmother? That's a lie.
I'd never sign a contract like that. Marlon Brando's old
enough to be my father. Those women are imposters!
They're impersonating us.

MARIA. When I say they're threatening us . . .

DOLORES. Alright. We must join forces, forget our quarrels,
our different roots . . .

MARIA. Shhhh! Don't let Mamá hear.

DOLORES. You're right. Secrecy. She doesn't understand
we're grown up now and can make our own decisions.

MARIA. No. What she wouldn't understand is what you said
about our different roots.

DOLORES. Bah, fathers can be different.

MARIA. Yes, little sister.

DOLORES. Shhhh! Don't let them hear us . . .

MARIA. Mamá?

DOLORES. No, silly, the Fourth Estate, the gossip columnists.
What would they say?

MARIA. That it's time for tea.

DOLORES. To psyche ourselves up and deal with the stresses
of the day. It's a cute English tradition.

MARIA. It's also drunk in France, you know.

DOLORES. Are we going to start again?

MARIA. To each her spiritual motherland.

DOLORES. Well, I only speak English at teatime.

MARIA. And I only speak French.

MARIA *sits down beside the walnut Mexican table.*
DOLORES, *standing up, prepares the two cups and picks
up the teapot.*

DOLORES (*in Queen's English*). How do you like your tea,
with lemon or with milk?

MARIA (*in a French accent*). I preefur eet vizout limon and
vizout meelk.

DOLORES (*English accent*). I'm seau sorry. We deaun't have it with neither lemon nor milk . . .

MARIA (*French accent*). Alors, just vizout ze zugar, pleez.

DOLORES *pours the tea into* MARIA*'s cup.*

DOLORES (*English accent*). Without white sugar or without brown sugar.

MARIA (*French accent*). Non. I preefur eet hottur.

> DOLORES *pours herself a cup of tea. She drinks it.* MARIA *watches her with her own cup on her knees.* DOLORES *spits out the tea violently.* MARIA *covers her mouth like a naughty little girl.* DOLORES *wipes her mouth.*

DOLORES. Ash, ash . . .

> *She takes the lid off the teapot, puts her hand inside and takes out* MARIA*'s wet cigar.* MARIA *has moved downstage. She stops at the edge of the stage. She makes a movement with her hand and arm as if she were drawing back a curtain and she looks out into the distance.*

MARIA. Venice . . .

DOLORES (*with hysterical anger*). I'm talking to you! You dropped your cigar in my tea!

MARIA. What am I looking at? The Campanile of San Marco or an oil derrick?

DOLORES. You put a cigar stub in my brew.

MARIA. On what cupolas is the sun shining? Santa Maria Maggiore or Howard Johnson's motel?

DOLORES. I hate you! Ash in my breakfast! That's what you are! Ash dressed up as flame!

MARIA. Where are we, in Venezia or in Venice? Are we looking out on the Grand Canal or Centinela Boulevard?

> *Both possibilities frighten* DOLORES, *who pours herself another cup of tea and drinks it with an expression of bitter nausea.*

DOLORES (*with disgust*). It's all right. We're in Venecia, on the Grand Canal. Can't you hear the gondoliers singing? '*Bandera rossa, color' del vin . . .* '9

MARIA (*with cold insistence*). Finish your breakfast. You must build up your strength.

DOLORES (*swallows with her eyes closed, as if she were drinking a purge. She screws up her lips. She starts singing softly again.*) '*Chi non lavora, non mangierá, viva el communismo e la libertá*'.

DOLORES *screws up her lips again.*

MARIA. Very good, Lolita. I thought I heard another song wafting through the open window. (*Sings softly*) 'When orchids bloom in the moonlight, and lovers vow to be true . . .'[10]

DOLORES (*makes an abrupt but smooth gesture, recognising she is in* MARIA'*s power*). All right. It's still all right . . .

MARIA (*stepping back from the balcony*). All right. Now we've built up our strength, what are we going to do with those imposters?

DOLORES. Report them.

MARIA. What for?

DOLORES. They . . . they . . . you know . . . they are . . .

MARIA. Say it. They are us.

DOLORES. You say it, you say it.

MARIA (*as a serious joke*). Shhhh . . . Don't let Mamá find out.

DOLORES *shudders.* MARIA *arranges her black veils in front of the mirror.* DOLORES' *gaze wanders around the apartment. She goes toward the paper flowers and strokes them. She picks up a clay piggy bank and sits on the floor downstage holding it in her arms like a peasant in a village market.*

DOLORES (*to the piggy*). Shhhh . . . Don't let Mamá find out.

MARIA. Don't worry! I make the newspapers disappear every day.

DOLORES. What do you do with them? That's not true. You leave them lying about. I told you to flush them down the toilet.

MARIA. Don't worry. I don't collect them. She doesn't see them. She doesn't know who's been dying.

DOLORES. That's good. It would make her so sad to read about the deaths of her contemporaries.

MARIA. No, it's not that. It's to stop her reading about the
people who die younger than her. It's to make her suffer *not*
knowing there are younger people dying the whole time.

DOLORES. But surely you'd only make her suffer if you also
let her know there are people dying of her own age?

MARIA. I think she'll really suffer *not* knowing that people are
dying and then finding out one day that there's nobody left
in the world except her: Mamá, alone.

DOLORES (*afraid*). Nobody? Not even us?

MARIA *starts playing with her black veils, dancing like a
funereal Salome.*

MARIA. Nobody. Our revenge will be to die before she does.

DOLORES. But . . . but don't you think she already treats us
like we're dead?

MARIA (*raising her eyebrow melodramatically*). She's not the
only one who's done that, baby. Or else what have we been
talking about all this time?

MARIA *has become a whirlwind of black veils.*

MARIA. Nobody remembers us, nobody remembers us,
nobody remembers us . . .

DOLORES. You cried, María. You said it. we're not desirable
any more, bulls and boleros aren't dedicated to us any more
. . . (*Sings softly*) 'Acuérdate de Acapulco, María bonita,
María bonita, María del alma . . . '[11]

Covered with black veils MARIA *moves towards*
DOLORES. *She dances around her sister, wrapping the
veils around her.*

MARIA. Quiet! That's not what I'm talking about. It's Mamá.
For her we died the day the first hair appeared in our
armpits.

DOLORES. How disgusting. I don't know why I stick around
with you.

*She wraps herself in her shawl without letting go of the
piggy bank.*

MARIA. Yes! As soon as we had our first period, she stopped
talking to us. Remember? She hated us because we grew up,
because we couldn't always be her children, her babies. (*She
lifts her veils for a moment to mimic.*) Do you remember

how she imitated us, how she made fun of us to her friends? (*Mimics*). 'Lolita doesn't like being called *señorita*. She screams and shouts I not thenolita, me are stwong fat baby!'

DOLORES (*taking up the mimicry, but talking to the piggy*). 'This little piggy went to market, this little piggy stayed at home...'

MARIA. 'Me are big baby'

DOLORES. 'This little piggy . . . ' (*She abruptly changes the song and tone. Sings softly.*) '*Y al verme tan sola y triste cual hoja al viento, quisiera llorar, quisiera morir de sentimiento.*'[12]

Waving her black veils, MARIA *looks like a vulture descending on poor* DOLORES.

MARIA. Quiet! Don't sing that song! She hates us because we're no longer her little girls with pink ribbons and crumpled panties, crumpled but still unstained.

DOLORES *raises her hand to her head and touches her ribbons.*

DOLORES. I am! I am!

MARIA. Stupid! Don't you realise that she doesn't want to see us ever again . . . as long as we live?

DOLORES. But . . . but then she won't care if we die.

MARIA. Yes. Yes, she will care.

DOLORES. Why? Didn't you say . . . ?

MARIA. Trust me. Watch out. (*Points to herself.*) Be very careful that *she* doesn't vanish.

DOLORES. I don't understand. (*Sighs, gets up.*) But I agree that your intuition is better than mine, even if you are ignorant and badly educated . . . (*She leaves the piggy bank on the table.*) Life, you know, is very different when you've read books . . . (*Satisfied, she embraces herself.*) . . . when one has cultivated – how shall I say it – the garden of the spirit . . . (MARIA *has disappeared again behind the folding screens.*)

MARIA. Don't be pretentious. You've never read a book in your life.

Prolonged silence. DOLORES *stealthily goes over to the white telephone which is on top of the toilet lid.*

DOLORES. It's true. It makes me sad. That's why I rely on you. Because even if you know nothing you have a good memory.

Stretches out her hand towards the telephone. She becomes frightened and pulls it back.

MARIA (*laughs from behind the folding screens*). What would you do without me, bougainvillea? Really, how would you prove you existed?

DOLORES *hears this and dares to put her hand on the telephone.*

MARIA. Let's see. Who directed *Flying down to Río*?

DOLORES *hangs her head but leaves her hand on the telephone.*

DOLORES. Archie Mayo, of course. Who doesn't know . . . ?

MARIA (*incredulous*). Don't you know who directed that film where you dance . . . what was that song called, Lolita . . . the one you danced to in *Flying down to Río*?

DOLORES (*hesitant, unsure*). No. I don't remember . . . a bolero, 'María Bonita,' 'Canción Mixteca,' Archie Mayo, Busby Berkeley . . .

She picks up the handset as if clinging on to it for dear life, holds it up in the air without daring to listen to it.

MARIA (*laughs*). You are Dolores del Río, and you can't remember that, you can't . . . ?

DOLORES *presses the handset to her mouth.*

DOLORES. It was very hot on set, the klieg lamps, the confinement. They were the first talkies and they were afraid of noise on set. They isolated us. They suffocated us. The lights, the playback, the tango, the passion. We were orchids, suffocated and burnt out by the spotlights . . . Orson Welles and Ginger Rogers dancing the tango . . . What memories! What confusion!

Music: 'Orchids in the Moonlight.' MARIA comes out from behind the folding screens, dressed in white satin. tailored and loose-fitting, just like Dolores del Río in Flying down to Rio. DOLORES *lets go of the telephone without managing to replace the handset before* MARIA *has seen her. The handset remains off its hook and a very light humming can be heard beneath the music of the tango. The humming grows until it becomes unbearable and drowns out the music of the dance.* MARIA *moves over to* DOLORES *with stylised tango steps and takes her round the waist. They dance,* MARIA *fervently and joyfully,* DOLORES *with initial inhibition which is overcome by the happiness of the dance. The dance ends with an elegant spin made by* DOLORES, *her hand on high, held that way for a moment by* MARIA. *The humming of the telephone becomes unbearable.* MARIA *lets go of* DOLORES. DOLORES *does not change her position: a statue with her arm on high.* MARIA *goes towards the toilet and, routinely, hangs up the telephone.*

MARIA (*sharply*). What were you doing with that telephone in your hand? (DOLORES *remains in her statuesque position.*) You know the telephone is not to be touched. (*She approaches* DOLORES *threateningly.*) You know the telephone is put there like the apple in Paradise: as a temptation. The first one to make a call will be carried away . . . the madonna . . . You know? Remember? Understand?

DOLORES. A temptation . . .

MARIA. The devil will carry you away. *Capiche*? The illusion is shattered. We are no longer where we are, but in . . .

DOLORES (*pretending to be crazy in order to interrupt* MARIA's *thought process*). Did you say the devil? Don't you think he's got prettier names? Beelzebub. Mephistopheles. Lucifer. Asmodeus. Mandinga. Do you remember? Doña Barbara had dealings with Mandinga.

MARIA. Everything has more than one name. When will you call a spade a spade . . . ?

DOLORES (*in the same frivolously apologetic tone*). A spade is a dago is a spick is a . . .

MARIA. Spade, señora! A spade to dig your grave!

DOLORES (*frightened*). Yes . . .

MARIA. 'Orchids in the Moonlight.' That's what that tango's called. You don't remember it. You're not her.

DOLORES. No. You remember for me, Mariquita, You do me that favour. I depend on your good memory. It's not that I'm not her, it's not that I don't exist. No. I just forget things.

MARIA. At least say thank you.

DOLORES. Thank you.

MARIA. That's the way I like it, Wild Flower.

DOLORES (*aggressively*). Who directed *French Can-Can*? Quick!

MARIA (*with her back to the audience and* DOLORES, *amused*). Jean Renoir. My little white teddy bear.

DOLORES (*even more aggressively*). What's your son called? Quick!

Silence. MARIA*'s back is still turned. She hangs her head slightly.*

DOLORES. How many times did you see him as a child? Tell me! What games did you play with him? Did you ever play on all fours with your baby? Tell me! Here's an A, and there's a B. Mary had a little lamb. Did you teach him the first letters, ring-a-ring-a-roses, riddles? Rock a bye-baby, on the tree-tops. A cold mother, drunk with success, selfish, perverse. A Mexican woman who sold whores, her plum pussy, her apricot ass and her watermelon breasts. How many times did your stwong, fat Sweetpea find you in the arms of a man who wasn't his father? Come on, let's go and dance in the moonlight . . .

MARIA *remains motionless, her back to the audience.* DOLORES, *inflamed by her boldness, taking advantage of* MARIA*'s state of mind, goes over to the telephone lying on the toilet, lifts the handset without hesitation, and rapidly dials a number. She waits for the reply cheekily twirling the tassles on her shawl, her tongue nailed into the inside of her cheek – a grotesque image, somewhere between the main character in* Las Abandonadas *and the female half of the Chema and Juana couple, or else somewhere between Madame X and La Criada Malcriada.*

DOLORES. Hello? Who do I have the pleasure of . . . ? Ah, I see . . . May I speak to . . . ?

MARIA *comes out of her paralysis, moves forward violently and snatches the handset from* DOLORES *and threatens her with it.* DOLORES *covers her head, laughing mockingly.* MARIA *hesitates between putting the telephone to her ear and hanging up.*

DOLORES. Go on, be brave, listen . . . listen . . . It's her, it's María.

MARIA *hangs up hastily.*

MARIA. You don't have to hurt me like this. I was brave enough to have a child. I've cured my forgetfulness. I've purged my guilt.

DOLORES *makes gestures characteristic of a cinema director.*

DOLORES. Cut! Print it! Kill the jerk! That's a wrap!

MARIA. You poor baby, you don't have anything for which to be forgiven.

DOLORES. Wrong again. I shall tell you my story. So that my son could go to school, I took to the streets. I was a cabaret dancer, a lady of the night, a street-walker. Do you remember? To pay for my little boy's law studies I let myself get old, battered and run-down. But my boy grew in honour and promise, as tall and strong as an oak, as noble as a king, as beautiful as the sun. And he went off and married Señorita O'Higgins, if you please. Baby O'Higgins, a Puebla girl, descended from the Irish, related to generals and presidents, multi-millionaire heiress in rubber, bottled water and sporting tabloids. My child of the fog went off and entered Mexican society thanks to my sacrifice, María. I saw the wedding from the street, in the Lomas de Chapultepec, in the rain. Whore that I am, old, limping, poor, mean, screwed up, toothless, unwashed, without social security to fall back on, without an American Express card, the last of the rejects, watching my son get married to a Puebla girl descended from the Irish . . .

MARIA *(with one eyebrow raised high).* Ah the Irish . . . Do you know why Jesus wasn't born in Ireland? *(Pause)* Because they couldn't find three wise men and a virgin.

DOLORES *(reacting).* You border girl, Sonora girl, daughter of the desert! What do you know about creole purity? Cactuses and prickly pears!

MARIA. Durango girl.

DOLORES. I have class. I was chased by the finest gentlemen.

MARIA. Chased, but not chaste.

DOLORES. Let me finish! I let you tell all your nasty melo-dramas, your stupid adaptations of Sappho and Camille.

MARIA. But my soap operas end up differently every time. You just tell me the same one over and over again.

DOLORES. The police came up to me, pushed me and told me: 'You don't belong here, old hag, go and peel some potatoes, get out of here.'

MARIA. You don't belong here.

DOLORES. What?

MARIA. That's what they told us at the border.

DOLORES. What are you talking about?

MARIA. When we left Mexico.

DOLORES. Ah yes. When we retired to live our autumn years in Venecia.

MARIA. Venice.

DOLORES. Very good. That's the way it's pronounced in English.

MARIA. Venice, California.

DOLORES is terrified. Nervously, she takes down a dress at random and starts to iron it with her hands, masking her anguish in activity. MARIA *looks at her doing this with a smile, singing softly:*

MARIA. 'When orchids bloom in the moonlight, and lovers vow to be true...'

DOLORES. We can't complain, Mariquita . . . Venecia is . . .

MARIA (*brutally*). A suburb of Los Angeles.

DOLORES. María! I called you María. I didn't say you were . . .

MARIA. The same as me. A retired Chicana living in an L.A. slum . . .

She goes downstage and makes the gesture of drawing a curtain.

DOLORES. No . . .

She drops the dress. She stops without daring to touch MARIA.

MARIA. Here's your Venecia. A fake Venecia, invented by a crazy gringo to make other gringo suckers think they're living in the second Renaissance. look at those tacky columns. Look. Look at the canals buried in trash. Look at the gondolas next to the roundabout and the big dipper. Look at your screwed up Venecia. Keep dreaming, Dolores . . .

DOLORES. Dolores, yes. Venecia, no. But Dolores, yes. Please?

MARIA. Look at your Venecia. It's up for auction.

DOLORES. We came in search of Hollywood. Do you remember?

MARIA. Yes. Like two elephants in search of their cemetery. When nobody offered us work in Mexico, we decided to come and die in Hollywood. To be buried in the fresh cement of the Chinese Theater. (*Pause.*) Even there they didn't want us. Old Chicanas, old movie stars? Trash. Everything here is trash. There can't be anything here worth more than two sols.

DOLORES (*unthinking*). Orchids in the moonlight . . .

MARIA. Everything is old the moment it comes out. Cars. Foodblenders. TVs. Clothes. Hearts.

DOLORES. The stars.

MARIA. Look outside, Dolores: Venice, California, the same as Moscow, Texas; Paris, Kentucky; Rome, Wisconsin; and Mexico, Missouri: borrowed clothes, names for sale, illusions up for auction. Yes, you are Dolores del Río . . .

DOLORES. María!

She moves to go towards her. She stops.

MARIA. Dolores del Río Mississippi. María de Los Angeles Félix. Something else. Not them any more. Nor us. A mirage. Nostalgia. Two crazy Chicanas . . .

DOLORES *embraces* MARIA. *Both are standing.*

DOLORES. . . . who love each other, who comfort each other in the desert. Yes . . . Who came looking for something that never existed . . .

MARIA. Your Hollywood . . .

DOLORES. The dream factory . . . which dreamed us up . . .

MARIA. The centre of illusion . . . which turned out to be just another illusion . . .

DOLORES. Our mirror . . .

MARIA. Our mirage . . .

Embracing each other, they sing the 'Canción Mixteca' together:

MARIA and DOLORES.

> *¡ Qué lejos estoy del suelo donde he nacido!*
> *intensa nostalgia invade mi pensamiento;*
> *y al verme tan sola y triste cual hoja al viento,*
> *quisiera llorar, quisiera morir de sentimiento.*
> *¡ Oh tierra del sol, suspiro por verte!,*
> *ahora que lejos yo vivo sin luz, sin amor . . .* [13]

The song is brutally interrupted by a noise: half heartbeat,
half knock.

DOLORES. *Ay nanita*!

The two women embrace again.

DOLORES. Holy Mary, mother of God . . .

DOLORES *pulls away from* MARIA *and beats her chest.*

DOLORES. Holy, holy, holy.

The blows on DOLORES' *chest get louder and stronger:*
someone is knocking on the door. The two women embrace
each other again.

MARIA. (*Pulling herself together and gulping*) Who can it be?

DOLORES. Mamá . . .

MARIA. She's forgotten us, I've already told you.

DOLORES. And what if she suddenly remembered us?

MARIA. Which are you more afraid of, her remembering us or
her forgetting us?

DOLORES. I don't know, I don't know . . .

The knuckles rap on the door.

MARIA. Did you tell anyone?

DOLORES. Me? How could I if . . .

MARIA (*with cold anger*). You just made a phone call,
stupid . . . Didn't I tell you . . . ?

DOLORES. No. I swear. I was pretending. It was another
number.

MARIA. Another number . . . ? *Oye*, who have you been talking to behind my back?

DOLORES. What are you thinking?

MARIA. What I am thinking.

DOLORES. Well, don't even think it.

MARIA. All right. I don't think it. I intuit it. I smell it and I smell a rat, I smell a slippery skunk . . . Who are you fooling around with, Xochimilco slut?

DOLORES. Ay, how can you bring that up? That was years ago.

MARIA. Aaaah, you admit it was years ago . . . How many?

DOLORES. My God, keeping track of all the years . . . spent together . . . what torture . . . or rather what indulgence . . . Anyway, I'm talking about that movie, *María Candelaria*, which was made years ago . . . (*Insistent drumming on the door.*) Can you hear it? It's not my heart, is it?

MARIA. I can hear it. I can't hear your heart. I can hear him, no?

DOLORES. He wouldn't dare. I told him to blow.

MARIA. Blow?

DOLORES. Yes, with the whistle, the horn, like this. (*She imitates the sound of a car horn.*) That's all I need to know it's him. He has no reason to come up here and worry you.

MARIA. Ah, how chic. He's coming by car.

DOLORES. Yes. He drives.

MARIA. Doesn't he have a chauffeur?

DOLORES. No. He drives on his own.

MARIA. He drives on his own. His own car?

DOLORES. Not exactly his own.

MARIA. He doesn't drive his own car?

DOLORES. No, no.

MARIA. Is it lent to him by his friends?

DOLORES. He does business in his car.

MARIA. In the car lent to him by his friends?

Increasingly insistent drumming. DOLORES *looks nervously at the door.*

DOLORES. Yes, that's it, lent to him.

MARIA. Is he a professional racing driver?

DOLORES. Yes, a professional. Who isn't in this traffic!

MARIA. I mean like Taruffi or Fangio or Stirling Moss. A profe-ssio-nal racing driver.

DOLORES. No, much riskier.

MARIA. Does he drive on special tracks?

DOLORES. No. Only on the Pasadena Freeway.

MARIA. The Pasadena Freeway?

DOLORES. And on the Golden State sometimes as well. (*Pause.*) He knows the Temescal Canyon very well.

MARIA. How cute. (*Violently*) Is your lover a cab driver?

DOLORES (*embarrassed*). Oh, what an idea.

MARIA. Cabby.

DOLORES. He drives people from one place to another, if that's what you mean.

MARIA. For free, of course.

DOLORES. In exchange for a modest fee.

MARIA. Whatever the meter says. (*Pause.*) Cab driver.

DOLORES. He's very brave. He drives blindfold through the tunnels of Arroyo Seco.

MARIA. You've fallen into the hands of a scummy little taxi driver . . .

DOLORES. He gives special rates to Newport . . .

MARIA. A road hog . . .

DOLORES. . . . to see the fairy lights on the beach . . .

MARIA. . . . a Genghis Khan of the freeways.

DOLORES. He wants to meet you.

MARIA. What for? To give me multiple orgasms looking for the exits on the Pasadena Freeway? What does your taxi driver smell like? What does his joystick smell like?

DOLORES. It's a Mercedes! He's coming in a Mercedes!

MARIA. An old banger, I bet. A rust bucket, a total mess, with a rubber Mickey Mouse hanging over the dashboard, and a little altar to the Virgin, and a ball autographed by Pelé. I can see it now and I wish I were blind.

Fists hammer on the door. MARIA *moves assertively towards the folding screens.*

MARIA. You were born to be carried in a litter by Ethiopian slaves . . . (*She pulls a Cleopatra costume out of the wardrobe and holds it up to herself.*) You, who should have been carried by barge down the Nile. You, woman: age cannot wither you, nor custom stale your infinite variety . . . [14]

DOLORES (*dreamily*). 'I will praise any man that will praise me.'

MARIA. Woman, divine woman . . .

She throws the Cleopatra costume on the folding screen. The knuckles rap again.

MARIA. There's your cut-price Mark Anthony.

DOLORES. No. I swear. It wasn't his phone number.

MARIA. What do you mean?

DOLORES. It was another number, not his.

MARIA. Another number?

DOLORES. A random number. The first one that came into my head. I swear on this . . .

She makes the sign of the cross with her forefinger and kisses it. MARIA moves away from DOLORES.

MARIA. Then . . . it could be anyone knocking at the door. The first one that came into your head, you dickhead . . .

DOLORES. How could he know...? I didn't give him the address . . . He couldn't have found out . . .

MARIA. Do you know what promiscuity is, Cleopatra?

DOLORES. Yes, yes, but I didn't give him our address. You heard me, I didn't.

MARIA. Listen: you can call the police and trace the number of someone who's just called and then put an address to that number, even a name . . .

DOLORES. But why would this man go to the trouble of looking for two women he doesn't even know?

MARIA. Two old Chicanas languishing in a Venetian suburb of a Hollywood which does not exist . . .

DOLORES. Which never existed. *Ay!*

MARIA. Two retired lunatics. Two stars which are burning out.

DOLORES. Oh, we're not that. Don't say that. Our movies live on, they don't burn out, Madame du Barry, Bird of Paradise. You said so . . .

Decisively, MARIA *interrupts* DOLORES *and marches over to the door. Her courage seems to falter for a moment. She takes a deep breath, stretches out her hand and opens the door. A slim bespectacled young man stands holding a bouquet of flowers in the same hand with which he was about to knock again. He is dressed like a respectable young man of the 1940s: striped shirt, bowtie, a double-breasted Prince of Wales suit, a diamond-patterned sweater underneath, black shoes and a hat with the brim raised in the style of a 1940s reporter. It is the only thing which reveals him. In fact, he is an unnerving mixture of Harold Lloyd and James Cagney. Under his arm he carries a canned film reel and in his hand he holds a cinema projector.* MARIA *and* DOLORES *look at him in astonishment. They look at each other.* MARIA *asking by moving her head whether he might be* DOLORES' *taxi-driver boyfriend,* DOLORES *shaking her head, indicating that she has never seen him before and enquiring whether, on the contrary, he might be one of* MARIA's *secret lovers. The young visitor does not have enough arms to protect the flowers – a bouquet of forget-me-nots – as well as holding the movie can under his arm, the projector and now the newspaper that he picks up with the bouquet hand and puts under his chin. He has still not entered or been invited to enter.*

FAN. Sorry. I don't have enough hands.

He offers the flowers to DOLORES *but the newspaper slips from his chin and falls to the floor. The* FAN *is most concerned about his canned reel, guarding it from any possible damage. He puts the projector on the floor and finally takes off his hat.* DOLORES *nervously stoops to pick up the paper. The* FAN *stoops as well and they bang their heads.* MARIA *stops* DOLORES *from picking up the paper by stepping on her hand.* DOLORES *stifles a cry. The* FAN *tries to help her and drops his hat. He keeps a firm hold of the reel.*

MARIA (*to* DOLORES). Don't be so curious. Go and look after your driver friend who takes people from one place to another for a modest fee.

The FAN *picks up and shakes his hat.*

DOLORES (*nursing her trampled hand*). I wanted to find out. I wanted to read about his death. (*Looks at their visitor*) Anyway, it isn't him.

FAN. Sorry?

MARIA. It isn't him? But he's giving you flowers. Go on, take them.

But before DOLORES *can touch them, even before she has timidly put her hand out,* MARIA *stops her.* DOLORES *stands up.*

MARIA (*to the* FAN). Where did you park your car, young man. Because if you're parked in front of the neighbours' garage, we'll get into big trouble.

FAN. Sorry . . . I came by bus . . .

MARIA. Ah, your day off . . .

FAN. Sorry, I don't understand you.

MARIA. Don't fool around. I know everything. She . . . (*half-winks at* DOLORES *conspiratorially*) . . . has told me everything. She's never been able to keep her mouth shut.

DOLORES. I have the right! I have the right to my own lover. (MARIA *looks at her scornfully.*) I don't have to spend my whole life going to the supermarket on the corner of Rialto and Pacific or traipsing all the way to Olvera to look for your favourite snacks. You're not a man eater, you're a taco eater, a tortilla-chip eater.

MARIA *takes no notice of her. She turns to the* FAN.

DOLORES. I have a right to my own secrets.

MARIA. Go on, *señor*, give her the weeds before they dry up.

FAN. They're forget-me-nots. (*He hands the bouquet to* DOLORES *and blushes.*) Ever since I saw you in *The Jungle of Fire*, I haven't been able to get you off my mind, ma'am.

DOLORES (*ecstatically*). A fan!

MARIA. A fan?

DOLORES. A fanatic, you idiot. An enthusiast, a supporter, an admirer . . . (*She sniffs the flowers primly.*) A dedicated follower of my artistic labours.

FAN. That's right, ma'am. At your service. I've seen every movie you've made, except one.

DOLORES (*flirting*). Well you've seen more than I have . . . Come in, come in. Make yourself at home.

The FAN *comes centre-stage.*

FAN. I didn't expect anything less from your proverbial hospitality. When in *The Little House* you invite Roberto Cañedo to visit you in . . .

DOLORES (*to* MARIA, *authoritatively*). Girl, will you please close the door?

FAN. Exquisite! That's like how you treat your Indian maid in *Bougainvillea.*

Unruffled, MARIA *closes the door. The noise of it closing is metallic, like that of a prison. We hear a clang and even the hint of locks and chains.* MARIA *leans against the door, her hands joined behind her back. But nothing distracts* DOLORES *and the* FAN *from their courtship rituals of courtesies and reminiscences.*

DOLORES. And what might that gap in your education be?

FAN (*bewildered*). I beg your pardon?

DOLORES. I mean the movie I made which you still haven't . . . admired.

FAN. Ah! Well, I'm talking there about *Carmen*, directed by Raoul Walsh in 1926, based on Mérimée's homonymous novel and Bizet's famous opera. (*Draws breath*) The only surviving copy is in the archives of the Film Library in Prague, capital of Czechoslovakia.

DOLORES (*grinning*). Aaaaah!

She pulls a flower out from the bouquet and puts it between her teeth. We hear the 'Seguidilla' from Bizet's opera. The actress imitates the vibrant ferocity of Dolores del Río playing Carmen: her hair down and dishevelled, thrown forward to cover her face, then flung back to reveal it: she moves like a wild tiger until, exhausted, she plants herself like a bullfighter centre-stage. The music reaches a triumphant climax with the 'Toreador Song' and the FAN *shouts:*

FAN. Olé! Olé!

Still leaning against the door, MARIA *makes the sign used during the Roman Empire to indicate the death sentence: the right thumb pointing downwards. But nothing can dampen the enthusiasm with which* DOLORES *and the* FAN *have infected each other.*

FAN. *Ramona*, 1927.

> DOLORES *wraps herself in an Andalusian shawl walking with the dainty steps of a virgin girl from a Catholic town. Music: the song 'Ramona'.*

FAN. *Bird of Paradise*, 1932.

> DOLORES *hangs a lei around her neck and dances the hula-hula to Hawaiian music.*

FAN. *Flying down to Río*, 1933.

> *Music: the tango 'Orchids in the Moonlight'.* DOLORES *starts to dance it alone. She sees* MARIA *and stops. She runs over and hugs her. She tries to draw her away from the door, almost sobbing.*

DOLORES. I'm sorry, I'm sorry . . .

> *The two women take each other in their arms and adopt the stylised but motionless stance of tango dancers. The* FAN *watches them entranced, without ever letting go of the can.*

DOLORES. I'm sorry, I'm sorry . . .

> MARIA *holds* DOLORES *firmly. The music ends.*

MARIA. What for?

DOLORES. You know . . .

MARIA. You flatter me. I don't get it at all.

DOLORES (*looking flirtatiously towards the FAN*). I'm still remembered. I still have a fan in the world. He . . . came looking for me. (*Looks compassionately at* MARIA.) While you, lovely Mariquita.

> *Slowly and deliberately,* MARIA *steps away from* DOLORES, *picks up the newspaper from the floor and starts to flick through it. The* FAN *feels he is responsible for the tension and tries to ease it.*

FAN. Caramba! Please forgive me . . . I didn't know you . . . two . . . of all people . . . like lived here together.

MARIA (*sighs as she picks up the newspaper*). The odd couple, in its original version.

FAN (*laughing*) *The Odd Couple*? In an L.A. suburb . . .

MARIA. The Venuses of Venice, *sí señor.*

FAN. Had I known, I would not have neglected to bring you flowers too, ma'am . . .

Pretending to be taken aback, MARIA *stops reading the newspaper.*

MARIA. How very kind of you . . . *señor.* (*To* DOLORES.) You see. You've found an admirer. But we've both gained an audience.

FAN (*to* MARIA). Believe me, there's also a very exclusive club of your admirers, your true fans.

MARIA. How exclusive? More than two members?

FAN. Not many, it's true, but select.

MARIA. Die-hards, eh?

With these words she dismisses the FAN *and walks over to* DOLORES *holding the newspaper open.*

MARIA. You should know, baby, that obituaries are prepared well in advance. As soon as you stand out in an activity – as a politician, a banker, a gangster, an au pair girl, a child prodigy, a medium, a matricide – the newspaper opens a file with all the facts of your life in case you suddenly kick the bucket. If you're not lucky enough to die young, the facts just keep piling up. Dates, prizes, film titles, the years in Alcatraz, the gossip, the photographic proofs that you're no longer the same and can only blame yourself . . . your self.

DOLORES, *listening to* MARIA, *has again taken the elaborate rococo-framed handmirror identical to the one she used in the movie* Madame du Barry *and stares at herself in it. The* FAN *cannot stop himself from exclaiming.*

FAN. *Madame du Barry*, 1934!

DOLORES (*looking at herself in the mirror*). After reaching forty, we're all responsible for our own face.

MARIA. Marcel Proust, 1913. (*Sighs*) The end of the Belle Epoque! Who was preparing the obituary for a whole era?

FAN (*with less enthusiasm*). *La Belle Otéro*, 1952, no?

MARIA. Thank you, young man. Thank you for being my cheerleader. The point is that *before* we were only responsible for the mask we saw in our own mirror. There was no other proof that we were who we were.

FAN. Unless you were lucky enough to be painted by Rubens or Titian.

MARIA. *Ay!* That was like winning the lottery, pal. But if that didn't happen to you, tell me what mask you'd leave? I'll tell you. None. The mask of millions and millions of women who died leaving nothing to be remembered by . . .

FAN. They left no trace of their faces.

MARIA. That's right. Now we're not just responsible for the face we see in our own mirror . . .

DOLORES (*gazing into her mirror*). . . . but also to our public who know our face better than we do because we've all been photographed . . .

MARIA. And a movie star more than anyone, and photographed in motion, from the past and for the future.

DOLORES. Eternal phantom and passing flesh. Ah!

MARIA. A dirty trick, Lolita, a dirty trick. Think about what I'm saying when we're both pushing up daisies.

Awkward silence. The FAN *breaks it.*

FAN. The Arabs say the face is the portrait of the soul. (*Gulps and adds*) That's why they don't let themselves be photographed.

MARIA. Nor do the Yaquí Indians. So what?

FAN. The first men didn't need to talk and certainly didn't represent themselves in drawings. They just looked at each other, without talking, without painting.

DOLORES *is still looking at herself in the rococo mirror.*

DOLORES (*to* MARIA). Diego Rivera told us not to worry about age because we had beautiful skulls. Do you remember?

FAN. What I'm saying is that the first men lived in lands of the sun and could look at each other. It was their gestures which mattered. Friend or foe. Peace or danger. A simple gesture.

MARIA (*impatiently*). And the first women?

FAN. I include them in the generic, ma'am. (*Smiles*) In the credits, you know?

MARIA. I'm glad to hear it. (*To* DOLORES) You and I are very different. You know why? You only love me and you only love yourself through the public.

FAN. But the South became hotter and hotter . . . An inferno.

DOLORES (*without taking her eyes off her reflection*). Don't tell me the only reason you don't love yourself more is because the public adores you . . . sorry, adored you.

FAN. And the North became cooler. Men, women and children migrated.

MARIA (*ignoring the FAN*). Yes. But I love you for yourself, not for the public. (*Pause*) I'm the only person who's loved you for yourself, and that includes yourself.

FAN (*obsequiously*). Excuse me . . . I hate to contradict you . . . but . . . I . . .

Now MARIA *does concentrate her attention on the FAN.*

MARIA. You are the public, popcorn boy! You're the pale reflection of what you see in a dark cinema. Just look at yourself, paleface. (*She advances threateningly towards the FAN.*) You're like an asshole: the sun never shines on you.

FAN. In the North the nights are longer and the light is weaker . . .

MARIA. You kill a bullfighter in the sun, the real sun, howling, swearing, throwing bottles at him.

FAN. There wasn't enough light, so men and women couldn't see themselves or communicate in gestures any more.

MARIA. You murder a lover under cover of the night, the real night, using the weapons of the flesh and deception and tender words and the weary sleep of heroes . . .

FAN. Since there was no light, they had to speak.

MARIA. But this love and this crime of the public, in the artifical darkness, in the false night of a cinema . . .

FAN. Since they couldn't see each other any more, they had to speak.

MARIA. In the artificial darkness, in the false night of a cinema . . .

She stops, looking for words that she does not find.
DOLORES *lowers the mirror like a fencer lowering her guard.*

MARIA (*to* DOLORES). I love you for yourself, little sister, not because you're a star and have a public.

DOLORES *is on the verge of getting up and kissing* MARIA. *But the FAN rapidly intervenes to stop her.*

FAN (*to* DOLORES). Don't listen to these spiteful arguments.
I . . .

MARIA (*to the FAN, furiously*). You? Who the hell are you?
How did you get here? Who gave you our address?

The FAN *is physically attacked by* MARIA.

FAN (*fending off* MARIA*'s anger*) I'm sorry. It was an
accident.

MARIA. An accident? An accident is to be born or to die. You
don't even deserve a sympathy fuck.

FAN. I'm her fan. You don't offend me.

MARIA. Listen, Mister unoffendable, I asked you a polite
question. How did you manage to . . . dig us up?

FAN (*flattered that they are paying attention to him again*).
This morning when I settled down in front of my desk and
my files to begin my daily tasks . . .

MARIA (*ironically*). You were going to work.

FAN. Correct. Alexander Graham Bell's great invention rang
in my office . . .

MARIA. The telefunken.

DOLORES. Ah, Hollywood, Hollywood, you've invented
everything. Spencer Tracy discovered electric light, Greer
Garson the radio, Don Ameche the telephone and Paul Muni
pasteurised milk.

FAN. That's right. The phone rang and I picked it up. I was
fortunate. It's the public telephone in the company where I
lend my services and anyone could have . . .

MARIA. We understand.

FAN (*in adoration of her style*). It was her. (*He turns to*
DOLORES *and walks over to her.*) It was her. Saying:
'Hello . . . '

The FAN *and* DOLORES *now talk in a duet, holding
imaginary telephones.*

DOLORES and FAN. 'Hello? Who do I have the pleasure
of . . . ? Ah, I see . . . May I speak to . . . ?'

DOLORES *falls silent.*

FAN. Silence. Then she hung up. But how could I not
recognise her voice, the voice of *What Price Glory* . . .

MARIA. Don't be a jerk. That was a silent movie.

FAN. The voice of *La Otra*, *Pensativa* and *Evangeline* . . .

DOLORES (*dazed*). My love . . .

MARIA. Careful. Get him to tell us what profession he
practises.

FAN (*to* MARIA). I don't understand your fancy way of
talking. I must be living in a different age.

MARIA starts circling around DOLORES *and the* FAN,
looking at him as though he were a strange insect.

MARIA. Desk . . . files . . . public office.

FAN. Correct. A bureaucrat. A civil servant.

MARIA continues rotating.

MARIA. Lots of telephones, you said . . .

FAN (*nervously*). Yes. Lots. Going ring . . . ring-ring?

DOLORES (*sings softly*). 'Ring-a-ring-a-roses . . . '

MARIA (*to the* FAN). Working?

FAN. Perfectly.

DOLORES. 'Ring-a-ring-a-roses . . . '

MARIA stops.

MARIA. Then it can't be a public office. The telephones there
never work.

DOLORES. 'A pocket full of posies . . . '

MARIA. A hospital?

FAN. Colder.

DOLORES. 'Ah-tish-oo...'

MARIA. The telephone company?

DOLORES. 'Ah-tish-oo...'

MARIA. Nobody would answer there. A company, you said?

DOLORES. 'We all fall down.'

MARIA. A newspaper? Warmer?

MARIA looks at the FAN *inquisitively. She picks up the
newspaper. She starts to flick through it.* DOLORES *uses
the pause to try and stop her.*

DOLORES. *Ay*, that's enough. No more unnecessary cruelty. Don't read the newspaper now. I'm not interested in who died today. I'm not interested in whether the dead are younger or older than me. I don't care if Mamá finds out, if Mamá suffers if they're older then her or is pleased if they're younger . . .

The following scene should be played in a very stylised manner, almost like an operatic trio. Even so, DOLORES' *voice dominates the chorus, without drowning it out. This stylisation has been prepared by the previous verbal trios between* DOLORES, MARIA *and the* FAN. *It should be extremely obvious that the* FAN *is moving his lips while* MARIA *reads the newspaper, repeating exactly but silently what she is reading out loud.*

MARIA (*reads assertively*). 'Born May 6, 1915 in Kenosha, Wisconsin, USA...'

DOLORES (*to* MARIA). Do you realise what you're doing. You're stopping us celebrating. Today, today when the thing we've wanted so much has happened, the thing we waited for for years, for ever. And you don't even stop and celebrate.

MARIA. 'Son of an inventor and pianist...'

DOLORES. Today I was recognised! I woke up, had breakfast and nobody . . . (*She points violently at the audience.*) Nobody . . . none of you . . . recognised me . . . But lo and behold just after midday an admirer arrived with a bouquet of flowers in his hand, and he said to me: I admire you. You are she.

MARIA *goes on reading the newspaper. The* FAN *mouths* MARIA'*s words.*

MARIA. 'He studied painting at the Chicago Arts Institute.'

She pronounces it in a French accent: Chicageau.

DOLORES (*to* MARIA). Do you understand? You are she. He said it to you too. You are she.

MARIA. (*reading*). 'Aged fifteen he had his acting debut in Dublin. He directed Shakespeare's *Julius Caesar*.'

FAN. We are all honourable men.

DOLORES. Don't you realise? We don't have to prove to anyone any more that we are them.

MARIA. 'He devised and directed a black *Macbeth* for the Federal Theatre during the Great Depression of the 1930s.'

FAN (*in syncopated rhythm*). When shall we three meet again, yeah man.

DOLORES. We have a witness.

MARIA. 'He directed and starred in a fascist version of *Julius Caesar.*'

FAN. We are *all* honourable Menschen.

DOLORES (*pointing to the* FAN). He doesn't lie! He's seen all our movies. He doesn't lie!

MARIA. 'In October 1938, he terrified thousands of listeners with his radio adaptation of H.G. Wells' *War of the Worlds . . .*'

FAN. We are all honorary Martians.

DOLORES (*very sad*) Wells . . . He doesn't lie . . .

MARIA. 'In 1940 he reinvented the art of film-making with *Citizen Kane.*'

FAN. We are all honourable *tycoons.*

MARIA. 'His name entered the Hall of Fame alongside Griffith, Chaplin and Eisenstein . . .'

DOLORES (*increasingly uncertain*). He doesn't lie . . .

MARIA. 'In 1942 he dressed Dolores del Río as a leopard and used her in *Voyage au pays de la peur . . .*'

DOLORES (*desperate*). No, *Journey into Fear.* Its name is *Journey into Fear.* You can't read English . . .

MARIA (*still going through the paper*). Gringa. Pains of the River.

DOLORES. Frog. Marie Joyeuse.

MARIA. Douleurs de la Fleuve.

FAN. We are all honourable tributaries.

DOLORES. María de los Angeles Félix! Happy Mary of the Angels!

FAN. Mary had a little angel, its cock was black as coal, and everywhere that Mary came, the cock was sure to grow . . .

DOLORES. You only came to Los Angeles because your name is María de los Angeles, you vain bitch. We could have gone to live in Rio, we could have flown down to Rio. Oooh, my youth!

MARIA. Or to the village of Dolores, to ring the bell of independence. (*She goes on reading*) 'And in 1941 he did not film *The Road to Santiago* with . . .

DOLORES. 'Dolores del Río.'

Sadness. The trio breaks up. MARIA *throws the newspaper far away from her.*

MARIA (*to* DOLORES, *but looking at the* FAN). May I introduce the author of the *Los Angeles Times* obituaries. (*To the* FAN.) We've been reading it for years, honourable sir. The obituary page is the first thing we look at every day. Nothing interests us more than finding out who died yesterday. You seem very young to devote yourself entirely to dead meat.

DOLORES. What are you saying? How do you know?

MARIA. I saw him moving his lips every time I read. Repeating his own memorable phrases about yesterday's celebrity death.

FAN (*correcting her*). Today's. What you read is the midday five-star final edition. My newspaper's proud to be the first with the latest.

MARIA. In love with what he writes.

FAN (*with sudden sarcasm*). Who's a clever dick then?

MARIA. Cleverer than you, you constipated ink-shitter. Sure, I'm very smart, a hundred times smarter than you. I'm the mother of Tarzan and all the rest of the chimps in the world. Get it? I am the top dog and you are the lowest and ugliest tramp who ever stepped on my fitted carpet. Go graze in another field . . . lambikins. This Big Bad Wolf is in charge here.

DOLORES. Holy Mary, mother of God! (*To* MARIA) You've offended my fan!

The FAN *makes as if to turn and walk out.*

FAN (*to* DOLORES). I'm sorry. I really am.

MARIA (*to* DOLORES). Don't be stupid. He's just a smart-assed hack who wants to hear your reactions to Orson Welles' death.

DOLORES. I don't care what he is. He recognised me, he
    admitted that I am she. You don't, you say you love me and
    you don't admit it.

MARIA. That's because I love you. Because I love you for
    who you are, Lola.

DOLORES (*not listening, insistent*). It's the same with Mamá,
    she says I'm crazy, we're both crazy, both of us: you María
    and me Dolores!

MARIA. She'll be happy today. Welles was younger than her.

DOLORES (*bewildered*). Wells? No, she cried a lot when he
    died, she said they were contemporaries, travellers in the
    same time machine, she said . . .

MARIA. Orson?

DOLORES. No, he's just a kid. Why should he die? I'm
    talking about Herbert George.

    MARIA *takes* DOLORES *by her shoulders.*

MARIA. Wake up, cutiepie. Come out of your trance. Orson
    died today. Orson. Your contemporary.

    DOLORES *is stupefied. She stares blindly at the audience
    in front of her. She murmurs.*

DOLORES. Wells. H.G. Wells. The author of *The Invisible
    Man.* Mamá says she met him once. On holiday in the
    Caribbean. On the island of Doctor Moreau. A very
    uncomfortable place, Mamá told us. The chambermaids ate
    the soaps and tore the sheets every morning. The waiters
    came through the window with bananas in their hands.

MARIA. You're getting it mixed-up. You're writing your own
    history.

DOLORES (*resuming a logical, mundane and serene tone of
    voice*). No. Welles adapted Wells to the radio and terrified
    the citizens of the state of New Jersey but he also fooled the
    newspapers of the Hearst chain who believed the Martian
    invasion dramatised by Welles to be true. So Welles stole
    the front page from Howard Hughes who was trying to go
    round the world in a wooden plane but found himself
    unpublicised because of Wells, Welles and the Hearst Chain,
    which is why Hughes then offered Welles Orson all the
    money in the world to make *Citizen Kane* and Welles
    responded by making the anticipated parody of Howard

Hughes' future life through a real-life parody of William
Randolph Hearst, thus making fun of them both. In other
words, Welles invaded Howard Hughes' future through
Hearst William Randolph's past and Wells Herbert George
invaded Hearst's future by offering him a little Martian
granddaughter who held up a bank with a machine-gun on
the same day that Hughes fled Managua Nicaragua in a
helicopter to die of starvation, surrounded by cellophane-
wrapped sandwiches and Coca-Cola bottles, isolated and
invisible. H.G. Wells wrote the invisible man who is
Howard Hughes, and Welles – which one? —adapted
Wells – which one? (*Pause.*) I cry for them both.
(*Anguished again, she goes over to* MARIA.) Who will
cry for us?

MARIA. *¿Quién?*

The FAN *imitates Orson Welles in the party scene in* Citizen
Kane.

FAN. *¿Quién?* Charlie Kane!

DOLORES *and* MARIA *continue acting out the scene with
the greatest intimacy, totally indifferent to the* FAN's *music-
hall buffoonery.*

DOLORES. Yes, will anyone cry for you and me?

FAN (*teasing*). The grateful public.

MARIA. Mamá . . .

DOLORES. No, she'll be pleased we went first.

FAN. Kane? *¿Quién?* Charlie Kane? Kane será será.

MARIA. The public . . . Our public . . . Our public will cry for
us . . . Listen . . .

*A murmur of applause and ovations: vivas, bravos. It
crescendos until it reaches an unbearable pitch.* MARIA
listens calmly, or rather sadly; DOLORES *becomes more
and more terrified until she puts her hands over her ears
and screams. Meanwhile, the* FAN *has gone over to the
toilet, his reel under his arm and the portable projector in
his hand. He takes off the white telephone and places the
projector on top of the toilet lid. While* MARIA *and*
DOLORES *are occupied downstage in the following scene,
the* FAN *prepares the projector upstage. He takes off his
coat and reveals his sleeveless, diamond-patterned jumper.
He takes the roll of film carefully out of the can, places it*

*next to the projector and starts rolling on the film. From
time to time, he interjects a pun from his dubious repertoire.*

DOLORES (*screaming*). No! Make them be quiet! No
applause! Applause pursues us like a ghost! Applause is
worse than a howl, a whisper or the clang of chains!
Applause is our Frankenstein: it created us, María, and it
killed us!

FAN. Citizen FranKanestein.

> DOLORES *leans against* MARIA. *They both sit down on
> the floor downstage,* DOLORES' *head leaning on*
> MARIA's *shoulder.* MARIA *strokes* DOLORES' *hair.*
> DOLORES *puts her arm round* MARIA's *waist.*

MARIA. I'll cry for you, little sister, if you go before me.

DOLORES. Together. Together.

MARIA. Will you cry for me?

DOLORES. No, together, please. Who would take care of me?
Who would take me on Sundays to Santa Monica beach to
show off my beautiful body in a bikini? Who would bury me
in the sand on my birthday and tie twenty candles from my
belly button? Who, little sister, who?

FAN. Kane or Abel?

MARIA. Do you need me?

DOLORES. You know I do. My memory . . . is you.

MARIA. Do you forgive me for not being like you . . . ?

DOLORES. The black sheep?

MARIA (*nods*). Black as pitch.

FAN. Lady Cain.

DOLORES. I think I was a bit jealous of your life.

MARIA. And I of yours, doll.

DOLORES (*with a pout*). Don't rub it in that we're different.

MARIA. No, I wasn't jealous of you. I'm not complaining
about anything. Who can take down the tapestry of our
lives?

FAN. An Amerikane in Paris, that's who.

MARIA. Do you regret not doing anything?

DOLORES. A child of my own?

MARIA. No. No. They would have taken it away from you. I didn't abandon mine. They took him away from me.

DOLORES. Everyone always says you abandoned him.

FAN. You ought to be Kaned.

MARIA (*in a hard voice, paying no attention to the* FAN). No. *They* took him away from me. The public. The producers. All of them. They came to an agreement. The soulless woman couldn't have a child. It would be a contradiction. The man-eater ate her child first.

FAN. Cainibal!

MARIA (*to* DOLORES). You know what I am jealous of you for?

DOLORES. What, my angel? What, my poor little *doña*?

MARIA. You never had to lie.

FAN. Hughes lying?

DOLORES (*with a flash of flirtatiousness*). Ooooh, if you only knew! One of the times I got married I was fifty and my husband was forty. He asked me before the ceremony to say we were both forty, you know, to be like the perfect couple. When the judge asked his age, he replied very seriously. 'Forty years old.' When he asked mine, I replied very cheerfully: 'Twenty years old.'

They both laugh and hug each other happily, their great intimacy restored.

MARIA. That's nothing. When they launched me, they made up an official biography that wasn't mine. Not my origins, not my husbands, not my son, nothing. I couldn't believe it when I read it. I was another woman. My life had been wiped out.

FAN. Hughes who?

MARIA. My husbands . . . my son . . . my lovers . . . were hidden away, taken out of the photos in which I appeared with them.

DOLORES. Jesus! Like poor Trotsky.

FAN. Whose? Hughes, that's whose.

MARIA (*with a sour smile*). Wiped out. They never existed, you see.

FAN. Jesus! The Cruci Fiction.

DOLORES. Why did you put up with it?

MARIA. Because I wanted to be wanted. I wanted to be admired. I deserved it. Half my life has been used by other people. The other half I sold to success to get back the life that the others took away from me.

FAN. You Kane take it with you.

MARIA. I've done everything to be wanted and admired. First comes the admiration, I told myself, and then love will come.

FAN (*playing pat-a-cake, pat-a-cake*). Patty Hearst, Patty Hearst, where are you?

MARIA. But some of what I'm saying isn't true. The truth, then and now, is that I want to be wanted, I want to be loved, Lolita, and for that I was and I am prepared to pay any price, first the humiliation, then the glory and now the forgetting.

DOLORES. Now the forgetting . . .

MARIA. Yes, because now we have to be forgotten, Lolita, so our movies can be remembered. Our movies are timeless, you know, they are eternal.

DOLORES (*in a dream*) They're like the perfume that's left of our lives . . .

MARIA. Yes, only our movies can laugh at our generation and survive it: to escape a sad childhood, a movie . . .

DOLORES. No, it was very happy . . . dolls and hoops and roundabouts.

MARIA. To escape poor and insecure adolescence, a movie.

DOLORES. No, no, dances and boyfriends and moonlit serenades . . .

MARIA. Yes, to escape smutty, decadent and humiliated youth, a movie . . .

DOLORES. No, Hollywood: the contract with Warner Brothers, the invitation to Pickfair, the swimming pool, the greyhound, the silk parasol and the organdie hat . . .

MARIA. Yes, Guadalajara: the invitation to Chapala, the little contract with the producer who demanded the goods up front, the sleazy motel, the hungry dogs barking, the mariachis falling silent.

DOLORES *kisses* MARIA *passionately.*

DOLORES. Not any more María. We're both royalty now, queens, floating for ever in our gondolas down the Grand Canal of Venecia towards the palace where our doges await us. (*Pause.*) Two queens of a single kingdom. We shall be remembered. Nothing has been forgotten.

FAN. Nothing has been forgotten.

The FAN *turns on the projector. The light should blind the audience, physically hurt them as if to supplant the vision they are about to be denied. What the* FAN *projects will be seen by him,* MARIA *and* DOLORES, *and imagined by the audience, since the screen supposedly occupies the audience's place.*

MARIA. Any price. First the humiliation, then the glory and now the forgetting.

FAN. Sorry. I told you I've got all the movies you've made, girls. Pardon me. Of your films, Lolita, I'm only missing *Carmen.* (*To* MARIA) But I'm not missing *anything* of yours, not even this one . . .

As the FAN *projects the movie,* DOLORES *watches first with alarm, then with embarrassment, finally covering her eyes and sobbing, shaking her head repeatedly, incredulous.* MARIA *stays calm, neither sad nor happy, but grave and severe as if she were watching a dance of death.*

FAN. It's incredible what you can find in the files of an old newspaper like the *Los Angeles Times.* These are things that the guys in editorial inherit from the executives: executed images, you know? A bit clichéd, overplayed, and passé . . . well, even the hardest pornography gets boring if you look at it more than twice. Sex is so mechanical, twice is too much, but once is always great, the first time's always surprising and exciting. Holy Mother, we tell ourselves, this time it'll be better, this time it'll be true. Truth? Truth? Didn't I tell you that when the tribes migrated to the north they couldn't see each other because the light was so weak, and they had to invent the lie of language to recognise each other in the darkness. But movies . . . movies. Could they be the truth? Because in the darkness they take us back to the world of pure gesture before language, when you didn't have to talk to say I love you, I hate you, I'll save you, I'll kill you, run away, come here . . . (*Pause*) You weren't

listening. You were too preoccupied with your dumb lies.
Truth? No. Just look at them monkeying around. He really
looks like a monkey, a gorilla, and no woman disobeys a
gorilla. He says: run away because there's danger. And
every woman runs away without hesitation. And she . . . she
looks like she's going to tear the sheets apart and eat soap.
Good God, how vulgar. Was it for this that we were created
in His own image, etcetera? To behave like this, worse than
wild beasts and in a bed . . . Ooooh! Maybe in the same bed
where we were born and where we'll die, the cradle and the
grave of our dirty pleasures. (*The* FAN *stops rolling the film
and furiously walks over to* MARIA *who is sitting
downstage next to* DOLORES. *The play of white, blinding
light and the shadows of the bodies comes across like an
hallucination and the struggle between the* FAN *and*
MARIA *projects itself like a bitter parody of the sexual act.
He takes her by the wrists and tries to lift her up.*) I'm sorry
not to let you forget. Look. (*He takes* MARIA *roughly by
the neck, forcing her to look at the images.*) Remember?
Remember when you made that? What year was it . . .
thirty-five, thirty-six? Look at how primitive the technique
was . . . they didn't even use sound . . . seriously gross. (*As
she tries to break free from the* FAN, *a negative, moaning
pain can be heard in* MARIA'*s voice. The* FAN *picks her up
by her armpits.*) The reel was forgotten in the oldest file of
the *Los Angeles Times.* You ran away from Mexico to run
away from your lost youth. You crossed the desert and the
Grim Reaper didn't appear to you. What appeared to you
was your forgotten, rotten, stinking youth: look at it. Who
would want to watch a 1930s porn movie, with a forgotten
little girl who today would be an old hag. Ughhh. No-one
likes to think his mother screwed too, his grandmother
opened her legs, his sister sucked the milk of human
kindness, his daughter will also go on vacation to the island
of Doctor Moreau . . . that they all howled with pleasure
with *another man*, that those women said the same to the
other man as what you did: fuck me . . .

MARIA (*struggling, defensive*). Macho . . . you disgusting
macho . . .

DOLORES (*her eyes covered*). No more, that's enough!

MARIA. Doesn't a man open his legs too? Doesn't a man suck
and get sucked? Doesn't a man screw and get screwed? Isn't
he screwed when he screws?

DOLORES (*in supreme self defence, sings softly to transform reality*). '*No me platiques ya, déjame imaginar que no existe el pasado y que nacimos el mismo instante en que nos conocimos.*'[15]

MARIA (*to the* FAN). So only you can be master of your own body, you macho bastard? A woman can't? (*Screams*) *A woman can't*?!

She throws the FAN *to the floor. Kicks him. The movie ends; the projector stops giving out light. The loose end of the film turns round and round on the reel.*

MARIA. I'm going to castrate you, faggot.

FAN (*from the floor*). Dyke!

MARIA. I would be if all men were like you. (*She gives him a final, spectacular kick.*) I may be a woman, but I'm more macho than you. I may be an old woman, but I still excite you. Eunuch!

DOLORES *stands up and puts herself between* MARIA *and the* FAN.

DOLORES. No more. Forgive him.

MARIA (*shrugs*). You're right. This nobody isn't good enough to be my errandboy.

DOLORES (*strangely conciliatory*). Anyway. We owe him something very important, you know.

MARIA. Sure, I know. He recognised us. But at what a price.

DOLORES. What we've dreamed of all our lives.

MARIA. Since we were little girls. Since we went together to the double bill at the Balmori cinema: *Doña Bárbara* and *María Candelaria*. Popcorn, chewing gum, chocolates.

DOLORES. Yes, ever since then.

MARIA. And you think today we finally triumphed?

DOLORES (*forcing herself*). Yes. Thanks to him.

Slightly disconcerted, MARIA *prefers to look contemptuously at the* FAN *lying on the floor.*

MARIA. What do you want, worm?

FAN. Can I get up?

MARIA *mimics his good education.*

MARIA. Make yourself at home, tramp.

The FAN *gets up painfully, shaking the dust off his knees
and shoulders, adjusting his bowtie. He does something
unexpected: he takes* DOLORES' *hand.*

FAN. I want her to come with me.

Diverse, conflicting feelings appear on DOLORES' *face.
Incredulity, disgust, resignation, the will to sacrifice herself.
She opts for the comic attitude of a young virgin.*

DOLORES. Me?

MARIA (*to the* FAN). What do you need, a nanny or a nurse?

FAN. No. I want her for myself.

MARIA. I warn you. She can't sew and she has no dowry.

DOLORES (*faking a trance*). Me?

FAN (*to* MARIA). I want to marry her.

DOLORES (*looking at the* FAN *with delight*). You?

At this moment, DOLORES *seems to have been persuaded
by her own dramatics.* MARIA *corrects her with incredulity
and ridicule.*

MARIA (*to the* FAN). *Oye,* don't ask me for permission. *La
señora* is a grown woman now.

FAN (*to* DOLORES). Yes? Since *The Jungle of Fire,* directed
by Fernando de Fuentes starring Arturo de Córdova?

MARIA (*jokily, but with a defensive humour*). Go on, Lolita,
don't forget he'll write your obituary. You'd better suck up
to him.

DOLORES (*confused*). Oh God!

MARIA. He is nigh.

DOLORES (*hands to her temples*). What am I thinking of?
This dick came here to insult you . . . to dishonour both of us
with his filth . . . his canned trash . . .

MARIA (*increasingly sure of what is about to happen, claps
her hands and chants like a soccer chant*). Lola . . . Lola . . .

DOLORES *adopts her most accentuatedly melodramatic
attitude.*

DOLORES (*to the* FAN). Out! Get out of here, sir! Have
respect for our age and our artistic status! (*Points to*
MARIA.) This woman and I . . . we're queens.

FAN (*calmly*). Well, one of you will be deposed when I release that short film of Popeye and Olive Oyl that I just showed you. .

DOLORES (*hands on her hips*). Bah. It sat for half a century in an archive and nobody was interested . . .

MARIA. Because nobody knew it was *her*.

DOLORES. Nobody will recognise her.

FAN. As soon as they're told it's her, everyone will say it's her, even if they don't recognise her. They'll want to recognise her. That's the way people are.

DOLORES. Don't get fresh with me.

FAN. That's cool. But I've completed that woman's filmography. They thought it was complete and it wasn't. I'm like Champollion: now the public can know what the mummies were saying . . . (*Pause.*) I mean. what the mummies were *doing*, when they were little girls. (*Laughs vulgarly.*)

DOLORES (*decisively*). All right. How much do you want for the reel?

FAN. Huh? There are lots of them, I warn you.

DOLORES. We'll buy them all. Won't we, María?

FAN. No. It's you or nothing.

DOLORES (*with a flash of flirtatiousness*). Me?

MARIA (*to DOLORES*). You. You or nothing.

FAN. You or nothing. It's that simple. Easier than spelling Zbigniew Brzezinski. (*Pause.*) You.

> DOLORES *is disconcerted. Silence.* DOLORES *goes over to her little altar. Like in the classic Mexican movies, she kneels down to ask advice from the Virgin Mary.*

DOLORES. Hail Mary.

MARIA (*conceitedly and seriously*). Conceived in sin . . .

DOLORES. Full of Grace, the Lord is with you . . .

MARIA (*smiles*). Because if we women didn't conceive in sin, what fun would we have?

DOLORES. Blessed art thou amongst women . . .

MARIA. The Lord is with thee but only to conceive in sin the son of misfortune . . .

DOLORES (*her arms open*). Alleluia! Alleluia! Alleluia!

MARIA (*her arms crossed*). I don't repent. Did you all hear me? I don't repent anything. Certainly not!

> DOLORES *crosses herself. She gets up. She picks up her piggy bank. She strokes it sadly.* MARIA *lights her black cigar.*

MARIA. Don't torment yourself over me, honey. (DOLORES *raises her head, awkwardly hopeful.*) I want to say something to you: this is your decision and yours alone. For me, a little scandal makes me . . . it's like the wind in Columbus' sails.

DOLORES (*murmurs*). Chores.

MARIA. The top dog.

DOLORES. What I've been to you for years.

MARIA. Division of labour. I took you out for walks, remember?

DOLORES. A man to do chores for . . . iron his shirts . . . sew his buttons on . . . cook his beans. I've never done it before. There was always a butler in the house.

MARIA. Then here's your break, my swallow.

DOLORES (*trembling*). No, María, no, how can you think . . . ?

MARIA. That you could leave me? *Oye*, the same way I'd leave you.

DOLORES. You . . . me?

MARIA. Sure. Not for this blind toad, but for a poet-musician, for a singing cowboy, even for a well-hung mariachi, why not?

DOLORES (*inquisitive, reflective*). Because *she* had them . . . because that was part of *her* life, so you could lead your life imitating *her* life.

MARIA. No. As far as I know, no. That would be a novelty. You were too decent.

> *The* FAN *intervenes to hurry things up, also hiding considerable alarm.*

FAN. Right, make up your minds. It's almost three o'clock. I have to get back to the newspaper. My corpses await me.

MARIA. Can nobody die without you, slimeball.

FAN. No, nobody important, no.

MARIA. Ah.

Impulsively, DOLORES *kneels down in front of* MARIA, *hugs her legs and presses her cheek against* MARIA's *knees.*

DOLORES. You don't get upset by scandal, but I do, I do . . . (*She looks imploringly at* MARIA, *her eyes filled with tears.*) We're queens, both of us, if one stumbles the other falls, if one's wounded the other dies, don't you see?

MARIA. But only through the public, remember Lolita. You only love yourself and me through the public. (*She looks at the* FAN. *She introduces him with an elegant flourish as if he were Prince Charming out of a fairy tale. The* FAN *adjusts his bowtie and takes his jacket.*) And there is your public.

DOLORES. Do you love me?

MARIA. Nobody, not even yourself, loves you more, because nobody, not even yourself, loves you alone, without your public, except me . . .

DOLORES. So?

MARIA. So you decide, litle sister.

DOLORES (*imprisoned by doubts*). Doña, Doña, Doña . . . [16]

She covers her head with the shawl. She strokes the piggy. The FAN *puts on his jacket.* DOLORES *speaks in the accent of an Indian girl.*[17]

DOLORES. *Ay,* our piggy. Remember Lorenzo Rafaíl, don't let them take our piggy away . . . it's the only thing we have . . . (*She puts it back in its place. Looks at* MARIA.) Don't leave me alone. I won't do anything bad. It's better to kill our piggy. Kill the pig. (*She changes her tone, feigning haughtiness. She stretches her hand out to the* FAN, *who takes it eagerly.* DOLORES *turns round to* MARIA *again.*) It's true, my love. I know you won't stop loving me because of this. (*Shrugs her shoulders.*) After all . . . a man . . . I was one less for all the others. I'll be one more for him.

The FAN *has opened the door with a faint sound of creaking hinges. The* FAN *and* DOLORES *exit quickly, leaving the door open. For a few seconds,* MARIA *stares at the door. Once again she drops her black cigar into the*

*teapot. Then she throws herself at the door and closes it.
The same prison-like, metallic sounds are heard as when the
FAN came in. MARIA leans against the closed door and
stifles a sob, biting her knuckles. She runs over to
DOLORES' altar, picks up the piggy bank and looks at it
disdainfully.*

MARIA (*mimicking*). 'We don't have anything else in the
world, Lorenzo Rafaíl.'

*Violently, she smashes the clay object on the ground. She
gasps. She composes herself. She goes over to the telephone.
She dials a number nervously.*

MARIA. Hello? The *Luz del Día* Restaurant? This is Lupe
Vélez[18] . . . No, not the usual, thank you . . . What? No, not
the usual lunchbox, no, listen to me. This is a special
occasion. I want to order . . . Yes, get your thing out . . . No,
not that thing, your pencil, don't be a jerk. You dirty old
man, as if anyone was interested in that Toltec ruin. Look, I
want to talk to the boss. Yes, to Don Pancho Cáceres, and
quick . . . Hello...? Hey, *patroncito*! Look, this is a very
special occasion . . . Yes, I know . . . But you know what?
I've been left all alone, don Panchito, and I'm hungry . . .
Ay, I know, *patroncito*, you were sent to me from heaven
above. Look: for starters, your soup with herb tea and baby
chilis, then your mushroom and cheese tortillas, two of
them, yes, and two with pumpkin flowers . . . Ah,
wonderful. Yes, lettuce sliced very fine and juicy, I don't
want those shrivelled up things you send me sometimes –
they're like eating old gloves . . . No, hold on, I've only just
begun . . . Then eggs, very well seasoned, and a side helping
of almond sauce, not too heavy, I don't want to die of
indigestion . . . Live to the full, *si señor*. Let's have the tacos
then, very fine and smooth, the tortillas cooked gently but
please not fried, you know I can't stand greasy food . . .
Stuffed chillis, sure, as long as the pomegranates are good, I
want them to really crack between my teeth, you know? Last
time you sent them all watery, ah, how could you do that to
me, my little merchant, aren't I your best client? Let me see:
some green *enchiladas*, only the green ones, so I know the
filling is fresh. And now for the main course. What can you
recommend? *Mole*, no . . . or, I don't know, maybe, yes . . .
but I want it in a marinated oriental sauce. Have you got that
marinated oriental sauce, with onion and green peppers,
which I can feel melting on my tongue, which doesn't even

touch my palate. *Ay, patroncito*, you know what nostalgia
for our country is. How could you not know it? You came to
California twenty-five years ago to pick lemons and stayed
to feed all us Chicanos. Just look, *patroncito*! No, no don't
go over the top, a tamal at this stage . . . you'll kill me with
love . . . I want something to wash down the banquet. Is the
pulque fresh? . . . 'Oh land of the sun, I long to see you!' . . .
Some hot fudge, just a spoonful. And lots of fruit. All the
holy Mexican Republic in the colours of its fruits for my
banquet: yellow mangos and pink papayas and dark zapotes
and ochre mameys and white custard apples and black
quinces and green pears and red pomegranates. And tequila,
patroncito, lots of tequila, with lots of salt, lots of lemon and
blood of the widow, blood of Jalisco . . . What? No it's not a
party, it's for me, boss, I'm all alone . . . I'm free. Don't let
me down Don Panchito, if you let me down today, you've
let me down for ever, I swear to you on your holy mother's
head. Thank you. You're a good man.

*She hangs up the telephone. Motionless for a moment. She
stretches. She hurries over to her personal altar. She opens
a drawer. She takes out a medicine bottle. It must be
understood from the size and the colour of the bottle and the
pills that they are sleeping pills.* MARIA *takes out a pill,
another and another and another, up to a dozen, and puts
them in her mouth as if they were sweets. She stops. A
moment of alarm. She tries to hear or feel something.
Nothing happens. She walks over to the folding screen. She
takes down the Cleopatra costume. She walks downstage
centre with it in her hands. A white curtain falls behind her
to hide the slight change of scenery upstage. The music of
the bolero 'María Bonita' is heard. On the white curtain
can be seen a montage of films in which close-ups of María
Félix and Dolores del Río alternate: movies of all ages and
all costumes, but always the alternating faces of the two
women: two eternal faces and two faces which in some way
are one. Slowly,* MARIA *picks up Cleopatra's ceremonial
baton. When she finishes doing this, the song and the images
also stop. The initial trumpet call of the mariachi 'La
Negra' is heard. The curtain which had served as a screen
opens. The original set, without losing any of the details
which we know – it is still* DOLORES *and* MARIA*'s
apartment in Venice, California – now takes on a harmony
from the absence of the folding screens and the pile of*

*clothes in the centre. Instead, the central space is occupied
by a banqueting table heaped with dishes and Mexican
antojos, barrels of pulque and bottles of tequila, clay pots,
plates overflowing with fruit. There is a great ceremonial
Pharaonic chair in the middle of the table, behind which the
Mariachi band is playing. The* NUBIAN SLAVE GIRLS
*appear, two beautiful girls dressed like Aida in Verdi's
opera, with large fans in their hands, half-naked, with no
shoes on, singing the verses of the zarzuela 'The Court of
Pharaoh' in counterpoint to the* MARIACHIS *who are now
playing 'Las Olas de la Laguna':*

NUBIAN SLAVES (*singing*). *Ay Ba, ay Ba, ay Babilonio que
marea, Ay Va, Ay Va, Ay Vámonos para Judea . . .*

MARIA *walks serenely to her throne, followed by the slaves
who fan her and then leave the fans to move back the throne
while* MARIA *takes her place. Next one of the* NUBIAN
SLAVE GIRLS *crowns* MARIA *with the ostentatious
headdress of the Egyptian queen and another one offers her
the Ptolemaic insignias which* MARIA *places over her
breast. The* NUBIAN SLAVE GIRLS *start serving the meal
to* MARIA. *They feed her as if she were a child. Her lips
become smeared with black chili sauce, her chin with beans,
but* MARIA *does not lose her hieratic, imperial composure.
In her eyes, however, a mortal terror appears. She sits up
with an air of desperation.*

MARIA. Thank you, my people. Thank you for accompanying
me in my solitude. You have understood our sacrifice.

The NUBIAN SLAVE GIRLS, *like cybernetically
synchronised automatons, hum the aria from* La Traviata,
'Conosca il Sacrifizio'. MARIA *raises her cup of pulque.*

MARIA. If they had seen us, defending *them* from blackmail!
If *they* had seen Dolores telling that pig: 'How much, how
much for the copies?' In the name of *them*, loyal to them, to
their movies, because without them we have no way of
returning there, to the land that we lost, Dolores . . . (*The*
MARIACHIS *play and the* NUBIAN SLAVE GIRLS *sing
the 'Méjico lindo y querido, si muero lejos de ti'.*[19] MARIA
drops the cup and slumps heavily into the chair, sick.) Oh
land of the sun, I long to see you, now I live so far from
light, from love, and seeing myself so alone and sad, like a
leaf in the wind, I want to cry, I want to die of feeling![20] We
left the land of the sun to come and live in the dark cave of

the north. *Ay,* Dolores! And the condition was that we would never part. The two beasts never part. When one man eater goes out in search of food the other accompanies her. It's not possible to part . . . That's the condition for living. Do you understand? Alone, each one of us returns to the jungle of fire, not to God but to the jungle: all the dead in the world are younger than God, don't forget that. Don't forget me, oh my land of the sun, I yearn for you . . . [21]

MARIA loses movement in her head. She drops her sceptres into a pot. Her head rolls uncontrollably. She raises her hands to her breasts. The headdress falls. MARIA gets up. The MARIACHIS fall silent.

MARIA. No! I don't want to die. Not yet.

Everyone makes way for her. She staggers round the banqueting table. When she reaches the edge she takes hold of the tablecloth, yanks it and overturns everything. The NUBIAN SLAVES try to run and help her. One of the MARIACHIS – suspiciously resembling Jorge Negrete – stops them. MARIA walks forward in silence. The white telephone rings. It is, as always, on the white toilet. MARIA turns, leans against the table, falls to her knees and crawls over to the telephone – and the toilet. She tries to get hold of the telephone. She drops it. DOLORES' voice can be heard from the handset:

DOLORES (*off*). Hello? *Hola?* María? María? Answer me! (*MARIA tries to speak, but cannot: the sleeping pills are taking effect.*) María . . . What's wrong, my love? Listen to me. I have something to tell you.

MARIA. Tell . . . tell your boyfriend . . . he has an errand to do tomorrow . . .

DOLORES. *María Bonita, María del alma* . . .

MARIA. To prepare a cute farewell for me, tell him . . .

DOLORES. María! I'm coming over. María, María de los Angeles!

MARIA. Let them bury me in the land of the sun . . . let them say that I'm sleeping, and . . . [22]

DOLORES. I'm going to hang up . . . I'm coming . . .

MARIA. Dolor . . . Dolor . . . es . . . I don't want to die, my love . . . (*A click is heard as DOLORES hangs up. MARIA keeps hold of the handset.*) I love you too. I am

you, didn't you know? We are both Dolores and María
so that we don't have to be us . . . I'm going . . . I'm going
to be sick, Lolita . . . maybe that way it'll go away . . . maybe . . . *ayayay* . . . Now you'll all see who is Doña Diabla! [23]

During this scene, the NUBIAN SLAVES *leave the set and
the* MARIACHIS *turn and exit playing 'Las Golondrinas.'
When* MARIA *lifts the lid of the toilet to be sick, she is
alone on the set which is unlit except for the light which
shines on her, kneeling, prostrate in front of the white toilet,
trying to be sick until, exhausted, she sticks her head into
the bowl. A frightening sound of drowning is heard, a
deathly spasm, a terminal asphyxiation. The* MARIACHIS,
*off, play and sing the complete 'Canción Mixteca.' The
music gradually fades. The sound of feet running up stairs is
heard. A bunch of keys nervously inserted. At last the door
opens and* DOLORES *appears, now dressed soberly in a
black raincoat, stockings and modern shoes, but with a
1940s hat. She screams when she sees bold* MARIA, *her
head inside the toilet, runs over to her, takes out her
dripping head, screams, weeps, rocks it in her arms, looking
at it straight in the face. Then she drops it in her lap.*

DOLORES. María, María Bonita, you should have trusted me.
That asshole won't write another line. He won't threaten
anyone ever again. Do you understand me, Mariquita? Why
didn't you understand me? I told you as I was leaving. I'll
kill the bastard, we'll kill the pig . . . I did it for you, my
holy sister, love of my life. *Ayayay!* Why didn't you wait
for me. *Ayayayayay* . . . (*Suddenly, as if she had remembered something, she puts her hand over her mouth. She
looks around suspiciously. She has left the door open. She
looks at it in terror.*) But don't make a noise, María de los
Angeles, Mamá can hear us. It would give her so much
pleasure to know that you died younger than her, you
know? She mustn't find out . . . How wonderful . . . How
wonderful . . . that gentleman . . . now won't be able to tell
the world . . . about your death . . . because nobody must
find out . . . least of all Mamá . . . nobody has to know..
Everyone must believe that you never died, that you are
beauty immortal . . . There will be no funeral ceremony,
María Bonita. Nobody will be present at your burial . . .
Except me . . . Your burial is today . . . this is the ceremony . . . nobody must know . . .

MARIA *and* DOLORES *make up a female Pietá.*
DOLORES *recites Luis Sandoval y Zapata's sonnet 'To a
deceased actress'.*[24] *This is the funeral ceremony.*

DOLORES. 'Here lies the sleeping purple, / Grace and charm
and beauty, / And here lies that clarion of gentleness /
Whose voice was lent to life's sweet songs...' (*She
alternates between the sonnet and asking* MARIA
questions) What did you say to me this morning? I'm trying
to remember, María. Something we should remember now, I
know. Trust me, you said. It'll upset Mamá if you and I die.
Trust me. (*Hesitates a moment*) Trust me? You didn't . . .
You thought that I . . . I and that . . . that . . . (*Puts her hand
over her mouth, holding back nausea*) You should have seen
it. He offered me some third-rate champagne. Californian.
Me! I broke the bottle. He laughed. With the smashed neck
of his bottle of undrinkable champagne I slit his throat so
that he could only drink his own blood . . . (*She holds back
her nausea. She composes herself quoting the sonnet, her
voice strained*) 'Thou mad'st life's loveliness surer...' He
won't laugh any more. (*She interrupts herself. She looks
around.*) Trust me, you said. It'll upset Mamá if you and I
die. Will it upset Mamá? How? How? (*She looks at the door
in terror. She saves herself again in poetry.*) 'Verses owed
thee their performance, and / Thou mads't life's loveliness
surer; / Loving, icy, elusive, thou didst feign / So well...'
(*She looks at the altars.*) Your altar. My altar. We've kept
them there since we were little girls. To store our memories,
our illusions, our prayers. Is that where the secret is? (*Her
attention is held by the* FAN'*s projector, which is sitting on
the porcelain cistern of the toilet.* DOLORES *gently lifts*
MARIA'*s head, lays it on the ground and gradually stands
up, reciting under her breath the sonnet, which culminates
in a requiem which is also an alleluia*). 'Thou didst feign /
so well that even Death was uncertain / if thou didst
simulate one dead or didst submit as one alive...' (*Pause.
Then suddenly*) The camera, María? Isn't the camera our
salvation? Aren't all our prayers met by the movie camera?
Isn't the camera our common altar, my love? (*She goes over
to the projector. She puts it on. As in the previous scene, the
light blinds the audience.*) Ah, look at you, how beautiful
and in love, following Pedro Armendáriz to the revolution,
Enamorada, Flor Silvestre, life's loveliness. Look at me,
following Pedro Armendáriz to the firing squad,

Enamorada, Flor Silvestre . . . (She turns the projector to face the back of the set so that it projects the alternating images of the two stars on to the free space behind the banqueting table. Moving away from the projector) I'm going to let it run, María. Now I've understood you. Oh yes, my God I have understood you, grace and charm and beauty . . . Let our movies run forever, uninterrupted . . . Let Mamá hear us upstairs, let her hear our voices and die slowly, slowly, in her wheelchair, dressed like an Indian priestess, the old witch, thinking she can take away our lives because she gave them to us, that hypocritical whore who is older than all the dead. Let her die of anger listening to us and thinking we're still alive, performing, living life's loveliness, María de los Angeles, loving, icy, elusive, even Death is uncertain if thou dost simulate one dead or dost submit as one alive . . . *(She stops for a moment, with a victorious air. She exclaims)* 'Here lies the sleeping purple.' *(Without turning her back on the projector she draws closer and closer to the door. Her words, all of them names of movies, are drowned out by the sound of the dialogues from those movies which correspondingly grow in volume.) Resurrection . . . Hidden River . . . Wonder Bar . . . Mare Nostrum . . . Evangeline . . . Juana Gallo . . . The Loves of Carmen . . . La Escondida . . . In Caliente . . . Ash Wednesday . . . The Little House . . . Vertigo . . . Beyond all Limits . . . La Malquerida . . . The Dove . . . French Can-Can . . . The Power and the Glory . . . Amok . . . La Otra . . . Lancer Spy . . . Corona Negra . . . Madame du Barry . . . Mesalina . . . Doña Diabla . . . Heroes and Sinners . . . El Monje Blanco . . .* (DOLORES *leans against the door.) Resurrection.*

She closes the door. Metallic clanging is heard first. Then the sound of earth being shovelled. All mixed up with the dialogues and the images from the movies.[25] *Then silence.* DOLORES *walks back to her chair, stares at the audience, pours herself a cup of tea, groans.* MARIA *gets up and walks over to her.*

MARIA. It's very early. What's wrong?

DOLORES. They didn't recognise me.

MARIA. Again?

End.

Notes

1. María Félix has been a goddess of Latin American cinema since the 1940s, and is most famed for her aggressive sensuality, which attracted a string of lovers that included Jorge Negrete and Frida Kahlo. She inspired artists like Diego Rivera to paint her, composers to write songs like *María Bonita* (Agustín Lara) and *Je l'aime à mourir* (Francis Cabrel), and bullfighters to dedicate fights to her. In *machista* society she was a revolutionary, a Pancho Villa in skirts, becoming a role model for many Latin American women yearning for independence. As an actress she worked with top international directors like Luis Buñuel and Jean Renoir but was never a convincing character actress, leaning heavily on vampy melodrama. She became typecast as a fierce, castrating woman in movies like *Man Eater* (1946), *Peak of Dead Souls* (1942), *Doña Bárbara* (1942), *Soulless Woman* (1943) and *Doña Diabla* (1943). Gossip columnists jeered at her ugly hands and accused her of disowning her own son because she was frightened he would undermine the myth of her eternal youth. Born in 1915 in Alamo, Sonoras, Mexico, Félix divided her time in 1996 between Paris, 'my external exile', and Mexico, 'my internal exile.'

2. Dolores del Río was a pioneer, the first Latina actress to gain Hollywood fame. She was born in 1905 in Durango, Mexico, and educated in a convent. In 1921, she married the writer Jaime del Río. Director Edwin Carewe was struck by her dark beauty at a Mexico City tea party and invited her to Hollywood to appear in his film *Joanna* (1925). This launched her movie career, which had two distinct stages. The first was in 1930s Hollywood, where she became a universal symbol of beauty, elegance and mystique, playing an exotic Polynesian maiden in King Vidor's *Bird of Paradise* (1931), dancing with Fred Astaire in *Flying down to Rio* (1933) and starring in movies like the screen adaptation of Tolstoy's *Resurrection* (1927), Raoul Walsh's *What Price Glory?* (1926), *Ramona* (1927), *Madame du Barry* (1934) and finally Orson Welles' *Journey into Fear* (1942). The second stage of her career was in the 1940s during the 'Golden Age' of Mexican cinema. Under the direction of 'El Indio' Fernández, she became a symbol of *Mexicanidad*. Her simple beauty and forceful personality brought a lyrical power to movies like the classic *María Candelaria* (1943), in which Dolores is persecuted by a villainous landowner who kills the little pig that she is rearing for the village

market. Other films of this era include *Enamorada* (1946) and *Flor Silvestre* (1943). She was married twice and was romantically linked to Orson Welles before his involvement with Rita Hayworth. She died aged 78 in Newport Beach, California, while rehearsing the part of Dolores in this play.

3. Orson Welles died after the play was written, on October 10, 1985, of a heart attack, while writing at his house in Hollywood.

4. A reference to the scene in *Casablanca* in which Ingrid Bergman reassures Humphrey Bogart that 'we will always have Paris'.

5. A reference to a bolero by Lucho Gatica.

6. Porfirio Díaz was President of Mexico from 1877 to 1880 and from 1884 until 1911 when Madero's revolution forced him to resign and flee into exile. He was a believer in the European Enlightenment ideas of progress and science. Octavio Paz describes him as 'the most illustrious dictator in Spanish America'.

7. La Malinche was the Indian woman who seduced and then married the Spanish conquistador Hernan Cortés. To Mexicans she is more than just an historical figure; she is the symbol of an ongoing conflict of identity. Many of Mexico's great painters, musicans and writers have taken her as a principal subject, including José Clemente Orozco who depicted her as the Mexican Eve. *Malinchista* is now a politically loaded adjective describing those who want Mexico to open itself to the outside world, but also used contemptuously, to denounce all those corrupted by foreign influences.

8. From a traditional *son*, originally from Santiago de Cuba, called *Mamá, quiero saber de donde son los cantantes.'*

9. This and Dolores's next line are from the Italian version of the Internationale. If an English version is preferred, a translation would be: 'Then comrades come rally, the last fight let us face'; and then, in the next line: 'The Internationale unites the human race'.

10. Different versions of this tango are available on the soundtrack to *Flying down to Rio* and on collections of songs by Rudy Vallée, including *Sing for your Supper* (Conifer, 1989).

11. An extract from the song *María Bonita*, written for María Félix by the Mexican singer and songwriter Agustín Lara.

12. An extract from *The Mixtec Song*, translated in note 13.

13. The literal translation of this traditional Mexican mariachi song, *The Mixtec Song*, is: 'How far I am from the land where I was born! / Intense nostalgia invades my thoughts; / and seeing myself so alone and sad, like a leaf in the wind, / I want to cry, I want to die of feeling. Oh land of the sun, I long to see you, now I live so far from light, from love, / and seeing myself so alone and sad, like a leaf in the wind, / I want to cry, I want to die of feeling.' If the director or the performers feel it poses too great a vocal or audience challenge, they might con-

sider replacing the song with the nostalgic 'Orchids in the Moonlight':
'When orchids bloom in the moonlight / And lovers vow to be true; /
I still can dream in the moonlight / Of one dear night that we knew. /
When orchids fade in the dawning / They speak of tears and goodbye; /
Tho' my dreams are shattered, / Like the petals scattered . . . '

14. From Shakespeare's *Antony and Cleopatra*, Act 1, scene 5.

15. From a bolero by Lucho Gatica.

16. 'La Doña' was María Félix' nickname in the media, and was the
title for Paco Ignacio Taibo's comprehensive biography of Félix,
published in 1991.

17. A reference to Dolores del Río's role in *María Candelaria*.

18. In the published Spanish version, María introduces herself as
Maclovia, the character played by María Félix in the eponymous
movie, directed by Emilio Fernández in 1948. In my discussions with
Fuentes, we changed Maclovia to Lupe Vélez. Like Dolores del Río,
Vélez was a Latina star in Hollywood. She was Douglas Fairbanks'
fiery leading lady in *The Gaucho* (1927), and subsequently played
various tempestuous leads, for example in Griffith's *Lady of the
Pavements* (1929) and De Mille's *The Squaw Man* (1931). She was as
volatile in her personal life as she was on screen. After being ditched
by Gary Cooper, she married Tarzan actor Johnny Weissmuller in
1933. They divorced in 1938, and she had a string of unhappy affairs.
In 1944, Vélez had a long session with her make-up man and
hairdresser, swallowed a bottle of barbiturates, adorned her room with
flowers, slipped her head into the toilet and drowned herself.

19. An excellent version of this nostalgic Mexican song is by Jorge
Negrete, highly appropriate considering María Félix' romantic
involvement with Negrete. The Spanish chorus, which is quoted later,
is: *México lindo y querido, / si muero lejos de tí, / que digan que estoy
dormido / y que me traigan aquí.* The translation is: Beautiful and
beloved Mexico, / If I die far from you / let them say I am asleep / and
let them bring me here.

20. A translation of a direct quote from *The Mixtec Song* – see note 13

21. Another quotation from the *The Mixtec Song*.

22. A quotation from *México lindo y querido*– see note 19.

23. 'Doña Diabla' refers to the nickname given to the character of
Angela played by María Félix in the eponymous film, a melodrama
about a Catholic high-society lady living a double life as a prostitute,
directed by Tito Davison in 1948. Fuentes suggested that Doña Diabla
should be translated as 'the Devil's own cunt.'

24. I have sought to find a 17th-century English equivalent to
Sandoval y Zapata's language. I have also tried to translate the
imagery and musicality of Sandoval y Zapata's poem, fragments of

which Dolores uses and adapts at the end of the play. The cast and
director may, however, wish to revert to the original Spanish of '*A una
cómica difunta*':

Aquí yace la púrpura dormida;
Aquí el garbo, el gracejo, la hermosura,
La voz de aquel clarín de la dulzura
donde templó sus números la vida . . .
La representación, la vida airosa
Te debieron los versos y más cierta,
Tan bien fingiste – amante, helada, esquiva –
Que hasta la Muerte se quedó dudosa
Si la representaste como muerta
O si la padeciste como viva.

25. Fuentes changed the play's conclusive and linear ending in July
1992 while we were discussing the translation. He said an oneiric and
ambiguous ending was most suitable to both the style and the structure
of play. From this point in the text, the previous end had gone: '... *All
mixed up with the dialogue and images from the movies. Then total
darkness. Music: 'Orchids in the Moonlight'.*

INTERVIEW WITH CARLOS FUENTES

SD: How has *Orchids in the Moonlight* been performed?

CF: It was originally taken by the American Repertory Theatre at
Harvard where Robert Brustein liked it very much. It was well cast,
with two black actresses. But it didn't work because the director saw it
as a feminist, realistic, psychological play, which it isn't. It also had an
interval, which it should not have had; and the magic of the play – the
ambiguity, the oneiric, fantastic, Latin American, baroque overtones –
was driven out. Then there was a Mexico City production which had
two men playing María and Dolores which, for me, is the best so far
because of its fringe, outsider quality. That was very baroque,
grotesque, cartoon-like at times, and very funny. It worked as a
comedy very well. Both of the actors have since died of AIDS, which
is rather dramatic. Then there was a very serious production done in
Madrid with two of Almodóvar's favourite actresses, including Marisa
Paredes. That had more of a dream-play dimension. Then there was an
excellent radio production done by National Public Radio in New
York, with very good sound effects: you can hear the play very well
there.

**SD: You once criticised the 'artifice of English acting'. How would
you advise British performers to prepare for these roles?**

CF: The play has a great degree of artificiality built into it because of
the nature of the two women, who are artifice incarnate. But there are
ways of being artificial. This is a very baroque artifice. Baroque means
horror of the vacuum, filling in the vacuum, desperation, abundance
born of necessity, of not having anything, and having to invent the
abundance. This plays into the ambiguity of the play, of the question:
who are these women? Are they really two film actresses who are
recreating their lives? Are they two fans, admirers of these women,
who throughout their lives have wanted to take on the role of the two
women they admire? This ambiguity has to play throughout, so that
the ambiguity becomes the nature of the play; it becomes the natural
and truthful aspect of the play, whereby any artificiality, baroqueness,
or caricatured aspects of the play are finally dissolved in the ambiguity
which is nurturing the play. As long as the ambiguous fluid is there,
bathing the play and the actresses, I think it works. If that is lost, if you
see it as a realistic play, then it fails. If it's purely a cartoon, it doesn't
work either.

**SD: How do the performers communicate the oneiric, or dream-
like, quality to the audience?**

CF: It is established right from the first moment, when Dolores points
at the audience which is there and is not there, saying 'they are not
looking at us', when the audience is doing nothing else, of course.
That is an invitation to accept what is going to happen as a dream

world, as an unreality in a naturalistic sense, but as a reality on its own terms, that is, the reality of dreaming. So the opening moments of the play are very important. The audience must be shocked, made to feel uncomfortable because of the length of time in silence. At the same time, they must be drawn into the play while being alienated from it, in a Brechtian sense. This is difficult to achieve, but it is what I had in mind.

SD: How would you describe the relationship between the two women?

CF: I think they are almost on a desert island. Any two people on a desert island are going to have to be many things to each other: sisters, lovers certainly, and there will be a master-slave relationship as well. They will run the gamut of relationships. Nevertheless, what is important is the relationship between two individuals – man and woman, two men, two women – which clamours to be so many things. This always gives us the dimension of absence, of the absence of someone else, of a third party, another eye. Who's watching us? Is it their mother? Her nature I think you can play with, and come up with an approximation of your own. I really don't know who *la mamá* is? But she is the absent one, the dimension of absence that you inevitably get in a claustrophobic relationship in which two persons are everything to each other, they interpret every single role, every single possibility of relationship between two individuals; yet no matter how fulfilling or exhausting it is, inevitably there is the question of the *other*, the absent one, our Arab, our Jew, our God, whatever. That, for me, has always been the mystery of the play.

SD: Did you have any specific real-life figures in mind when you were writing the characters?

CF: Yes. Any screen goddesses could have done the roles. You could have multiplied them into a maze of mirrors, with each part being played successively by another actress. At a certain stage in history, the image of the sex goddess is interchangeable. It is a mould and you can shuffle them easily. In the 1930s and the 1940s it is very easy to play with many other names of other actresses. In this play, there is the added element, which is that they come from a poor, underdeveloped country. They aspire to reach a metropolis, which is Hollywood or Paris; I don't think Dietrich or Garbo ever wanted to reach Mexico.

SD: Maria Félix once described you as a *mujerujo*, a man with a woman's heart. You've had a mysterious relationship with her, haven't you?

CF: Yes. We were very close friends. I have a novel in which she is the principal character, *Holy Place*. Then I told her about the play at a dinner party and she was very amused and thought it was great. I told her I would send it to her when I had finished it, and did so, asking her what she thought about it. She never gave me an answer. I got an indirect answer through Dolores del Rio who was already rehearsing it and wanted to do it for Mexican television, but then she died. Maria Félix banned me and started saying I was a horrible individual for writing this, that I had smeared her. Which isn't true: it's a homage to a myth, a goddess, which goes beyond biography. She didn't take it that way. She made some comments about me in *Vanity Fair*. She would not mention me by name, calling me 'Mr. X'. She said my only unhappiness about our relationship was that I never went to bed with her. Then she invented the word *mujerujo*, and called me it on television. I find that very flattering, almost a description of Flaubert: *Madame Bovary, c'est moi*. You have to be a woman when you're writing about a woman. I had to become María Félix to write this play. It makes me unhappy, because I had no intention of offending her. I like her very much.

SD: Your father has been a great influence on your theatre, hasn't he?

CF: My father was my educator in a very broad sense. He took me to the theatre at a very early age. One of the first plays I saw was in 1937 when I went to see Helen Hayes and Vincent Price in Maxwell Anderson's *Victoria Regina*. In my father's home in Vera Cruz, there was a large gymnasium and he and his brother and their friends would stage and invent plays, and do *The Three Musketeers* and *The Count of Monte Cristo*. This gave him great joy. When he was 18, he fled home and joined a theatrical troupe in Mexico, was picked up by my grandfather at the next railway station where the troupe went. He always had an enormous sensitivity and love for the theatre which he handed down to me.

SD: What playwrights have influenced you?

CF: The two most influential plays in my education were *Life is a Dream* by Calderón and *The Prince of Homburg* by Kleist. Those are the two plays which I would have liked to have written and I come back to them constantly. They are dream plays and they speak very deeply about imagination, and the possibilities of words, and the hidden invisible reality that art finally reveals, that no other medium can reveal. I have also been greatly influenced by the dramatists of the Spanish Golden Age, and of the Elizabethan and Jacobean era. Those plays are very Latin American, I think, because of the atrocious and extremely violent things that happen on stage.

SD: You once confessed that you were really only a frustrated actor. What appealed to you about acting?

CF: I really loved character parts. I greatly admired character actresses. When I acted, I was very small and imitated Charles Laughton, Claude Rains, Sydney Greenstreet, Peter Lorre, Conrad Veidt. I even have a novel dedicated to the four character actors in *Casablanca*. That is what I would have loved to done, if I had been an actor. I couldn't stand romantic leads.

SD: Latin American theatre is almost unknown in Britain and the USA. Why do you think that is?

CF: It is very mysterious and difficult to understand the stages of literary development in any given country. Why didn't we have good novels until the 1930s and 1940s, whereas we have had a long, uninterrupted and continuous brilliance of lyric poetry? There have been lyric poets writing in Latin America since colonial days: Sandoval y Zapata or Sor Juana Inés de la Cruz. We have never ceased to have great poets. But we did not have great novelists or narrators until Borges, Asturias, Carpentier, Onetti and Rulfo appeared on the scene in the 1940s. Why haven't we had good theatre? Well, I think one thing grows out of another but it takes time. We the novelists grew out of the poetry of Latin America. We finally assimilated the poetical culture of Latin America and therefore we could write novels. I don't know if future dramatists will have to assimilate the novels and the poetry in order to write really first-class theatre. There are very good individual dramatists in Latin America in almost every country. What there is not is a general movement of brilliance comparable to that of poetry or the novel. I have sometimes wondered if this has something to do with political life, with the nature of political language, with the rhetoric that has characterised the political language of Latin America. Poetry is a way of breaking away from that language. The novel became great, too, when it discovered it could get away from the rhetoric of politics and of official language and create its own language. But the theatre is very difficult because it shares with political language the fact that it is said out loud, in the public square, under the sun, like María Félix's bullfighter in the play. There the competition is much greater. When you are writing for a secret audience which will read in silence, that is one thing. When you are writing to declaim in public, it's another. What is happening is that films have finally been able to break through the artificiality – the pomposity, the rhetoric, the melodramatic stance – that identified politics with the theatre in Latin America. We are now hearing dialogues which are spontaneous, natural, well-said in very good films from Mexico, Cuba, Argentina and Chile. This gives me heart that finally this breakthrough in film will lead quickly to a real renaissance in theatre. Or rather a 'naissance' because it would be the first time that we have had a full-blown theatrical movement.

SD: Do you see any particular proponents of this movement?

CF: There is a history of modern Latin American theatre, probably beginning with Florencio Sánchez, the Uruguayan dramatist. Usigli is another important figure there. And then you have a number of younger people like Emilio Carballido in Mexico, the novelist Luis Rafael Sánchez in Puerto Rico, who would be very worth putting on. But these are isolated figures, and do not form part of a movement the way we form part of a movement with Mario Vargas Llosa, Julio Cortázar, Gabriel García Márquez and José Donoso.

SD: Do you see any shared characteristics between the prominent dramatists?

CF: All of them identify themselves as Latin American, but I see no strong current, no structured movement which you could identify as a Latin American theatre.

SD: What social function has the theatre had in Latin America over recent years?

CF: There is a form of theatre which has had an enormous social function which is satirical theatre: skits, the *teatro de carpas* as we call it in Mexico and from which Cantinflas arose, what Pinti does in Buenos Aires. Pinti does a one-man show, a tour de force which has being going on non-stop every day for several years, in which he furiously comments on all the foibles of Argentina. A fantastic monologue. There is this immediate satirical function, and you can gauge a country by how much it respects that kind of theatre. But it's very specialised and it provokes an immediate cathartic response from anyone who sees it. It's not the same as Molière or Shakespeare.

SD: It's very ephemeral?

CF: Very ephemeral. It's not written down, it's improvised, based on daily occurrences. Nobody knows a year later what was said. There are no scripts, it's a jam session, which makes it very beautiful and interesting but it goes with the wind. There are political plays which are important such as Ariel Dorfman's *Death and the Maiden*. This was a play that curiously flopped in Chile and then had a big success outside the country. I saw a play in Santiago called *Pablo Neruda is Flying Towards Us* and one in Mexico City called *Sexo, Pudor y Lágrimas* which is very funny, frank, and liberating. But they seem to be isolated instances. They haven't linked into a significant chain like poetry and the novel have been able to do. And the greatest social effect has been this kind of theatre, but sometimes when you get political theatre going beyond the burlesque, the skit, the cathartic experience, the everyday commentary with something like Dorfman, then the local audiences will not accept it. Dorfman's play had to get a showing outside. In Chile, it proved too irritating, too offensive. It didn't work. There you have the case of a play which finds an international audience because it deals with a political subject, yet cannot find a national audience for that very reason. So the question is: are there no audiences for theatre in Latin America? Is that the reason we have to continue addressing our audiences in silence, through the medium of the book, the written word?

SD: What could audiences find particularly attractive in Latin American theatre?

CF: The same that they are finding in films. They see imagination, real people, real language, real conversation. This is the way you start a theatre. At the same time, even the success of the films is because they are in the dark, because they are not live. The presence of a live stage production, of a live actor is impressive. It invades you, it takes over your life, it forces you into something very direct, material, and corporeal. That is what people are afraid of. It's like being afraid of touching someone's hand. I find there is a reticence in the Latin American audience which can only express itself bestially, in a burlesque show where you have naked women and they can scream their heads off in a bestial manner. Or they fall back on the convent and they want to be absolutely quiet, intangible and holy: nothing shall touch me and I shall touch nothing. So there are these two extremes and I think theatre exists between the two of them. In its extremity, it is the brothel or the convent.

This verbal interview was conducted in English, in London in July 1992.

MISTRESS OF DESIRES

by Mario Vargas Llosa

Truth is rarely pure and never simple.

Oscar Wilde

Author's Note

The plot of this play can be summed up in a few sentences. The action takes places in a small bar near the Stadium in Piura, a city surrounded by sand in northern Peru. The bar is run by La Chunga and is frequented by the poor and the shady. One night, one of the regulars, Josefino, comes in with his latest conquest, Meche, a young woman of strong and attractive features. La Chunga takes an immediate fancy to her. Josefino goads Meche to provoke La Chunga in order to amuse himself and his friends, a group of layabouts who call themselves the Boys. In the course of the evening, Josefino loses all his money at dice. To carry on playing, he hires out Meche to La Chunga. The two women spend the rest of the night together in La Chunga's little room next to the bar. After that night, Meche disappears and nothing has been heard of her since. So what happened between the two women? The play begins a long time after that episode. At the same table in the bar, still playing dice, the Boys try in vain to persuade La Chunga to reveal her secret. As she won't tell, they invent. Each Boy's fantasies materialise on stage. They are, perhaps, fleeting images of the truth. Above all the Boys reveal their most secret desires. In La Chunga's house, truth and lies, the past and the present co-exist, as they do in the human soul.

The play develops or touches upon several distinct themes as the story develops: love, desire, taboos, the relationship between man and woman, the fashions and customs of a particular sector of society, the status of women in a primitive and male-dominated society and the way that all of these objective factors are reflected in the realm of fantasy. I think that the play shows that real life does not condition and enslave desire; on the contrary, even the simplest man can use his imagination and his desires to break the bars of the prison that confines his body.

As in my two earlier plays, *The Young Lady from Tacna* and *Kathie and the Hippopotamus*, I have tried in *Mistress of Desires* to project through dramatic fiction the human totality of acts and dreams, facts and fantasies. The characters in the play are both themselves and their fantasies. They are creatures of flesh and blood whose destinies are conditioned by precise limitations – of being poor, marginalised, uneducated etc. In spite of their coarseness and the monotony of their existence, they have souls which can always escape to the relative freedom offered by man's greatest gift: fantasy.

I use the expression 'human totality' to underline the obvious fact that man is an unbreakable unity of acts and desires; also, because this unity ought to be shown in performance, confronting the spectator with an integrated world, in which the man who speaks and the man who fantasises – he who is and he who imagines he is – make up an uninterrupted continuum, an obverse and an inverse which are easily confused, like those garments which can be worn either way round, making it impossible to tell which is the right side out.

I do not see why the theatre cannot be a suitable medium to represent the marriage, or rather the wedding, of human objectivity and subjectivity. Through stubborn prejudice, however, people tend to consider that a world which is ambiguous, evanescent, made up of sudden, timeless and arbitrary shades and movements, revolving around the imagination, and driven by desire cannot co-exist on stage with the world of objective life without creating insuperable difficulties for the director. I do not think that there is any explanation for this scepticism other than laziness and a fear of taking risks, that same fear which cripples any creative endeavour.

It is simply a question of creating theatre that plays deeply on theatricality and people's aptitude for pretending and for multiplying themselves through situations and personalities different from their own. In the scenes in which the characters live out their dreams, they must indulge themselves, embody themselves, make a double of themselves like actors do when they go on stage, or as men and women do when they call on their imagination to enrich their existence, illusorily enacting what real life forbids or denies them.

Finding a technique of theatrical expression for this universally shared activity – enriching life through the creation of images and fictions – should be a stimulating challenge for those who want to renovate the theatre and explore new avenues, rather than continue cacophonously reworking the three canonical models of modern theatre which are starting to show signs of sclerosis: Brecht's epic didacticism; the amusements of the theatre of the absurd; and the threats posed by the happenings and other variants on the text-bereft show. Theatre is, I am sure, a genre whose imagery is exceptionally good at portraying the disturbing labyrinth of angels, demons, and marvels in which our desires abide.

MVLl, Florence, July 9, 1985.

Note

The Spanish title, *La Chunga*, is a word used in northern Peru to refer to a strong woman at the bottom of the socio-economic pyramid. There is no equivalent in English. Vargas Llosa and I discussed an English title during our interview and, following various proposals, he agreed that *Mistress of Desires* was an appropriate English title.   S.D.

La Chunga's House

Piura, 1945.

La Chunga's bar-restaurant is near the Stadium, in that slum of
planks and matting which sprang out of the sands not long ago.
It is located between the road to Sullana and the Grau barracks.
It is large and square and, unlike many of the flimsy buildings
in the neighbourhood, it has been properly constructed with
adobe walls and a calamine roof. On the ground floor there are
rough tables, benches and seats where customers sit, and a
counter made of wooden beams. Behind the counter is the
sooty, smoky kitchen. On a higher level, reached by a staircase
which has only a few steps, is the room which no customer has
ever seen: the boss' bedroom. From there, La Chunga can
watch through a window, concealed behind a floral-patterned
curtain, and see everything that is happening below.

The customers in the bar are from the neighbourhood: soldiers
on leave from the Grau barracks, football or boxing fans who
have dropped in on their way to the Stadium, or construction
workers from Buenos Aires, the new white neighbourhood
which is making Piura into an expanding city.

La Chunga has a cook who sleeps in front of the stove and a
boy who comes during the day to serve at the tables. She is
always at the bar, usually standing. On a night like tonight,
when there are few customers, just the four layabouts who call
themselves the Boys and have been playing dice and drinking
beer for some time, La Chunga can be seen rocking gently in
her straw rocking-chair, creaking rhythmically, her eyes lost in
the void. Is she submerged in her memories? Or is she just
existing, her mind a blank?

She is a tall and ageless woman, with a hard face, smooth and
taut skin, firm bones and forceful gestures. She looks at others
unblinkingly. She has a mop of dark hair, tied back with a
band, a cold mouth with thin lips which speak little and smile
rarely. She wears short-sleeved blouses and skirts so
unseductive that she looks like she could be wearing the

uniform of a college for nuns. Sometimes she goes barefoot, at others she wears flat sandals. She is an efficient woman; she runs the place with an iron hand and she knows how to command respect. Her physical appearance, her severity and her terseness are intimidating, and hardly ever do drunks try and take liberties with her. She does not listen to confidences, nor is she susceptible to charm. She is not known to have a boyfriend, a lover, or even a friend. She seems determined to live always alone, dedicated to her business, body and soul. Except for the very brief episode with Meche – which confused the customers a great deal – nothing or no-one is known to have upset her routine. For as long as the Piuranos who frequent the place can remember, she has been standing gravely and motionlessly behind the bar. Does she go occasionally to the Variedades or the Municipal to see a movie? Does she ever take an afternoon walk in the Plaza de Armas to listen to an open-air recital? Does she go out to the Eguiguren waterfront or to the Puente Viejo to bathe in the river – if it has rained in the Cordillera – at the beginning of every summer? Does she watch the military parade on Fiestas Patrias among the crowd standing at the foot of the Monumento Grau?

She is not an easy woman to engage in conversation; she answers in monosyllables or gestures and if someone tells her a joke she will respond with a curse. 'No flies on Chunguita', say the Piuranos.

The Boys know this very well. They roll their dice, toast each other and joke around. Their table is right beneath a beam from which hangs a kerosene lamp, and insects flit around the light. Although they come here two or three times a week, the Boys could not be described as La Chunga's friends. Acquaintances and customers, nothing more. Who in Piura could boast of knowing her intimately? The elusive Meche, perhaps? La Chunga has no friends. She is a wild and solitary being, like a cactus in the sands around Piura.

182

La Chunga was written in 1985 and first staged on 30 January 1986 in the Teatro Canout, Lima, Peru, by the Grupo Ensayo, with the following cast:

LA CHUNGA	Delfina Paredes
MECHE	Charo Verástegui
JOSEFINO	Gianfranco Brero
MONKEY	Alberto Isola
LITUMA	Cipriano Proaño
JOSÉ	Ricardo Velásquez

Director Luis Peirano

Designer Javier Sota

This translation of *Mistress of Desires* was first staged on 18 February 1992 in Christ's Theatre, Cambridge University by The Southern Development Trust, with the support of Mario Vargas Llosa and the following cast:

LA CHUNGA	Gabrielle Jourdan
MECHE	Ina Sarikhani
JOSEFINO	Edward Docx
MONKEY	Graeme Surtees
LITUMA	Mike Davis
JOSÉ	Rupert Tebb

Director Sebastian Doggart

Music David Knotts

To Patricia Pinilla

Act One

I

A Game of Dice

MONKEY (*before throwing the dice, his hand above his head*).
Come on, boys! Bring me some luck, let's sing the song.

JOSE, LITUMA, JOSEFINO, MONKEY (*in chorus, with
very exaggerated gestures*).
The four of us are called the Boys
We get our kicks from simple joys.
And throughout Piura it's been said
Every girl needs a Boy in her bed
So don't tell us to get off our asses
We're doing just fine in front of our glasses.

MONKEY. Now back to our vice of playing the dice! (*Blows
on and kisses the dice, then throws them onto the table. The
black and white cubes roll, bounce, ricochet off the half-full
glasses, are blocked by a bottle of Cristal beer and lie still.*)
Ahahai! Double threes! That makes me really happy. I'll
double the stake, gentlemen. Who's game? (*No-one answers
and no-one adds anything to the pile of notes and coins that
sits by* MONKEY's *glass.*) Come on, you faggots. (*Picks up
the dice, rocks them like a baby, blows on them, shakes them
above his head, but doesn't yet throw them.*) Here go the
knockers again. Five and a one, four and a two, or double
threes – or else this boy's going to chop his todger off.

JOSEFINO (*handing him a knife*). It won't help you much, but
you can use my knife. Go for it – chop it off.

JOSE. Toss the dice will you, Monkey. Tossing's one thing you
can do.

MONKEY (*making funny faces, fooling around*).
Huhuhuhuuuu! Three and a six. (*Crosses himself*) Now, give
me a six, Holy Whore!

LITUMA (*turning towards the bar counter*). Hey Chunga,
don't you think Monkey's getting very crude?

LA CHUNGA *doesn't stir. She doesn't condescend to look at the Boys' table.*

JOSE. Why don't you answer poor Lituma, Chunguita? He's asking you a question, isn't he?

MONKEY. She's probably dead. It's just her corpse rocking there. Are you dead, Chunguita?

LA CHUNGA. I'm sure that would make you happy. Then you could run off without paying for your beers.

MONKEY. Ahaha! I've brought you back to life, Chunga Chunguita. (*He blows on and kisses the dice, and throws them.*)

Now, give me a six, Holy Whore! (*Their four faces follow the journey of the dice through the glasses, bottles, cigarettes and matchboxes. This time the dice land on the damp earthen floor.*) One and three is four, Boys. I only need a two. The bank is still open if anyone's got the balls.

LITUMA. So what happened that time with Meche, Chunga? We're all alone tonight. You can tell us.

JOSE. Yeah, go on, tell us, Chunga Chunguita.

LA CHUNGA (*ever indifferent, sleepily*). Go ask your mother.

MONKEY (*throws the dice*). Siiiix! Suck on that and swallow, all of you! Hahahai! (*Turns towards the bar counter.*) It must be your cutting words that are making me lucky, Chunguita. (*Raises the pot and kisses the notes and coins extravagantly.*) Another couple of cold beers. This time they're on me. Hahahai!

LA CHUNGA *stands up. The chair continues to rock, creaking at regular intervals, while the owner of the Bar goes and takes out a couple of beers from a bucket full of ice that she keeps under the bar. Nonchalantly, she carries them to the Boys' table and puts them down in front of* MONKEY. *A forest of bottles covers the table.* LA CHUNGA *returns to the rocking chair.*

JOSE (*in a mischievously high voice*). Won't you ever tell us what you did that night with Meche, Chunga?

JOSEFINO. Shut up about Mechita right now or I'll strip one of you and do it to you right here. Just her name makes me horny.

MONKEY (*making eyes and mimicking a woman's voice*). Does that happen to you too, Chunga?

LA CHUNGA. That's enough, you sonofabitch. I'm here to serve beers, not to listen to your filth, or be laughed at. Watch it, Monkey!

MONKEY (*starts trembling. His teeth chatter. His shoulders and hands shudder, he becomes white-eyed with terror, hysterically possessed*). Uy, I'm so scared.

Roaring with laughter, the Boys slap him on the back as if to calm him down.

LITUMA. Don't get mad, Chunga. We may get on your nerves sometimes, but you know we really love you.

JOSEFINO. Fuck! Who's bloody idea was it to mention Meche? It was you, wasn't it, Lituma? You've made me all sentimental. (*Raises his glass solemnly.*) Let's drink to the hottest pussy that ever walked on Peruvian soil. To you, Mechita – in heaven, in Lima, in hell, or wherever the fuck you are.

II

Meche

While JOSEFINO *toasts and the Boys drink,* MECHE *enters, slowly and rhythmically, like someone coming into the real world out of the world of memory. She is young and very feminine, with a balanced and full figure. She wears a light, tight-fitting dress and high-heels. She walks flirtatiously.* LA CHUNGA's *eyes widen and brighten as she enters. The Boys do not notice her presence. By contrast,* LA CHUNGA *is now so entranced by* MECHE *that she feels that the present has lost all consistency and stopped. The voices of the Boys become fainter.*

MONKEY. I'll never forget your face when Meche came in that time, Chunga Chunguita. You were totally awestruck.

LITUMA. You're the only person in the world who knows where she is, Chunga. Go on, girl, what does it matter? Satisfy our curiosity!

JOSE. Or even better, tell us what happened that night between you and Meche, Chunga. Fuck! I lie awake every night thinking about it.

MONKEY. I'll tell you what happened. (*Sings, monkeying around as usual*)
Chunga and Meche
Meche and Chunga
Cheche and Menga
Menga and Cheche
Che Che Che Che Che
Chu Chu Chu Chu Chu
And long live Fumanchu!

LA CHUNGA (*in a faint and distant voice, mesmerised by* MECHE *who is now standing beside her*). Hurry up and finish your drinks, I'm closing.

JOSEFINO *stands up, unnoticed by the other Boys. Stepping out of the present into the past, from reality into dream, he goes over to* MECHE *and takes her arm as if he owns her.*

JOSEFINO. Good evening, Chunguita. May I introduce Meche.

MECHE (*holding out her hand to* LA CHUNGA). Pleased to meet you, señora.

The Boys wave greetings to JOSEFINO *and* MECHE, *remaining absorbed in their game of dice.*

LA CHUNGA (*devouring her with her eyes and holding on to* MECHE'*s hand. She speaks emotively*). So you're the Meche I've heard so much about. Welcome. I didn't think he'd ever bring you. I've wanted to meet you so much.

MECHE. So have I, señora. Josefino's always talking about you. (*Pointing to the table.*) So do they – the whole time. About you and about this place. I've been dying to come. (*Pointing to* JOSEFINO.) But he didn't want to bring me.

LA CHUNGA (*resigning herself to releasing* MECHE'*s hand. Making an effort to compose herself and look natural*). I've no idea why. I haven't eaten anyone up as far I know. (*To* JOSEFINO.) Why didn't you want to bring her?

JOSEFINO (*joking coarsely*). I was afraid you might steal her away from me, Chunguita. (*Putting his arm round* MECHE'*s waist, displaying her proudly.*) Worth her weight in gold, don't you think?

LA CHUNGA (*admiring her and nodding*). Yes. This time I have to hand it to you. You must be the Don Juan of Gallinacera. She's worth more than all your other conquests put together.

MECHE (*slightly embarrassed*). Thank you, señora.

LA CHUNGA. Please, call me Chunga. You don't have to be formal with me.

LITUMA (*calling from the table*). We're starting another game, Josefino. Are you in?

JOSE. Come on, Josefino, it's Monkey's turn with the dice. There's easy money to win from this sucker.

MONKEY. Sucker? Holy Whore, come to me! Tonight I'm going to clean you all out. Hahahai! And Josefino, you're going to lose so much, you'll have to pawn Mechita to me.

JOSEFINO (*to* LA CHUNGA). How much do you think I could get for this little doll, Chunguita?

LA CHUNGA. Anything you asked for. It's true, she's worth her weight in gold. (*To* MECHE.) What can I get you? It's on me. Beer? Vermouth?

JOSEFINO. I don't believe it . . . Did you hear that, Boys, drinks are on Chunga.

LA CHUNGA. Not for you they're not. You're a regular. It's Meche's first time here. That's why I'm buying for her – so she'll come back.

Uproar from the Boys' table.

MONKEY. Hahahai! I must be dreaming!

JOSE. Order a whisky and enjoy, Mechita.

JOSEFINO (*going over to the table and taking his seat again with the Boys*). Right, let's roll!

MECHE. I thought you were taking me to the movies?

JOSEFINO. Later. First I'm going to earn some hard cash off these three wankers. The night is young, my love.

MECHE (*to* LA CHUNGA, *pointing to* JOSEFINO). I can see already we won't be going to see a movie. They've got one on at the Variedades with Esther Williams and Ricardo Montalbán. In colour. With bullfighting and music. What a pity Josefino likes that game so much.

LA CHUNGA (*handing her the vermouth which she has been preparing*). He's mixed up in every game. He's the biggest bastard of the lot. What do you see in him? What could any woman see in a bum like him? Tell me, Meche. What's he got?

MECHE (*half blushing, half pretending to blush*). Well . . . I don't know. He's got . . . He's charming; he knows how to say lovely things. And also he's so good-looking, don't you think? And . . . and . . . Well, when he kisses me and strokes me, I tremble all over. I see little stars.

LA CHUNGA (*with a mocking smile*). Really? Little stars?

MECHE. Well, that's just an expression. You know what I mean.

LA CHUNGA. No. I don't know. I don't know how a woman as beautiful as you could be in love with a pathetic devil like that. (*Very seriously.*) You realise where you'll end up if you stay with him, don't you?

MECHE. I never think about the future, Chunga. You have to take love as it is. For the happiness it gives now, this moment. Drink the juice while the fruit's still ripe. (*Suddenly becoming alarmed.*) Where will I end up if I stay with him?

LA CHUNGA. He'll make you see a few more little stars. And then he'll put you in the Casa Verde, so you can earn him a living. By whoring.

MECHE (*scandalised*). What are you talking about? You must be joking. You think I could do that? Obviously you don't know me. Do you think I'm capable of...?

LA CHUNGA. Of course you're capable. Just as capable as all the other stupid girls who have seen little stars with that pimp. (*Stretches out her hand and caresses* MECHE's *cheek.*) Don't look so frightened. I like you much better with a smile on your face.

III

A Gallinazo and Three Mangaches

At the Boys' table, the game starts to heat up.

MONKEY (*Very excited*). Three and a four is seven! Hahaha! So I'm a sucker am I, José? Down on your knees and pray, pencil-dick! When in your stupid life have you seen anything like it: seven whole games in a row. And the money's still all there, for anyone brave enough. Who's game?

JOSEFINO (*taking out some banknotes*). I am. You think you can scare me. Let's see how much there is. Two hundred, three hundred. Here's three hundred. Throw the dice, Mangache.

JOSE. That's a big wad, Josefino! (*Lowering his voice.*) Have you already put Mechita out to work then?

JOSEFINO. Shut it, or you'll give me a hard-on. What are you waiting for, Monkey?

MONKEY (*as if he were casting a spell, he passes the dice across his eyes and his lips, cradling them in his hand*). Just making you suffer a little, Gallinazo. And they're off, huhuhuhuuu . . . (*Excitedly, everyone watches the dice.*) Eleven! Suck on that and swallow, again! Eight in a row! Fuck! You're really gagging now! More beers, Chunga. We have a miracle to drink to.

JOSEFINO (*stopping* MONKEY *as he reaches to collect the money he has won*). The pot stays on the table.

The three Boys watch him, surprised.

MONKEY. You want to carry on losing? Fine by me, brother. There's the money. Six hundred sols. You could get rich on that. But are you betting that all on your own?

JOSEFINO. All on my own, señor. (*Takes out more banknotes from his pocket and counts them ostentatiously. He places them in the pot, slowly and theatrically.*) There. Six hundred. Gallinacera against Mangachería.

LITUMA. Holy Shit! Has he robbed a bank, or what?

JOSEFINO. Mangaches rob banks, not Gallinazos. We may be bastards to our women in Gallinacera, but we're not thieves.

JOSE. Get real, Josefino. Gallinacera's the worst part of Piura.

LITUMA. I'd stay quiet about being a Gallinazo if I were you, man. With your slaughterhouse, your corpses, your flies, your vultures.

JOSEFINO. At least we've got paved streets and real toilets. Mangachería doesn't even have that. Just donkeys and beggars. You Mangaches shit on the floor next to your bed. I don't know why I hang around with you. One of these days I'm going to start smelling like shit too. Wait, Monkey, don't throw the dice. Mechita! Come here and bring me luck.

MECHE *goes over to the table at the same time as* LA CHUNGA, *who brings two more beers.* JOSEFINO *puts his hand round* MECHE's *waist and forces her to bend over and kiss him on the mouth. He is obviously showing off and takes pleasure from the laughter and applause of the Boys.* LA CHUNGA *looks on, her eyes shining.*

JOSEFINO. OK, Monkey. Now you can throw the dice.

JOSE (*to* JOSEFINO). You know the saying, don't you? Lucky in love, unlucky at dice.

MONKEY (*throwing the dice*). They're away, and this boy's a rich man!

JOSEFINO (*happy and exuberant*). Double ones! Dig your grave, Monkey! (*To* JOSE.) You got that saying wrong, brother. It's actually: lucky in love, luckier at dice. Here's to Mechita who brought me luck. Thank you, my love. (*Once again he forces her to bend down and kiss him. As he does this, he looks askance at* LA CHUNGA, *as if he were mocking her.*) Cheers, Chunguita.

LA CHUNGA *does not reply and returns to the bar counter.*

MONKEY (*stretching out his hand to* JOSEFINO). Congratulations. You had to be brave to bet the whole pot after I'd won eight in a row. You may be from Gallinacera, but you still deserve to be one of the Boys.

JOSE (*aroused*). Did you see Chunga's face when Josefino was kissing you, Mechita? Her eyes were on fire.

LITUMA. She was dying of envy.

JOSEFINO (*raising his voice*). Did you hear what these Mangache faggots are saying about you, Chunga?

LA CHUNGA. What?

JOSEFINO. That when I was kissing Meche, your eyes were on fire. That you were dying of envy.

LA CHUNGA. Perhaps it's true. Who wouldn't feel envious of a woman like that?

Laughter and exclamations from the Boys.

JOSEFINO. And you haven't even seen her naked, Chunga. Her body's even better than her face. Eh, Meche?

MECHE. Be quiet, Josefino.

LA CHUNGA. I'm sure that for once in your life you're telling the truth.

JOSEFINO. Of course I am. Pull up your skirt, my love. Show her your legs, just to give her an idea.

MECHE (*more embarrassed than she really feels*). Josefino, the things you say sometimes!

JOSEFINO (*raising his voice slightly. With a firmness that is not quite brusque, but which hardly conceals his sense of superiority. Flaunting his authority in front of his friends.*) Listen to me. If you and I are going to keep getting along together, you have to do what I ask you. Show Chunguita your legs.

MECHE (*looking upset but deep down finding the game quite appealing*). You can be so moody and pushy sometimes, Josefino.

Lifts up her skirt and displays her legs. The Boys applaud.

JOSEFINO (*laughing*). What do you think, Chunga?

LA CHUNGA. Lovely.

JOSEFINO (*beaming, arrogantly*). I can show my woman naked to all of you because you're my friends – my soulmates. I can trust you. (*Starts to gather up the money he has just won.*)

MONKEY. Hold it right there, pal. Only a coward withdraws his winnings if someone still wants to take him on.

JOSEFINO. You want to bet the whole pot? There are twelve hundred sols here, Monkey. Have you got enough?

MONKEY (*rummages through his pockets, takes out all the money he has and counts it*). I've got five hundred. I'll owe you the other seven hundred.

JOSEFINO. It's bad luck to borrow money in the middle of a game. (*Gesturing to* MONKEY'*s wrist-watch.*) Wait. You can put your watch down. I'll accept that instead of seven hundred.

LITUMA. Your watch is worth more than that.

MONKEY (*taking off his watch and placing it in the pot together with his five hundred sols*). But I'm going to win, my friend. OK, Josefino, throw the dice and, please, lose!

JOSEFINO (*pushes MECHE towards the bar counter*). Go and keep Chunga company while I win this cash and his watch. When I've got the dice, I don't need anyone else to bring me luck. I make it myself.

JOSE. Watch out Chunga doesn't try and seduce you, Mechita.
She's creaming her pants over you.

MECHE (*exposing a rather morbid curiosity, in a low voice*).
She's not one of them, is she?

LITUMA. No-one knew what she was until now. We always
thought she was nothing.

JOSE. But she's lost her cool since she saw you. Her cover's
blown. she's a dyke.

MECHE. No! Really?

JOSEFINO. Whooaa, Chunga! If you knew what they were
saying, you'd let fly at them with these bottles and ban them
from ever setting foot in here again.

LA CHUNGA. What are they saying?

JOSEFINO. José says you've been creaming your pants over
Meche, and you've blown your cover as a dyke. And Meche
wants to know if it's true.

MECHE. He's lying Chunga, don't believe him. You're
pathetic, Josefino.

LA CHUNGA. Why doesn't she come and ask me herself. I'll
whisper in her ear.

Laughter and ribaldry from the Boys.

JOSEFINO (*to* MECHE). Go on, my love. Go and flirt with
her. Let her think she stands a chance.

MONKEY. Get on with it and throw the dice, Josefino.

MECHE *walks over to the bar counter where* LA CHUNGA *is
standing.*

IV

Dykes and Women

MECHE (*confused*). You didn't believe him, did you? You
know Josefino's always fooling around. I didn't say that
about you, really.

LA CHUNGA. Oh, forget it. I couldn't care less what people
say about me. (*Shrugs her shoulders.*) If that's what amuses
them, let them be amused. As long as I don't hear them . . .

MECHE. Don't you care if they say nasty things about you?

LA CHUNGA. I only care if there are fights or if they don't pay for their drinks. As long as they don't get violent or try and rip me off, they can talk about what they like.

MECHE. Don't you even care if they say you're a . . . a...?

LA CHUNGA. A dyke? (*Takes* MECHE's *arm.*) What if I am? Would I frighten you?

MECHE (*with a nervous giggle, half feigning, half feeling what she says*). I don't know. I've never met a real one before. I've heard there are masses of them around, but I've never actually seen one. (*Scrutinises* LA CHUNGA.) I always imagined they'd be butch and ugly. You're nothing like that.

LA CHUNGA. What am I like?

MECHE. A bit tough maybe. But I suppose you have to be to run a place like this, with all the weirdos and drunks who come in. But you're not ugly. If you fixed yourself up a little, you'd look attractive, beautiful even. Men would like you.

LA CHUNGA (*with a chuckle*). I don't care if men like me or not. But you care, don't you? It's the one thing that's really important to you. Fixing yourself up, getting all made up, looking pretty. Making their heads turn, exciting them. No?

MECHE. Surely that's just being a woman?

LA CHUNGA. No. That's being an idiot.

MECHE. Then all women are idiots.

LA CHUNGA. Most of them are. That's why things are the way they are for them. Women let themselves be badly treated, they become slaves to men. Why? So that when men get tired of them, they get thrown out in the rubbish, like dirty rags. (*Pause. She strokes* MECHE's *face again.*) I'm sorry to think of what will happen when Josefino gets tired of you.

MECHE. He'll never get tired of me. I know how to keep him happy.

LA CHUNGA. Yes, I've seen: by letting him twist you round his little finger. Don't you feel humiliated when he pushes you around like that?

MECHE. I enjoy doing whatever he asks me to do. That's what love is for me.

LA CHUNGA. So you'd do anything that poor devil asked you to do?

MECHE. For as long as I'm in love with him, yes. Anything.

Pause. LA CHUNGA *watches her silently, revealing, in spite of herself, a kind of admiration. They are both distracted by the uproar coming from the Boys' table.*

V

Hard Cash

MONKEY (*euphorically, holding up fistfuls of banknotes*). Jeeeesus Christ! Fuck, this is classic! Pinch me, Boys, I must be dreaming.

JOSE (*patting* JOSEFINO). The game's not over yet, Monkey. Leave the money on the table.

MONKEY (*to* JOSEFINO). What have you got left to bet with? You've already lost two thousand sols, plus your watch, and your fountain pen. What else have you fucking got?

Pause. JOSEFINO *looks all around him. He watches* LA CHUNGA *and* MECHE *for a moment. His mind made up, he gets to his feet.*

JOSEFINO. I have got something else. (*Strides towards* LA CHUNGA. *His eyes shine like a man ready to go to any extreme to get what he wants.*) I need three thousand sols to win the game, Chunguita.

LA CHUNGA. Over my dead body. You know very well I never lend anything to anyone.

JOSEFINO. I've got something worth far more than the three thousand sols I'm asking you for. I've got some really hard cash. (*Grabs* MECHE *round the waist.*)

MECHE (*taking it half as a joke, uncertain how to respond*). What are you saying?

LA CHUNGA *bursts out laughing.* JOSEFINO *remains deadly serious. The Boys have fallen silent and stare at them, spellbound by what is happening.*

JOSEFINO (MECHE's *lord and master, grips her next to his body*). You heard me. You love me, don't you? I love you too. That's why I'm asking this of you. Didn't you swear to me that you'd always be obedient? Well, now you're going to prove it to me.

MECHE (*incredulously*). But, but . . . Are you crazy? Do you realise what you're saying? Or have all those beers gone to your head?

JOSEFINO (*to* LA CHUNGA). There's no use pretending, Chunga. I know you've been drooling over Meche ever since you first set eyes on her. So what do you say?

MONKEY. Holy Whore! This is getting serious, Boys.

JOSE. Fuck! He's actually selling her to Chunga.

LITUMA. Why don't *you* buy her, Monkey? Or don't you think Mechita's worth three thousand sols?

JOSEFINO (*not taking his eyes off* LA CHUNGA *and still embracing* MECHE). No. I wouldn't lend her to Monkey for all the gold in the world. Or to any man either. (*Kissing* MECHE.) It'd make me jealous. I would tear the guts out of anyone who laid a finger on her. (*To* LA CHUNGA.) But you don't make me jealous. I'll lend her to you because I know you'll give her back to me unspoiled.

MECHE (*sobbing, confused, and exasperated*). Let go of me! You monster! How could you do this? I want to leave now.

JOSEFINO (*releases her*). You can leave. But if you do, don't ever come back. Because you'd be betraying me by leaving now, Meche. I could never forgive you for letting me down when I needed you.

MECHE. But, Josefino, do you realise what you're asking me to do? What do you think I am?

LA CHUNGA (*mockingly, to* MECHE). You see, it wasn't true what you said. You wouldn't do *anything* this bandit asked you to do.

JOSEFINO (*putting his arms around* MECHE). Did you really say that to her? Did you? Then it's true! (*Kisses* MECHE.) I love you. You and I will be together until the end of the world. Don't cry, stupid. (*To* LA CHUNGA) So what do you say?

LA CHUNGA (*she has become very serious. Long pause.*) Let Meche say she accepts by herself. Let her say she'll do anything I want from now until daybreak.

JOSEFINO (*to* MECHE). Don't let me down now. I need you. She won't do anything to you. She's a *woman*, what can she do to you? Say it.

Ecstatic pause, during which the Boys and LA CHUNGA *watch the struggle going on inside* MECHE, *who squeezes her arms together desperately and looks at everyone around her.*

MECHE (*to* LA CHUNGA, *stammering*). I'll do anything you tell me to, from now until daybreak.

LA CHUNGA goes to fetch the money from beneath the bar counter. JOSEFINO *whispers in* MECHE's *ear and strokes her. The Boys start to recover from the surprise.* LA CHUNGA *hands the money over to* JOSEFINO.

MONKEY. Holy Mother of Whores! I don't believe this. It's happening in front of my eyes, but I still can't bloody believe it.

LITUMA. I would even marry a woman like that.

JOSE. Fuck! Let's sing the song for Mechita. She deserves it.

MONKEY. The song and a toast, in honour of Mechita, Boys.

MONKEY, LITUMA, AND JOSE (*singing*).
The four of us are called the Boys
We get our kicks from simple joys.
And throughout Piura it's been said
Every girl needs a Boy in her bed
So don't tell us to get off our asses
We're doing just fine in front of our glasses.

MONKEY. And to wind up our boast, let's make a toast: To you, Mechita!

They raise their glasses to MECHE *and drink.* LA CHUNGA *takes* MECHE's *hand and leads her towards her room. The two of them climb the little staircase.* JOSEFINO, *counting the money, takes his place again at the gambling table.*

End of Act One.

Act Two

I

The Boys

As the curtain rises the actors are in exactly the same position as they were at the beginning of the first act. We are in the present, a long time after the episode with MECHE. *The Boys are playing dice at their table, beneath the lantern hanging from a beam, and* LA CHUNGA, *in her rocking chair, her eyes lost in the void, lets time pass her by. The warm night carries the distant sounds of the city: the chir of crickets, a car travelling through the night, dogs barking, a donkey braying.*

JOSE. How much do you think I'd have to pay Chunga for her to tell me what happened that night between her and Meche?

LITUMA. She'll never tell you, not even for a million sols. Forget it, José.

JOSEFINO. If I wanted her to, she'd tell me. For free.

MONKEY. We already know what a naughty boy you are, Josefeenie.

JOSEFINO. I'm not joking. (*Takes out his knife and holds it up so it glints in the light.*) Chunga may be tough, but there's no man or woman alive who wouldn't squawk like a parrot with this at their throat.

MONKEY. Did you hear that, Chunga?

LA CHUNGA (*indifferent as ever*). Hurry up and finish your drinks. I'm closing.

JOSEFINO. Don't be frightened, Chunguita. If I felt like it, I'd make you tell me about that night. But I don't feel like it, so you can stuff your secret up your ass. I don't want to know. I couldn't give a toss about Meche. For me, a woman out of sight is a woman out of mind. There's not a girl alive who could make me run after her.

JOSE *has stood up and, without the Boys noticing, approaches* LA CHUNGA*'s rocking chair, staring with his mouth half open, like a sleepwalker. Throughout the following scene the Boys behave as if* JOSE *were still sitting in the empty seat: they chink glasses with the invisible* JOSE, *take his bets, pass him the dice, slap him on the back, and joke with him.*

JOSE (*in a heavy, feverish voice*). Something in my life changed that night, Chunga, although nobody knows about it. (*Taps his head.*) It's up here, as clear as if it were still happening. I remember everything you and Meche said. When you took her arm and led her up there to your room, I thought my heart would leap out of my chest. (*Makes* LA CHUNGA *touch his chest.*) Can you feel it? Do you see how strongly it's beating? As if it were trying to burst out. It gets like that whenever I think about the two of you up there.

LA CHUNGA *moves her lips to say something, but no sound comes out.* JOSE *leans closer, trying to hear but suddenly recoils, wishing he hadn't. For several seconds* LA CHUNGA *continues mouthing the same word.*

LA CHUNGA (*finally speaking, with great serenity*). You're a wanker, José.

JOSE (*haunted, impatient, pointing to the bedroom*). Tell me. Please, tell me, Chunguita. What happened? What was it like?

LA CHUNGA (*lecturing him, but without severity, as if to a naughty boy*). You don't like real women, José, women of flesh and blood. You like the ones up here. (*Touching his head, as if caressing it.*) Memories, fantasies, the ones you've invented. Isn't that right, José?

JOSE (*trying to make* LA CHUNGA *get up from the rocking chair, increasingly excited*). You took her arm and led her over there. As you climbed the stairs, you never let go of her arm. Were you squeezing it? Were you stroking her gently?

LA CHUNGA *stands up and* JOSE *takes her place in the rocking chair. He shifts it in order to see better.* LA CHUNGA *pours a glass of vermouth, goes up the little staircase and enters the little bedroom, which is lit with a reddish light.* MECHE *is there.*

II

The Voyeur's Dream

MECHE (*with a nervous giggle*). Now what happens. What game is this, Chunga?

LA CHUNGA (*the cold woman of previous scenes seems to have been charged with life and sensuality*). No game. I've paid three thousand sols for you. And you're mine for the rest of the night.

MECHE (*defiant*). You mean I'm your slave?

LA CHUNGA. Yes. For a few hours, anyway. (*Holding out the glass.*) Here. It'll calm your nerves.

MECHE (*takes the glass, then takes a long drink*). Do you think I'm nervous? You're wrong. I'm not scared of you. I'm doing this for Josefino. If I wanted, I could just push you aside and run out the door.

LA CHUNGA (*sits on the bed*). But you won't. You said that you would obey me and you're a woman of your word, I'm sure. Anyway, you're dying of curiosity, aren't you?

MECHE (*finishes her drink*). Do you think you're going to get me drunk on two vermouths. Dream on! I've got a hard head. I can drink all night long and not even get tipsy. I can handle more than Josefino.

Pause.

LA CHUNGA. Do to me what you do to him when you want to excite him.

MECHE (*with the same nervous giggle*). I can't. You're a woman. You're Chunga.

LA CHUNGA (*suggestive and domineering*). I'm Josefino. Do to me what you do to him.

Soft tropical music – boleros by Leo Marini or Los Panchos – breaks out in the distance. It evokes images of couples dancing close in a place full of smoke and alcohol. MECHE starts to undress, slowly and rather clumsily. Her voice sounds forced and tense.

MECHE. Do you like watching me undress? Slowly, like this. That's what he likes. Do you think I'm pretty? Do you like my legs? My breasts? I've got a firm body, look. No blemishes, no spots, no flab. None of those things that make people so ugly.

She has stripped down to her skirt. She feels faint and screws up her face.

I can't, Chunga. You aren't him. I can't believe what I'm doing or what I'm saying. I feel stupid; it all seems so fake . . . so . . . (*She collapses on to the bed, abashed and confused, wanting and not wanting to cry.*)

LA CHUNGA (*gets up and sits next to her. She now acts attentively and tenderly, as if* MECHE*'s discomfort moved her*). The truth is, I admire you for being here. You surprised me, you really did. I didn't think you'd go along with it. (*Smooths* MECHE*'s hair.*) Do you love Josefino that much?

MECHE (*whispering*). Yes, I do love him. (*Pause.*) But I don't think I did it just for him. It was also what you said. I was curious. (*Looks at* LA CHUNGA *again.*) You gave him three thousand sols! That's a fortune.

LA CHUNGA (*stroking her cheek, drying away non-existent tears*). You're worth more than that.

MECHE (*showing a glimpse of flirtatiousness behind her anxiety and shame*). Do you really like me, Chunga?

LA CHUNGA. Of course I do. You must have noticed?

MECHE. Yes. You looked at me like no woman's ever looked at me before. You made me feel . . . strange.

LA CHUNGA *puts one hand around* MECHE*'s shoulders and draws her towards her. Kisses her.* MECHE *passively allows herself to be kissed. When they separate,* MECHE *laughs, faking a giggle.*

LA CHUNGA. Oh well, you're laughing, so it can't have been that awful.

MECHE. How long have you been like this? I mean, have you always been a . . . ? Have you always liked women?

LA CHUNGA. I don't like *women*. I like you.

LA CHUNGA *puts both arms around* MECHE *and kisses her.* MECHE *remains passive, allowing herself to be kissed but not responding to* LA CHUNGA*'s caresses.* LA CHUNGA *quickly draws away and, her arms still around her, orders:*

LA CHUNGA. Open your mouth, slave. (MECHE *lets out her forced giggle, but parts her lips.* LA CHUNGA *gives her a long kiss and this time* MECHE *raises her arm and puts it*

around LA CHUNGA*'s neck.*) Yes, that's much better. I
thought you didn't know how to kiss. (*Sarcastically.*) Did
you see little stars?

MECHE (*laughing*). Don't make fun of me.

LA CHUNGA (*holding her in her arms*). I'm not. I want you to
enjoy yourself tonight more than you've ever done with that
pimp.

MECHE. He's not a pimp! Don't say that word. He loves me.
We may be getting married.

LA CHUNGA. He is a pimp. He sold you to me tonight. Next,
he'll take you to the Casa Verde where you'll whore for him
– just like he does with all his conquests. (MECHE *tries to
break free, feigning more anger than she really feels. After a
brief struggle, she gives in.*) Let's not talk about that bum.
Just about you and me.

MECHE (*more docile*). Don't squeeze so tightly, you're
hurting me.

LA CHUNGA. I can do what I like to you. You're my slave
(MECHE *laughs.*) Don't laugh. Repeat after me. I am your
slave.

MECHE (*pauses, laughs, becomes serious*). It's just a game,
isn't it? All right. I am your slave.

LA CHUNGA. I am your slave and now I want to be your
whore. (*Pause.*) Repeat.

MECHE (*almost whispering*). I am your slave and now I want
to be your whore.

LA CHUNGA. And so you shall.

*The room gradually darkens and eventually disappears.
From the rocking chair, JOSE carries on watching the
darkened room, hypnotised. We begin to hear the noise the
Boys are making – toasts, singing, oaths – at the table
where they are playing dice.*

III

Speculations about Meche

*Throughout the following dialogue, the Boys continue playing
dice and drinking beer.*

LITUMA. Do you want to know something? Sometimes I think Mechita's disappearance is just another one of Josefino's little stories.

MONKEY. You'll have to do much, much better than that, because I don't know what you're talking about.

LITUMA. A woman can't vanish into thin air, overnight. Not in Piura. This town's no bigger than my hand.

JOSEFINO. If she'd stayed in Piura, I'd have found her. She's left town, I'm sure of it. Probably run to Ecuador. Or Lima, maybe. (*Pointing to the rocking chair where* JOSE *is sitting.*) *She* knows, but she'll take the secret to her grave. Won't you, Chunguita? Because of you I lost a woman, a woman who'd have made me rich. But I don't hold any grudge against you. Because I've got a heart of gold, you know.

MONKEY. Don't start on Meche again or José will start wanking off. (*Nudging the invisible* JOSE.) It drives you crazy imagining them up there. Eating hair pie, weren't they?

LITUMA (*continues unperturbed with his theory*). Someone would have seen her taking the bus or the *colectivo*. She'd have said goodbye to someone. She'd have taken some stuff with her. But she left behind her clothes, her suitcase. And no-one saw her go. That's why I'm not convinced about this escape story. You know what I think sometimes, Josefino?

MONKEY (*touching* LITUMA'*s head*). A miracle! He can think! I thought 'hee-haw' was the only thing asses could manage. (*Mockingly sympathetic.*) Aahh!

JOSEFINO. What do you think then, Einstein?

LITUMA. You beat her up every now and then, didn't you? Don't you beat every girl who's mad about you? I sometimes think you might have let things get out of hand, my friend.

JOSEFINO (*laughing*) Are you saying that I killed her? What a profound thought, Lituma.

MONKEY. But this little Gallinazo couldn't hurt a fly. He's all mouth and trousers. Just look at him, playing with his knife, acting like he's Mr Big. I could blow on him and he'd fall over. Look! (*Blows*). Fall over, will you! Don't make me look bad in front of my friends.

LITUMA (*very seriously, developing his idea*). You could have been jealous that Mechita spent the night with Chunga. You were furious. You'd been totally cleaned out that night, do you remember? You got home feeling like a wild beast. You needed to take it out on someone. Mechita was there and she took the rap. You could easily have let things get out of hand.

JOSEFINO (*amused*). And then I chopped her into little pieces and threw her in the river. Holy Shit, you're a genius, Lituma. (*To the absent* JOSE, *handing him the dice*.) At last, José, you've been chosen to win. The dice are yours.

LITUMA. Poor Meche. She didn't deserve a sonofabitch like you.

JOSEFINO. The things you have to put up with from your friends. If you weren't one of the Boys, I'd cut off your balls and feed them to the dogs.

MONKEY. Aahh! You big bully! What have the little doggies done to make you want to poison them?

   JOSE *returns to his seat, as discreetly as he left it. At the same time, and with the other three Boys equally unaware of any movement,* LITUMA *gets up and leaves the table.*

JOSEFINO. Why have you gone so quiet, pal?

JOSE. I'm losing and I don't feel like talking. OK, now my luck's going to change. (*Picks up the dice and blows on them. Puts a banknote on the table.*) There's a hundred sols. Who's game? (*Addressing* LITUMA*'s chair, as if he were still there.*) Lituma?

In the following two scenes JOSE, MONKEY *and* JOSEFINO *act as if* LITUMA *were still at the table. But* LITUMA *is now at the foot of the little staircase, looking up at* LA CHUNGA*'s bedroom, which is now lit up.*

IV

Pimping

LA CHUNGA *and* MECHE *are dressed. There is no trace of them having taken off their clothes and made love. Both behave very differently from the previous scene that they acted out.* MECHE *is sitting on the bed, slightly distressed, and*

LA CHUNGA, *who stands in front of her, no longer seems sensual and domineering but more enigmatic and Machiavellian.*

MECHE (*lights a cigarette and takes a deep drag, trying to conceal her uneasiness*). You must be dreaming if you think he's ever going to give you back those three thousand sols.

LA CHUNGA. I know he won't give them back. I don't care.

MECHE (*scrutinising her, intrigued*). Do you think I believe that, Chunga? That I don't know what a moneygrubber you are? You work day and night like a dog just to rake in more cash.

LA CHUNGA. I mean, *in this case*, it doesn't bother me. And it's helped you out, hasn't it? If I hadn't given him that money, Josefino would've taken out all his anger on you.

MECHE. Yes. He would have beaten me. Whenever something goes wrong, whenever he gets angry, I'm the one who takes the rap. (*Pause.*) One of these days he's going to kill me.

LA CHUNGA. So why are you still with him, you fool.

MECHE. I don't know . . . Maybe that's why. Because I'm a fool.

LA CHUNGA. Do you love him even though he beats you?

MECHE. I don't really know if I love him any more. I did in the beginning. Now perhaps it's only fear that stops me leaving him. Chunga, he's . . . a brute. There are times, even when I haven't done anything, when he makes me kneel in front of him like he were a god. He takes out his knife and presses it here. 'Be grateful you're still alive,' he says. 'Your life is only on loan, always remember that.'

LA CHUNGA. And you're still with him? Women can be so stupid. I'll never understand how anyone could stoop so low.

MECHE. Then you've never been in love.

LA CHUNGA. And never will be. I prefer to live without a man, alone, like a cactus. No-one's ever going to force me to my knees. Or tell me my life's only on loan.

MECHE. Ah, if only it were possible to break free from Josefino . . .

LA CHUNGA (*starting a game in which the spider lures the fly into her web*). But you can, you fool. (*Smiling*

mischievously.) Have you forgotten how pretty you are?
Don't you realise what you do to men when you walk past?
Don't their heads turn? Don't they flirt with you? Don't they
make passes at you when he can't hear?

MECHE. Yes. If I'd wanted to, I could have been unfaithful a
thousand times. I've had many opportunities.

LA CHUNGA. Of course you have. But perhaps you never
noticed your *best* opportunity.

MECHE (*surprised*). What are you talking about?

LA CHUNGA. Someone who's crazy about you. Someone
who would do whatever you asked him, just so he could be
with you. Because, to him, you're the most beautiful, most
precious woman alive – a queen, a goddess. You can have
him at your feet, Meche. He'll never treat you badly or make
you feel afraid.

MECHE. Who are you talking about?

LA CHUNGA. Haven't you noticed? I suppose it's possible.
He's very shy with women . . .

MECHE. Now I know why you gave Josefino those three
thousand sols. You're not a dyke. You're a pimp, Chunga.

LA CHUNGA (*laughing, cordially*). Did you think I was going
to pay three thousand sols just to make love to you? No,
Mechita, no man or woman's worth that much to me. Those
three thousand sols aren't mine. They belong to the man
who loves you. Just to have you, he's prepared to spend
everything he's got and more. Be nice to him. Remember
you promised to do whatever I told you. Now's your chance
to get your own back on Josefino for all those beatings.
Make the most of it. (*LITUMA has climbed the little
staircase and is standing in the bedroom doorway, not
daring to go in. LA CHUNGA goes out to get him.*) Go in,
go in. She's there waiting for you. She's all yours. I've
spoken to her, don't worry. Go on, Lituma, don't be afraid.
She's all yours, enjoy it.

*With a mocking little laugh, she goes down from the
bedroom to sit in her rocking chair. The Boys continue
gambling and drinking.*

V

A Romantic Love Affair

MECHE (*amazed*). You! You're the last person I expected.
Monkey or José, perhaps. They're always flirting with me,
and when Josefino isn't looking, they go even further. But
you, Lituma, you've never said a single word to me.

LITUMA (*profoundly troubled*). I've never dared, Mechita. I,
well, I've always hidden my feelings for you. But, but, I . . .

MECHE (*amused at his embarrassment and awkwardness*).
You're sweating, your voice is trembling. You're so
embarrassed, it's painful. Ay, you are funny, Lituma!

LITUMA (*imploring*). Don't laugh at me, Meche. For the love
of God, please don't.

MECHE. Have you always been frightened of women?

LITUMA (*very distressed*). Not frightened. It's more . . . I
don't know how to talk to them. I'm not like the others.
When they want a girl, they know exactly what to say. But
I've never known. I get nervous, the words don't come out
right.

MECHE. Have you ever had a girlfriend?

LITUMA. Not for free, Mechita. Only the harlots at the Casa
Verde. I've always had to pay.

MECHE. Just like you're paying for me now.

LITUMA (*kneeling down in front of* MECHE). Don't ever
compare yourself to a harlot Mechita, even as a joke.

MECHE. What are you doing?

LITUMA. I'd never make you kneel in front of me like
Josefino does. I'd spend my life on my knees before you.
You're a goddess to me. (*He crouches down and tries to kiss
her feet.*)

MECHE. You look like a dog in that position.

LITUMA (*still trying to kiss her feet*). Then let me be that for
you, too. Your dog, Mechita. I'll obey you. I'll be loving
when you want or I'll stay very, very quiet if you prefer.
Don't laugh; I mean it.

MECHE. Would you really do anything for me?

LITUMA. Try me.

MECHE. Would you kill Josefino if I asked you to?

LITUMA. Yes.

MECHE. But he's your friend?

LITUMA. You're worth more to me than any friend. Please believe me, Mechita.

MECHE (*runs her hand through his hair as if she were stroking an animal*). Come and sit down. I don't want anyone to grovel to me like that.

LITUMA (*sits beside her on the bed without daring to approach too close, let alone to touch her*). I've been in love with you from the first day I saw you. In the Bar Río, on the Puente Viejo. Do you remember? No, why should you remember. You never seem to notice me, even when you look straight at me.

MECHE. In the Río Bar?

LITUMA. José, Monkey and I were in the middle of a game and Josefino came in with you on his arm. (*Mimicking him*). 'Check out what I've found. What do you think of this little pussy?' And he lifted you up by the waist and showed you off to everyone. (*Frowns.*) I can't stand it when he treats you like that.

MECHE. Are you jealous of him?

LITUMA. It's more that I wish I could be like him. (*Pause.*) Tell me, Mechita. Does he really have one this big? Is that why all the girls are so mad about him? He never stops bragging to us: 'I'm hung like a donkey.' But I've asked the harlots in the Casa Verde and they say he's lying, that he's got a normal one.

MECHE. You're not going to get very far with me with filth like that, Lituma.

LITUMA. Sorry. You're right, I shouldn't have asked you about that. But don't you think it's unfair? Josefino treats girls like an animal. He kicks them around, wins their heart, and when they've become totally hooked on him, he turns them into whores. Yet he still gets any girl he wants. Then look at me: I'm a nice guy, I'm romantic, I'd treat a woman who loved me like cut glass. But girls don't even look at me. Is that fair?

MECHE. Perhaps it isn't fair. But is anything in life fair?

LITUMA. Is it because I'm ugly that they don't look at me, Mechita?

MECHE (*making fun of him*). Let's see, turn round, let me look at you. No, you're not ugly, Lituma.

LITUMA. Please be serious. I'm telling you things I've never told anyone before.

MECHE (*watches him for a moment, suspicious*). You fell in love with me the first time you saw me?

LITUMA (*nods*). I couldn't sleep all night. In the darkness, I kept seeing you and saying to myself: 'She's the loveliest woman I've ever seen. Women like that exist only in movies.' I got so worked up I started crying, Mechita. You don't know how many nights I lay awake thinking about you.

MECHE. And you say you don't know how to talk to women. What you're saying to me is lovely.

LITUMA (*puts his hand into his pocket and takes out a small photograph*). Look. I always carry you around with me.

MECHE. Where did you get this photo from?

LITUMA. I stole it from Josefino. It looks faded because I've kissed it so much.

MECHE (*strokes his head again*). Why didn't you ever say anything to me, silly?

LITUMA. We still have time, don't we? Marry me, Mechita. Let's get out of Piura. Let's start a new life.

MECHE. But you're broke, Lituma. Like all the Boys. And you've never done a day's work in your life.

LITUMA. That's because I didn't have anyone to push me, to make me change the way I lived. You don't think I like being one of the Boys, do you? Let's get married and you'll see how different I'll be, Mechita. I'll work hard, at whatever. You'll have everything you ever wanted.

MECHE. Would we go to Lima?

LITUMA. Lima, yes. Or wherever you want.

MECHE. I've always wanted to go to Lima. It's such a big city, Josefino would never find us.

LITUMA. Of course he wouldn't. Anyway, who cares if he does find us? Are you afraid of him?

MECHE. Yes.

LITUMA. With me, you wouldn't be. He's all bark and no bite. I've known him since we were little kids. He's not a Mangache like us – he's a Gallinazo. Gallinazos are all talk.

MECHE. He's not just talk with me. Sometimes he beats me unconscious. If I left him and went off with you, he'd kill me.

LITUMA. Rubbish, Mechita. He'd find himself another woman in no time. Let's go to Lima. Tonight.

MECHE (*tempted*). Tonight?

LITUMA. On the night bus from the Cruz de Chalpón. Let's go.

MECHE. Will we get married?

LITUMA. Once we're in Lima, I swear. It's the first thing we'll do. Are you game? Shall we go?

MECHE (*pause*). Let's go. We'll never come back to Piura. I hope I won't live to regret this, Lituma.

LITUMA (*kneels again*). You won't, Mechita, I swear. Thank you, thank you. Ask me for something, anything, tell me to do something.

MECHE. Get up, we're wasting time. Go and pack your bags and buy the tickets. Wait for me at the Cruz de Chalpón bus station. It's half way up Avenida Grau, isn't it? I'll be there by midnight.

LITUMA. Where are you going?

MECHE. I can't just leave without anything. I'm going to fetch my things. Some essentials anyway.

LITUMA. I'll come with you.

MECHE. No, there's no need. Josefino's in the Casa Verde and he never gets back till dawn. I've got masses of time. No-one must see us together. No-one must suspect a thing.

LITUMA (*kissing her hands*). Mechita, my darling Mechita. I'm so happy, it can't be real. (*Crosses himself, looks up to heaven.*) Thank you, God, thank you. Now I'm going to change, I'll stop being a bum, no more gambling, no more lazing around. I swear I'll . . .

MECHE (*pushing him*). Come on, hurry up, we're wasting time, Lituma. Run, run.

LITUMA. Yes, yes, anything you say, Mechita.

> LITUMA *gets up hastily, running, rushing down the*
> *staircase, but half-way down he loses momentum, slows*
> *down, and his frenzy is extinguished. Heavily, slowly and*
> *sadly, he returns to the gambling table without the Boys*
> *stirring. The dice, the toasts and the oaths are again the*
> *centre of attention.*

VI

Fantasies on a Crime

MONKEY. Why not? Lituma's right, it could have happened like that. Close your eyes and imagine Mechita. She rushes into the house, frantically looking this way and that. Her buttocks are stuck together, tight with fear.

JOSE. She starts throwing things into her suitcase, trembling all over, stumbling, packing all the wrong things, terrified Mr Big might come back. She's so scared the tips of her little tits have turned hard as rocks. Mmm, yummy!

JOSEFINO (*laughing*). And? Carry on. What happens then?

LITUMA. Then you get there. Before she's finished packing.

JOSEFINO. And I kill her because I catch her packing?

MONKEY. That would just be your excuse. Actually, you were pissed off with the whole world. Remember I'd won so much off you that night, you were cleaned out. Holy Whore! I hope I get dice like that again!

JOSE. Or maybe you had a fit of jealousy. Meche could've told you that Chunga had made her so happy, she was going to live with her.

JOSEFINO. I wouldn't have killed her for that. I'd have probably sent flowers to Chunga. And a card saying: 'You win. Congratulations.' After all, I am a fucking gentleman.

LA CHUNGA (*from her rocking chair, yawning*). It's nearly midnight and I'm tired. Last orders.

LITUMA. Quiet, Chunga, you're spoiling my line of thought. When you see the half-packed suitcase, you ask her: 'Travelling far, are we?' And she says: 'I'm leaving you.'

JOSEFINO. Why would she leave me? She was totally hooked on me.

LITUMA (*serious and concentrating hard, not listening to* JOSEFINO). 'I'm leaving you because I'm in love with a better man than you.'

JOSEFINO. Better than me? And where did she dig up this gem?

LITUMA. 'Someone who won't beat me, who'll be faithful and kind to me, someone who's not a bastard and a pimp, but who's decent and honest. HE also wants to marry me.'

JOSEFINO. How unimaginative, Boys. You can't even invent a good reason for me to have killed Mechita.

LITUMA. Because she betrayed you, Josefino. Like Judas betrayed his master. So you laid into her, like an animal. Perhaps you only meant to give her a beating. But you let things get out of hand and that was the end of the poor thing.

JOSEFINO. And what the fuck did I do with the body?

MONKEY. You could have thrown it in the river.

JOSEFINO. It was September and the River Piura was dry. So what did I do with the body? Come on! Guess how I pulled off this perfect crime.

JOSE. You buried it in the dunes behind your house.

MONKEY. You threw it to those German dogs that guard Señor Beckman's warehouse. They would have finished her off, bones and all.

JOSE. Well, I'm bored by these detective games. Let's go for a drink in the Casa Verde instead.

JOSEFINO. Why go so far when you've got Chunga right here. Go on, give him what he wants.

LA CHUNGA. Why doesn't your mother give him what he wants, Josefino.

JOSEFINO. Don't mess with my mother, Chunga. That's one thing I won't stand.

LA CHUNGA. Then don't mess with me.

MONKEY. Ignore him, Chunguita, you know he's not a Mangache like us – he's a Gallinazo.

JOSE. It's a pity you're always so tetchy, Chunguita. Even with us. You know we love you, you're like a lucky mascot to us.

MONKEY (*gets up, without his friends noticing, and goes over to* LA CHUNGA). These jokers are always giving you a hard time, aren't they Chunga? Forgive them for they know not what they do. But I am always well-behaved when I'm with you. I hope you've noticed that. I never get on your nerves and I don't make fun of you. I don't follow the pack when they're annoying you. I love you dearly, Chunga.

LA CHUNGA (*looking at him compassionately*). You don't have to play that good-little-boy game with me. What's the point? I'm going to give you a good time no matter what you do. Come on, give me your hand.

She takes his hand and leads him to the staircase. She goes up with him. MONKEY *is happy, his eyes sparkle like a little boy about to realise a great wish he has harboured for a long time. The Boys continue playing as though* MONKEY *is still with them.*

VII

A Naughty Little Boy

MECHE. Hi, Monkey.

MONKEY. Hi, Mechita.

LA CHUNGA. Come in, don't be afraid, we're not going to beat you.

MONKEY. I know you're very good people.

MECHE. Come and sit down, next to me.

MONKEY *sits down on the bed next to* MECHE *and* LA CHUNGA *sits down on the other side. The two women behave as if* MONKEY *were a spoilt child, and he too, in his gestures and expression, seems to have regressed to infancy. He lets out a sigh. Another one. It appears something is tormenting him, something that he wants to share with them, but doesn't dare.*

LA CHUNGA. Relax. You can trust us. What do you feel like doing? You're the boss here, you know. Ask anything.

MECHE. We're here to give you whatever pleasure you desire. What would turn you on?

LA CHUNGA. Do you want us to do a strip-tease for you, Monkey?

MECHE. Shall we dance naked, the two of us together, just for you?

MONKEY (*hiding his face, scandalised*). No! No! Please!

LA CHUNGA (*pointing to the bed*). Would you like it if we went to bed together, all three of us, with you in the middle?

MECHE. Shall we touch and stroke you until you shout 'Stop! Stop! I can't take any more.'

LA CHUNGA. Do you want us to pose for you?

MONKEY (*laughing, very nervous*). Don't joke like that! It embarrasses me. Please don't! (*Overcome by a fit of sadness.*) You're the best people I know, Chunga, Mechita. I'm sorry for getting like this, but I'm not like you. I'm . . . I'm a shit.

LA CHUNGA. Don't say that. It's not true

MECHE. A bit of a clown, perhaps. But deep down you're a good kid, Monkey.

MONKEY. You're wrong. I'm very bad. One of the worst little boys around. You can't tell me I'm not. You don't know me. If I told you . . .

LA CHUNGA. Well, tell us then.

MECHE. Do you want us to comfort you? Is that it?

MONKEY. I don't want to make you do anything. Only if you insist . . .

LA CHUNGA (*makes him rest his head in her lap. MONKEY curls up like a frightened child*). Come, rest your head here. Make yourself comfortable.

MECHE (*in a soft, caressing voice*). Tell us, Monkey.

MONKEY (*nervously, making a great effort*). I didn't even understand what I was doing. I was very small, just a boy in short trousers.

LA CHUNGA. Are you talking about what happened with the little girl? Doña Jesusa's little girl, your neighbour?

MONKEY. I was just a boy. Surely a boy can't reason for himself?

MECHE. Of course not, Monkey. Well, carry on. I'll help you. You were spying, waiting for Doña Jesusa to go to the market, to her vegetable stall . . .

LA CHUNGA. And when she'd gone out, you went into her house without anyone seeing you. You jumped over the cane fence by the banana plantation, wasn't that it?

MONKEY. Yes. And there was the little girl, crouching down, milking the goat. She was squeezing its little tits. Like this! And she didn't have any knickers on, Chunga! I swear to you!

MECHE. Of course we believe you. So you saw everything then?

MONKEY. It was more like she showed me everything, Mechita. Well, why else wouldn't she have had any knickers on? Why else? She wanted people to see her privates, she wanted to show them off to the boys.

LA CHUNGA. Do you mean she provoked you, Monkey? Then you're not to blame for anything. She asked for it, the little tart.

MECHE. Was that what you wanted to tell us? That it was all the little girl's fault?

MONKEY. Well, no. I suppose it was me too, a bit. After all, I did sneak into Doña Jesusa's house. That's what burglars do, isn't it?

LA CHUNGA. But you didn't go there to steal anything, Monkey.

MONKEY. I just went to see the little girl.

MECHE. Did you want to see her with no clothes on?

MONKEY. I was just a kid, you know. I didn't understand. I couldn't tell the difference between right and wrong.

LA CHUNGA. But you were carrying a knife, this long. Do you remember, Monkey?

MONKEY. I remember.

MECHE. Didn't you feel sorry for the little girl? Not even when she smiled at you, thinking you were just monkeying around.

MONKEY (*disturbed*). I *was* just monkeying around! And she didn't have any knickers on, Meche. She provoked me. She . . .

LA CHUNGA (*telling him off, without great severity*). Tell the truth, Monkey, tell the truth. She did have knickers on. You made her take them off.

MECHE. By threatening to kill her. Yes or no, Monkey?

MONKEY. Well, perhaps. It's a long time ago now. I've forgotten.

LA CHUNGA. You liar! You haven't forgotten. You ripped off her dress and ordered her: 'Take down your knickers.' And when she did, you saw everything you wanted to see. Yes, Monkey?

MONKEY (*ashamed*). Yes, Chunguita,

MECHE. And you also fondled her, didn't you? You touched the little girl's body all over. Yes or no?

MONKEY (*anguished*). But I didn't rape her, Meche. I swear to God I didn't rape her.

LA CHUNGA. You didn't rape her? Then what did you do? Doesn't it all come to the same thing?

MONKEY (*laughing*). What do you mean the same thing! Don't be silly, Chunga. (*Lowering his voice conspiratorially, placing a finger to his lips, and going 'Shhhh, Shhhh' as if he were about to tell a great secret.*) I put it up her the back way. Do you understand? She stayed intact *where it mattered*. I didn't even make a scratch there. Her husband could have broken it on their wedding night. That's a very, very important difference. Ask Padre Garcia if you want. He told me: 'If the hymen was undamaged, I absolve you. But if it was broken, then there's no magic cure, you wretched child: you must marry Jesusa's little daughter.' Well I didn't marry her, you see, so . . . You women have your honour in that little piece of skin, in the hymen, and that's what you must defend tooth and nail. But we men have our honour in our ass, and the man who gets it up the back way, wham! He's buggered for ever. (LA CHUNGA *and* MECHE *look at him, derisive and silent, and he becomes forlorn and remorseful. He sits up.*) Yes, it's true. I know what you're thinking, and you're right. What I did to the little girl was very bad. I could fool Padre Garcia, but not you. I know that when I die God will punish me for it.

LA CHUNGA. Why wait so long, Monkey?

MECHE. *We* can punish you right now.

MONKEY (*takes off his belt and hands it to them. He gets into a position to be whipped*). All right. Take away the filth, make me pay for my sins. Have no pity on me. Destroy my honour, Chunga, Mechita.

LA CHUNGA and MECHE (*while they whip him*). Naughty little boy! You spoilt child! Beastly boy! You vile child! Nasty little boy! You wicked child! Pervert!

MONKEY *moans as he receives the blows, his body straining, sweating, with an enjoyment that culminates in a spasm.* MECHE *and* LA CHUNGA *sit down and watch him. Satiated but despondent, he stands up, wipes his brow, puts on his belt again and combs his hair. Without looking at them, he goes out of the bedroom. Discreetly,* MONKEY *takes his place at the Boys' table.*

LA CHUNGA. Are you going, Monkey? Without a goodbye? Not even a thank you?

MECHE. Come back when you want to tell us more of your sins, Monkey.

VIII

Two Girlfriends

As soon as MONKEY *has disappeared from the room,* MECHE *and* LA CHUNGA *change their demeanour, as if the previous scene had not occurred.*

LA CHUNGA. Some men hide it better than others. But once you scratch the surface, the mask peels off and the beast comes out.

MECHE. Do you think all men are like that, Chunga? Do they all have something dirty to hide?

LA CHUNGA. Yes, all the ones I know do.

MECHE. Are women any better?

LA CHUNGA. At least what we have between our legs doesn't turn us into devils.

MECHE (*touching her stomach*). Then I hope it's a girl.

LA CHUNGA. Are you pregnant?

MECHE. My period's two months late.

LA CHUNGA. Haven't you been to see anyone?

MECHE. I'm scared they'll tell me I am.

LA CHUNGA. Don't you want it?

MECHE. Of course I do. But Josefino doesn't. If I am pregnant he'll make me have an abortion. He's not going to let any woman tie him down with a child.

LA CHUNGA. For once, I think he's right there. It's not worth the trouble of bringing more people into this world. What do you want a kid for? So he can grow up to be like one of *them*?

MECHE. If everyone thought like that, life would come to an end.

LA CHUNGA. It can end tomorrow morning, for all I care.

Pause.

MECHE. You know something, Chunga? I don't think you're really as bitter as you're trying to make me believe.

LA CHUNGA. I'm not trying to make you believe anything.

MECHE. If you were that bitter, I wouldn't be here. (*With a twinkle in her eye.*) You wouldn't have given Josefino those three thousand sols to spend the night with me. Besides . . .

LA CHUNGA. Besides what?

MECHE (*pointing to the bed*). When you were holding me just now, you said some very sweet things. That I made you feel as if you were in heaven. That you were happy. Were you lying?

LA CHUNGA. No. That was true.

MECHE. Well then, life isn't so ugly after all. It has its good things. (*Laughs.*) I'm glad to be one of those good things that life has to offer you, Chunga. (*Pause.*) Can I ask you something?

LA CHUNGA. If it's how many women have been here before, you'd better not. Because I won't tell you.

MECHE. No, it's not that. But, could you fall in love with me, Chunga? Like a man does with a woman? Could you love me?

LA CHUNGA. I wouldn't fall in love with you or with anyone else.

MECHE. I don't believe you, Chunga. You can't live without love. What would life be worth if you didn't love anyone, if you weren't loved by anyone?

LA CHUNGA. A woman who falls in love becomes weak. She allows herself to be dominated. (*Looks at her in silence for a while.*) *You* think it's something good now. Let's talk again when you see what Josefino does with your love. Let's talk again when you're in the Casa Verde.

MECHE. Why do you keep frightening me with that?

LA CHUNGA. Because I know where you'll end up. He's got you right under his thumb, he already does what he likes with you. He'll start by lending you to one of the Boys, on a night like tonight, when he's drunk. Then he'll tell you a fairy-story of what you could do together if you had more money – buy a little house, go travelling, get married. And he'll end up persuading you to whore for him.

MECHE. When you say things like that to me, I don't know if you're doing it out of kindness or cruelty. If you want to help me, or if you just like scaring me.

LA CHUNGA. I want to help you.

MECHE. Why? Because you're in love with me? You just told me you weren't. Why would you want to help me? You let everything wash over you. You couldn't give a damn about anyone else.

LA CHUNGA (*looks at her, pondering*). You're right. I don't know why I'm giving you advice. What should your life matter to me.

MECHE. Have you given advice to any of Josefino's other conquests?

LA CHUNGA. No. (*Watches* MECHE. *Takes her chin in her hand and forces her to look into her eyes, bringing her face very close to* MECHE's.) Perhaps I feel sorrier for you than I did for the others. Only because you're prettier. There's another thing that's unfair in life. If you didn't look the way you do, I certainly wouldn't give a damn about you.

MECHE. You're a monster sometimes, Chunga.

LA CHUNGA. That's because you won't see life as it is. It's life that's monstrous. Not me.

MECHE. If life's how you say it is, I'd prefer to stay the way I am. Not to think about the future. But just live for the moment. And let God's will be done. (*Deeply troubled, she looks down at her belly.*)

LA CHUNGA. Perhaps you'll work that miracle: make a 'new man' of Josefino.

MECHE. You know that won't happen.

LA CHUNGA. No. It won't happen.

MECHE (*lets her head rest against* LA CHUNGA'*s shoulder. But* LA CHUNGA *doesn't put her arms around her*). I'd like to be a strong woman, like you. To believe in myself, to be able to fend for myself. (*Pause. Half-smiling.*) But if *I* didn't have someone to look after me, I don't know what I'd do.

LA CHUNGA. You're not a cripple, are you?

MECHE. I can hardly read, Chunga. Who would ever give me work? Except as a servant. Working morning, day, and night, sweeping, ironing, washing the filth off those lily-whites of Piura? I just couldn't do it.

Pause.

LA CHUNGA. If I'd known you might be pregnant, I wouldn't have made love to you.

MECHE. Do pregnant women disgust you?

LA CHUNGA. Yes. (*Pause.*) Did it disturb you, what we did?

MECHE. Did it disturb me? I don't know. I don't . . .

LA CHUNGA. Tell me the truth.

MECHE. Yes, a bit, at first. I felt like laughing. After all, you're not a man, are you? I thought it wasn't for real, that it was a game. I was trying not to laugh, at first.

LA CHUNGA. If you had laughed . . .

MECHE. You'd have hit me?

LA CHUNGA. Yes, I might have hit you.

MECHE. And you said it was only men who were turned into devils by what's between their legs.

LA CHUNGA. Perhaps I *am* a man.

MECHE. No you're not. You're a woman. And a desirable woman, if you wanted to be.

LA CHUNGA. I don't want to be desirable. No-one would respect me if I were.

MECHE. Are you annoyed by what I said?

LA CHUNGA. That you were trying not to laugh? No, I asked you to tell me the truth. (*Pause*)

MECHE. I want you to know something, Chunga. Although I'm not a dyke – sorry – like you, I mean, I've become very fond of you. I would like it if we could be friends.

LA CHUNGA. Leave Piura, will you. Don't be a fool. Can't you see you're almost hooked? Before Josefino really savages you, get out of here. Go far away. You still have time. (*Takes hold of* MECHE's *face.*) I'll help you.

MECHE. Will you really, Chunga?

LA CHUNGA. Yes. (*Puts her hand to* MECHE's *face again, and strokes her.*) I don't want to see you rot in the Casa Verde, being passed from one drunk to another . . . Go on, take my advice, go to Lima.

MECHE. What will I do in Lima? I don't know anyone there.

LA CHUNGA. Learn to believe in yourself. But don't be stupid. Don't fall in love. Love distracts you, and there's no hope for a distracted woman. Let men fall in love with you. But never you with them. Look for some security, a better life than the one you have. And always remember: deep down, all men are like Josefino. If you start to give them affection, you've no hope.

MECHE. Don't talk like that, Chunga. You know, when you say things like that you remind me of him?

LA CHUNGA. Maybe Josefino and I are the same.

As if the mention of his name had been a summons,
JOSEFINO *gets up from the Boys' table. He goes up the little staircase.*

IX

Mr Big

Although MECHE *remains in the room and watches the following dialogue with interest,* JOSEFINO *and* LA CHUNGA *behave as if she is not there.*

JOSEFINO. Hi, Chunga. (*Looks around, casting his eye over* MECHE, *without seeing her.*) I've come for Meche.

LA CHUNGA. She's gone.

JOSEFINO. So soon? You could have held on to her a little bit longer. (*With a snigger*) Squeeze out all your money's worth. (LA CHUNGA *just watches him with that scolding and disgusted look she always gives him.*) So how was she? What was it like?

LA CHUNGA. What was what like?

JOSEFINO. Mechita. Was she worth it?

LA CHUNGA. You've been drinking all night haven't you? You stink from head to foot.

JOSEFINO. What else could I do, Chunguita? You'd taken away my baby. Well, tell me. How was Meche?

LA CHUNGA. I'm not going to tell you. That wasn't in the agreement.

JOSEFINO (*laughing*). You're right. Next time I'll have to put in a special clause. (*Pause.*) Why don't you like me, Chunga? Don't lie, I know you think I'm evil.

LA CHUNGA. I shan't lie to you. It's true. I've always thought you were a nasty piece of work.

JOSEFINO. Well, I've always had a soft spot for you. Seriously, Chunga.

LA CHUNGA (*laughing*). Are you going to try and conquer me as well? Go on. Show me what techniques you use on those poor idiots.

JOSEFINO. No, I'm not going to try and conquer you. (*Undressing her with his eyes.*) It's not that I don't want to, I assure you. I like you as a woman. But I know when I'm not going to get anywhere with a girl. I'd be wasting my time with you, you would never let me try it on. And I've never wasted my time with women.

LA CHUNGA. Right, then get out of here.

JOSEFINO. Let's talk first. I want to make you a proposition. A business proposition.

LA CHUNGA. Business? You and me?

JOSEFINO (*sits down on the bed and lights a cigarette. He has clearly thought long and hard about what he is going to say*). I don't want to stay the way I am, Chunga. Being one of the Boys and that. I've got ambitions. Fuck! I want to have cash, drink well, smoke well, wear lily-white Chinese silk suits. I want to travel the world, have my own car, a

house, servants. I want to live like the white folks do,
Chunga. That's what you want as well, isn't it? That's why
you work night and day like a slave, that's what you're
destroying your soul for. Because you want another life, a
life you can only enjoy if you have the cash. Let's become
partners, Chunguita. You and I could do great things
together.

LA CHUNGA. I already know what your proposition's going
to be.

JOSEFINO. All the better, then.

LA CHUNGA. The answer is no.

JOSEFINO. You're being narrow-minded. What's the
difference between a bar and a brothel? I'll tell you: here
you earn a few sols; in a brothel you would earn millions.
(*Standing up, gesturing, pacing round the room.*) I've got it
all worked out, Chunga. We can start with four little
bedrooms. They can be built out there, behind the kitchen, in
that yard where you leave the rubbish. We'll keep it simple,
just cane walls and straw mats. I'll take charge of the girls.
All first class, guaranteed. The Casa Verde takes fifty
percent off its girls. We'll only take forty; that way we'll be
able to pull whoever we want. Only a few to start with.
Quality rather than quantity. I'll take care of discipline and
you can do the administration. (*Anxious and vehement.*)
We'll get rich, Chunguita.

LA CHUNGA. If I'd wanted to set up a brothel, I'd have done
it already. Why would I need you?

JOSEFINO. For the girls. Call me what you like, but in this
field, haven't I proved myself? I'm the best there is. I'll get
first class girls who haven't worked before. Virgins even,
you'll see! Fifteen or sixteen year-olds. That'll drive the
clients crazy, Chunga. We'll attract all Piura's whiteboys,
ready to pay fortunes. Girls who can be initiated, brand new
ones . . .

LA CHUNGA. Like Meche.

JOSEFINO (*laughs lewdly*). Well, Meche isn't exactly brand
new . . . We'll make her the star attraction, of course. I
swear to you, Chunga, I'll get girls as good, even better than
Meche.

LA CHUNGA. And what if they don't want to work?

JOSEFINO. That's my affair. I don't know much, but I do know how to teach a girl that what God gave her is a winning lottery ticket. I've earnt the Casa Verde a fortune by bringing them women. What for? Fuck! For a few measly tips. Well, enough's enough, and now I want to be a capitalist as well. What do you say, Chunguita?

LA CHUNGA. I've already told you. No.

JOSEFINO. Why, Chunga? Don't you trust me?

LA CHUNGA. Of course I don't trust you. The day after we went into business together, you'd start fiddling the accounts.

JOSEFINO. I swear to God, I wouldn't, Chunga. You can handle all the money. I accept that. You can take charge of the agreements with the girls, and decide on the percentages. I won't touch a sol. You'd have a free hand. We'll do whatever you decide. What more do you want? Don't look a gifthorse in the mouth.

LA CHUNGA. You'll never be anyone's gifthorse, Josefino. And certainly not a woman's. In fact, you're a Trojan horse to any woman gullible enough to believe what you say.

JOSEFINO. So you're being self-righteous, Chunguita? I have never pointed a gun at any woman's head. I simply convince them of one truth. That in one night in the Casa Verde they can earn more money than working in the market for six months. Isn't that the truth? Fuck! Thanks to me, some of those girls live better than we do.

LA CHUNGA. It's not out of self-righteousness that I don't want to be your partner. I don't feel sorry for them. If they were idiotic enough to let you try it on, they deserve whatever they get.

JOSEFINO. I don't like the way you're talking to me, Chunga. I came here peacefully, to make you an honest business proposition. And you insult me. What if I lose my temper? Do you know what might happen if I lose my temper? Or do you think a dyke like you can put up a fight against me? (*He becomes increasingly angry as he speaks.*) The truth is I'm fed up with this high-and- mighty, jumped up, sonofabitch act you're playing. Fuck! Enough's enough. I'm going to teach you a lesson. You've had this coming for some time. No woman looks down her nose at me, let alone a dyke.

He takes out his knife and threatens LA CHUNGA, *as if she were still in front of him. But, in reality,* LA CHUNGA *has discreetly moved beside* MECHE. *Both look at* JOSEFINO *who carries on talking and threatening an invisible* LA CHUNGA.

JOSEFINO. Now how do you feel, dyke? Scared, aren't you? Pissing yourself, huh? Well, you're about to see how I deal with disobedient women. There's nothing I like more than a girl who's disobedient to me. It turns me on, you see. Down on your fucking knees! Fuck! Do what I say – unless you want a crossword drawn on your face. On your knees, I said! It's because you own this filthy pigsty that you're so jumped up, isn't it? Because of all the centavos you've scrounged exploiting us poor bastards who come and drink your beers and put up with your bad temper? Do you think I don't know who you are? Fuck! Do you think all Piura doesn't know you were born in the Casa Verde? Among the whores, the screwing, and the stink of douches. Keep still! Stay on your knees or I'll cut you to shreds, you shit. That's what you are, Chunga. A child of the Casa Verde. A whore's bastard. Don't put on airs with me, I know too well where you come from. Now, suck. Suck or die. Obey your man. Suck. Slow and gentle. Get used to being my whore. (*For some time,* JOSEFINO *mimes the scene, sweating, trembling, caressed by the invisible* LA CHUNGA.) Now, swallow what you've got in your mouth. It's my birthday present. (*Laughs, now satisfied, even a little bored.*) They say it's good for the complexion. Were you scared? Did you think I'd kill you? Don't be a twat. I'm not capable of killing a woman; deep down, I'm a fucking gentleman, Chunguita. I respect the weaker sex. It's a game, you see? It gets my blood flowing. I get a kick out of it. You must have your little games too. As we get to know each other better, you can tell me about them, and I'll indulge you. I'm not one of those guys who thinks a girl shouldn't have a good time, that if you teach them how to come, they'll start cheating on you. That's what José and Monkey think, for instance. But I don't. I'm fair. A girl has the right; well, why shouldn't she? Let's make it up, Chunguita? Don't be spiteful. Let's be friends. Shake on it, like the kids do. (LA CHUNGA *has materialised again next to* JOSEFINO.) So, you on for that deal? We'd get rich, I swear.

LA CHUNGA. We wouldn't get rich. We might do better than I'm doing now. But I'd certainly end up losing. Sooner or

later, you'd make me feel that you were the stronger, like
you did a moment ago. And whenever I disagreed with you,
you'd get out your knife, your fists, your boots. You'd end
up winning. I'd rather die poor than get rich with you.

JOSEFINO (*goes to rejoin the Boys at the gambling table*). My
God, women can be so stupid.

X

The End of the Party

Long pause while MECHE *and* LA CHUNGA *watch*
JOSEFINO *go down the staircase and take his seat again.*

MECHE. Chunga, can I go now? It's nearly daybreak. It must
be around six, no?

LA CHUNGA. Yes, you can go. Don't you want to sleep a
little first?

MECHE. If you don't mind, I'd rather go.

LA CHUNGA. I don't mind.

They go down the stairs together and head towards the exit.
They stop by the rocking chair. The Boys have finished their
beers and are playing, yawning occasionally, without seeing
the two women.

MECHE (*slightly hesitant*). If you want me to come back, to
stay here with you, at night, I mean . . .

LA CHUNGA. Of course I'd like to spend another night
together.

MECHE. Well, that's fine. I don't mind, Chunga. I even . . .

LA CHUNGA. Wait, let me finish. I'd like to, but I won't. I
don't want to spend another night with you, and I don't want
you to come back here, ever.

MECHE. Why Chunga? What have I done?

LA CHUNGA (*watches her silently for a moment and then*
draws her face towards her, as on previous occasions).
Because you're very pretty. Because I like you and because
you've made me care about you, and about your future.
That's as dangerous for me as falling in love, Meche. I've
told you before: I can't allow myself to be distracted. I'd
lose the war. That's why I never want to see you here again.

MECHE. I don't understand what you're saying, Chunga.

LA CHUNGA. I know you don't understand. Never mind.

MECHE. Are you angry with me about something?

LA CHUNGA. No, I'm not angry about anything. (*Hands her some money.*) Here. It's a present. For you, not for Josefino. Don't give it to him, and don't tell him I gave it to you.

MECHE (*confused*). No I won't tell him anything. (*Hides the money in her clothing.*) I feel bad taking your money. I feel like . . . (*Pause.*)

LA CHUNGA. A whore? Well, get used to it, in case you work in the Casa Verde. By the way . . . Do you know what you're going to do with your life? (MECHE *is about to reply, but* LA CHUNGA *puts her hand over her mouth.*) Don't say it. I don't want to know. It's up to you if you stay in Piura or if you go. Don't tell me. Tonight I wanted to help you, but tomorrow's another day. You won't be here and everything will be different. If you tell me where you're going, and Josefino sticks a knife to my neck, I'll end up telling him everything. I already told you I don't want to lose the war. But if I get killed, that's the end of the war. Go on, think about it, make up your mind and do what you think best. But if you do go, whatever you do don't even think about telling me or writing to me, or letting me know where you are. All right?

MECHE. All right, Chunga. Bye then.

LA CHUNGA. Bye, Meche. Good luck.

MECHE *goes out of the house.* LA CHUNGA *goes back and sits down in her rocking chair. She is in the same position as she was when the curtain rose at the beginning of the play. The Boys' voices can be heard, beneath their cigarette smoke. Long pause.*

LA CHUNGA (*emphatically*). Right! Pay up and go. I'm closing.

MONKEY. Just five minutes more, Chunga.

LA CHUNGA. Not a second more, I said. You're going right now. I'm tired.

LITUMA (*getting up*). I'm tired too. Anyway, I'm down to my last centavo.

JOSE. Yes, let's get out of here. The night's got sad.

MONKEY. But first let's sing the farewell song, Boys.

MONKEY, JOSE, LITUMA, and JOSEFINO (*singing, heavily, as at the end of a party*).
The four of us are called the Boys
We get our kicks from simple joys.
And throughout Piura it's been said
Every girl needs a Boy in her bed
So don't tell us to get off our asses
We're doing just fine in front of our glasses.

MONKEY. Enough of this shit, let's cough up and split.

MONKEY, JOSE, LITUMA, and JOSEFINO. Goodbye, Chunguita!

They get up and head towards the rocking chair. LA CHUNGA *stands up to take the money for the beers. Between them, they give it to her.*

JOSE (*before crossing the threshold, as if completing a ritual*). Tomorrow will you tell me what happened that time with Mechita, Chunga?

LA CHUNGA (*closing the door in his face*). Go ask your mother about it.

Outside the Boys laugh, celebrating crudely. LA CHUNGA *bolts the door. She puts out the kerosene lamp that hangs over the table where the Boys were playing. Sleepily, she goes up to her room. She looks very tired. She collapses on the bed, hardly taking off her sandals.*

LA CHUNGA'S VOICE. See you in the morning, Mechita.

Curtain.

INTERVIEW WITH MARIO VARGAS LLOSA

SD: What led you to write *Mistress of Desires*?

MVL: When I wrote *Mistress of Desires*, what I had in mind was a
minor character called La Chunga who was in one of my novels, *The
Green House*. I always felt I could have worked better and in more
detail on her character. That was the beginning. I then discovered that
I was dealing with a woman in a machista world, not only because
Peru and Latin America are very machista worlds, but also because the
social backgrounds of the characters are particularly machista.
Machismo is stronger at the base of every social pyramid. So it was
very exciting for me to tell a story about a woman having to face this
kind of world and fighting successfully to operate, survive, and even
succeed there. Another theme that was introduced was one that has
been appearing in all my plays and recent novels: the relationship
between fiction and desires. This theme has explored the way fiction
has roots in secret desires, in appetites that cannot be fulfilled in real
life – sexual, sensual and economic desires. I wanted to write a story
about stories themselves, how stories are linked and mixed with real
life; and it was a thrilling challenge for me to translate these themes
and problems to the very primitive, ignorant, and physical world of the
Boys. I had tried similar things in *Kathie and the Hippopotamus*, but
in another social class, of rich and educated people, where this kind of
subtlety was much more easily acceptable.

SD: *Mistress of Desires* pulls no punches on things which many people would find difficult to deal with. Did you consciously confront social and sexual taboos when writing it?

MVL: I have never planned any fiction in abstract or ideological ways.
The first stimulus for all my novels and plays has always been very
mysterious: some vague idea of a character, a situation, a relationship
between some characters; and I have then followed my instincts as
much as my reason and ideas.

SD: Some people might object to the strong sexual element, the erotic realism of this play. How would you respond to such criticism?

MVL: If you want to explore the realm of human desires, you must be
prepared to be shocked by some very nasty things. This is a very
complex world in which angels and devils are mixed in inextricable
ways. I don't think you can separate good, presentable themes in the
dimension of the real world. But this play is in no way complacent.
There is no deliberate exploitation of this subject. Nor does the play
make any moral statement. It is a very literary work, about what
literature is about and about some roots of fiction. But it is true that
some very nasty aspects of desires and of the secret personality of
human beings are explored and presented. I have tried very hard,

without being evasive, not to be excessively factual about all this. The literary element is always present. And I rely very much on the director and the actors to reduce anything that might be offensive or excessively brutal or vulgar.

SD: Would you describe this play as anti-moralistic?

MVL: Yes. I hate hypocrisy. Our moral world, particularly in countries like Peru is based much more on hypocrisy than on real principles. You can read the play from this point of view very easily. All real and important Latin American literature clearly shows that there is a great gap between what we say we should do, and what we really do. This gap is there in the play, particularly in its moral perspective.

SD: In your introduction to *Mistress of Desires*, you criticise the 'signs of sclerosis' in contemporary theatre. What exactly do you mean by this?

MVL: Since the 1960s it has been fashionable to neglect or reject the text. Although this has produced some beautiful formal achievements, in general it has led to the decline of the theatre. It has produced something very ephemeral. The omnipotence of the director as the only master of the game was not good for the theatre, which cannot survive without the text. The text is essential for what theatre is for. This is changing now, and we are seeing a move away from improvised theatre and happenings towards a reappearance, a vindication of the text. The text is as important as the actor and director are for the survival and enrichment of the theatre. I don't think the text limits the freedom, imagination or spontaneity of the director and actors. This is a prejudice. The text can be open to all kinds of initiatives and manipulations. An author must be modest and cannot claim any kind of privilege on his text. Unlike a novelist, who is an absolute, totalitarian sovereign, the playwright must be a very humble person who accepts that what he does is just a part of a very complex machine in which there are other factors as important as himself.

SD: How do you think Latin American theatre has developed over recent times?

MVL: I have always been very curious about the different evolutions of literary genres. I believe that the existence of literary genres is not arbitrary as people like Roland Barthes think. This was not something that was artificially imposed by 18th century literati. There is a very profound reason for the existence of different literary genres. You use drama, poetry or the novel to say very different things about the world, using words, fantasies, music or other elements in the case of theatre. I am also convinced that there are some links between literary genres and the social, historical, cultural and religious situation of a society. Each time someone has tried to describe this link in a scientific way the result has been very artificial and insufficient to get to the heart of the matter. It is true, however, that the theatre, which was the most important literary genre during colonial times, has been very poor in modern times in Latin America. There have been some exceptions but in general it has been very poor. I don't know the reason. It may have something to do with the decline of the theatre in general in the world. Or because the theatre needs something more than just individual talent. It needs a social structure, an economic and social support in order to exist: you need audiences, you need theatres, you need a whole machine in order to be able to produce theatre. With some exceptions like Argentina, this has not existed, which has discouraged the theatrical imagination. This is a great pity because the theatre is a very rich and useful way of using imagination and words, of reacting vis-à-vis the world, and I love the theatre. It was my first vocation and I hope to keep writing plays.

This was a verbal interview conducted in English, in Berlin in February 1992.